MW01110096

Jochen Felsenheimer and Philip Gisdakis

Credit Crises

Dr. Jochen Felsenheimer works in the Global Research department at UniCredit Markets & Investment Banking. He heads the Credit Strategy & Structured Credit Team. He holds a PhD in Economics from the LMU in Munich.

Dr. Philip Gisdakis works as a Senior Credit Strategist at UniCredit Markets & Investment Banking. He studied Mathematical Finance at the University of Oxford and holds a PhD in Theoretical Chemistry from the TU Munich.

Jochen Felsenheimer and Philip Gisdakis

Credit Crises

*From Tainted Loans
to a Global Economic Meltdown*

WILEY-
VCH

WILEY-VCH Verlag GmbH & Co. KGaA

Library of Congress Card No.:
applied for

British Library Cataloguing-in-Publication Data:
A catalogue record for this book is available from the British Library.

Bibliographic information published by the Deutsche Nationalibliothek
Die Deutsche Nationalbibliothek lists this publication in the Deutsche Nationalbibliografie; detailed bibliographic data is available in the Internet at http://dnb.d-nb.de

Typesetting: Steingraeber Satztechnik GmbH, Dossenheim
Printing and Binding: AALEXX Druck GmbH, Großburgwedel
Cover Design: Christian Kalkert, Birken-Honigsessen

Printed in the Federal Republic of Germany
Printed on acid-free paper

ISBN: 978-3-527-50375-9

Table of Contents

Foreword

The global financial system is experiencing one of the severest and most complicated credit crises in history. Events have come in rapid succession since the collapse of the US subprime mortgage market last summer. Following an all-time record first half year in 2007, financial institutions went from heaven straight to hell within just a few weeks. Initial hopes that the subprime disaster would be contained and not spill over to other sectors of the global financial system had to be buried as it became increasingly clear that the subprime turmoil was not the real cause of the crisis but just the trigger event for bursting an unprecedented credit bubble of mind-numbing dimensions. It is only five years after the bursting of the equity bubble that the stability of the global financial system is challenged again. Aggressive monetary easing and a sustained period of low interest rates in combination with rapid product innovation in structured credit markets were the catalyst for a dramatic increase in credit lending and in leverage. This excess lending and excess leverage as a reflection of excessive risk taking by credit investors took place against a background of a very benign macroeconomic environment characterized by the best of all worlds, strong global growth and low inflation. With the bursting of the US housing bubble and the US housing market now experiencing the most severe recession since the Great Depression in 1929, things have obviously changed. But it is not so much the recession in the US housing market that is causing headaches. It is rising systemic risk within the global financial system following the tsunami in structured credit markets which could potentially lead to a credit crunch with dramatic consequences for the real economy that keeps policymakers, central bankers and regulators on high alert. Banks across the globe have already started to tighten their lending standards significantly, according to central bank lending surveys. And rising risk provisions on the back of deteriorating asset quality and additional write-down needs on structured credit products continue to undermine the capital adequacy of banks. As a consequence, many financial institutions are under pressure to reduce risk weighted assets, get fresh equity capital and cut their lending activity. In addition, the lack of transparency in regard to the potential size of the losses and the distribution of those losses prevent a rapid recovery of confidence in financial markets. Early estimates of

Credit Crises. J. Felsenheimer and P. Gisdakis
Copyright © 2008 WILEY-VCH Verlag GmbH & Co. KGaA, Weinheim
ISBN: 978-3-527-50375-9

the IMF of USD 200 bn back in August 2007 have been superseded by G-7 estimates of up to USD 400 bn in January and now some analysts have even raised their loss estimates to a potential USD 1,000 bn.

Following the bursting of this gigantic credit bubble, the painful deleveraging process is now well under way. Week after week investors are confronted by new horror stories about esoteric structured credit products they never heard of before. The subprime virus shows no signs of abating and its negative impact on real economic activity cannot be accurately estimated at the present time.

Given that we are still far from a resolution of the credit crisis, this book comes at exactly the right point in time. The book does not only analyze the causes of the current credit crisis and its potential impact on the real economy, it also helps the reader to understand how he can profit from it. In addition, it explains all the instruments and all those special vehicles and entities most of us have never heard before, e.g., CPDOs, SIVs, ABCPs, etc. Hence, this book is not only a deep analysis of what happened in credit markets over the last few years, but also a useful guide which provides a deep insight into the structure of the credit market, helping to explain what a majority of investors still perceive as a market anomaly. After reading this book, it should become clear that the current situation is the logical consequence of the behavior of highly leveraged credit markets in a cyclical downturn rather than being a six-sigma event!

Thorsten Weinelt, CFA
Global Head of Research
UniCredit
Munich

Preface

At first glance, the structure of the book might appear a bit confusing. The book starts with the chronology of the subprime turmoil, turning to the widely used instruments in the credit markets afterwards, thus describing the players in the market before we discuss the most popular instruments used to implement these strategies. The final chapter shows the anatomy of credit crises in general, pointing out the similarities and differences between credit crises experienced in the past and the subprime meltdown and how such a crisis can be avoided. Indeed, the structure of the book could also be exactly the other way around. However, there is good reason for this composition: the book should be readable for outsiders but also for professionals working for years in the area of credit markets. Therefore, the book is designed to be read from the first until the last page, while those readers who are familiar with some topics may jump over single sections without losing sight of the central theme.

The first chapter covers the chronology of the subprime crisis and provides a detailed introduction to the complex topic of credit crises as it covers many of the credit-specific topics. All the relevant instruments (e.g., CDOs), players (e.g., hedge funds), and vehicles (e.g., Structured Investment Vehicles) are introduced, however, without explaining them in detail – this will happen in the following chapter. The course of the subprime crisis has proved to be a very good template for credit crises in general, and allows us to discuss the basic mechanism behind a credit crisis, and the accompanying spillover effects.

A detailed description of the most important instruments in global credit markets, including cash instruments like loans and bonds, and synthetic instruments, ranging from single-name Credit Default Swaps to complex credit structures and correlation products follows in Chapter 2. The analysis of the risk-return profile of these instruments is, indeed, a prerequisite to understanding the mechanism behind credit crises, which are closely linked to the "tail-event" character of credit-risky instruments. The chapter does not only include plain-vanilla instruments, but especially those innovative products from the structured credit and credit derivatives universe in the global credit market, which moved center stage during the subprime turmoil.

To understand the technical side of the market, with forced selling or the technical bid being the most prominent buzzwords, knowledge regarding the major players in the credit market remains a prerequisite. Therefore, Chapter 3 is dedicated to traditional players in the credit market but also to those who, at first glance, have nothing to do with credits, e.g. money market funds. Knowing the motivation and constraints of these players is crucial to understanding the emergence of credit crises and potential transmission channels.

The next logical step is to analyze the investment strategies of different players in the credit and structured credit market, which will be done in Chapter 4. The extensive use of leverage either through the unfunded nature of credit derivatives or through funding via short-term debt was one of the main reasons for the dramatic effect of the subprime crisis, not only on credit markets. In this respect, investments in Leveraged-Super-Senior (LSS) transactions and other highly leveraged instruments have been center stage during the subprime crisis. The technical bid, which was the major reason for the tight spread valuation in the run-up to the subprime turmoil, was accompanied by a shift of default-risky into mark-to-market risky instruments. A result of this strategy was the jump behavior of credit spreads during the subprime crisis.

In Chapter 5, the anatomy of a credit crisis, in general, will be discussed. There are many similarities between the crises we have experienced in the past, with excessive liquidity and excessive leverage being typical characteristics of a pre-crisis era. Moreover, the transmission effects between different segments of the credit market, as well as spillover effects onto other markets (e.g., equity markets) and the real economy are pretty similar. However, there are also major differences when analyzing previous credit crises. We briefly discuss broad crises like the savings & loan crisis in the US, the 2001/2002 credit crunch scenario, but also recent very credit-specific ones like the correlation crisis in the credit derivatives universe from 2005. The crucial questions are: What can we learn from analyzing these crises and are there crises models that help us to explain the mechanism behind them? In this respect, the book discusses overshooting models, financial panic, and moral hazard. One conclusion that can be drawn: crises have a cyclical character and are rather normal adjustment processes in case markets move too far away from fundamentally justified levels! The book ends with a discussion whether credit crises can be avoided in the future. The conclusion is as simple as it is important: In general not, but you can make money from it!

This book was written "live" during the crisis. The months of the turmoil have been times of extreme stress (and shortage of time), not only for credit researchers. The signs of stress can be seen in this book. We have included those bits and pieces that appeared most relevant and interesting to us. However, since there was so much news and so many (often quite complex) stories to tell, we had to be selective with the material we chose. Furthermore, as we are publishing this book in the middle of the crisis, it obviously cannot be complete; however, we plan to update it when more information becomes available. Finally, we have to admit that we continue to have a very distinct view on credit markets before ("negative") and during the crisis ("it will deteriorate even further"). Nevertheless, we hope to provide the reader with a fair and objective view, as we have tried to publish something that is more than "just another piece of market research".

Jochen Felsenheimer
Philip Gisdakis
Munich

Acknowledgements

This book would not have been possible without the support of many individuals. First of all, we are very grateful for editorial support from Edda Nee, Janine Fuchs and David Dakshaw. Moreover, we want to thank Thorsten Weinelt, Global Head of Research at UniCredit, who supported this project from the very beginning, while we continuously benefited from the challenging and inspiring environment at UniCredit's MIB division during these challenging times. Thanks go to all our colleagues from the trading, sales, structuring, and origination side, who provided us with very helpful comments and deep insights in their specific fields. This is especially true for all our colleagues within the Global Credit Research department, who answered all our questions with patience and endurance, while supporting us with their knowledge, their ideas and their practical help. In this respect, we also want to thank our colleagues Julia Wisser and Katharina Günther for their support in preparing the manuscript. Last but not least, we are particularly grateful for the immense support of our families who demonstrated patience and understanding as we spent many weekends and evenings writing this book. The authors assume full responsibility for mistakes in the text.

1

Prologue: Chronology of a Crisis

1.1 The subprime turmoil included all ingredients of a severe financial markets crisis

Every financial crisis has its own character, whether regarding the trigger event, the course of the crisis, or the impact on the financial system as a whole. There is no textbook-like financial crisis, although there are some similarities among market crises we have experienced thus far. We will discuss some interesting cases later. We now focus on the US subprime crisis, a near-perfect example of a financial market crises, as it includes all necessary features like excessive lending, excessive risk taking, excessive ignorance (regarding the sensitivities of structured investments), and excessive leverage. These are the basic ingredients of asset price inflation, which will, in general, end up in an asset price bubble. The bursting of the bubble is what we call a financial crisis. However, it is just the logical consequence of the preceding events. From a purely academic perspective, the market shake-out following a burst of a bubble is simply the adjustment towards a new equilibrium in the market. This adjustment is not a smooth one; it can be rather characterized as a jump process.

In this chapter we follow the chronology of the US subprime crisis, pointing out the major milestones and the step-by-step development from a housing market correction, initially limited to the United States, to a full-fledged liquidity and confidence crisis. It is a perfect example for studying first, second, and third-round effects, spillover mechanisms, and contagion also of financial market segments which are not linked to the US housing market at first glance. To highlight the course of the crisis, we depict the level of the iTraxx Crossover index. This synthetic index is based on Credit Default Swaps of 50 European High Yield and Crossover names and therefore reflects the most risky part of the European credit universe. This is reflected in a pretty high volatility of the index, which means that this index is a very good indicator for the systematic credit risk premium discounted even in the global credit market. In addition, the iTraxx universe is the most liquid segment in global credit markets. The Crossover was the preferred hedging tool at this time for many investors. It was used to eliminate directional risks in ABS books, to immunize complex

Credit Crises. J. Felsenheimer and P. Gisdakis
Copyright © 2008 WILEY-VCH Verlag GmbH & Co. KGaA, Weinheim
ISBN: 978-3-527-50375-9

structured credit books against spread swings, or simply to hedge plain-vanilla financial floater books.

This turned out to be a problematic idea for many market participants, as the Crossover developed a life of its own during the crisis, partly showing a decoupling from other credit-risky instruments. The problem for many investors was that their investment book (including, for example, cash credits) remained under pressure, because the Crossover tightened strongly after the record wides we have seen during the summer, while cash credits widened further. This means that many investors got hit twice: on their long cash positions and on their short hedge positions, aggravating the situation even further.

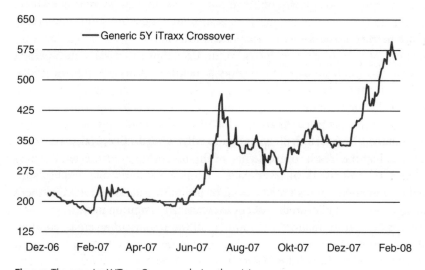

Fig. 1.1: The generic 5Y iTraxx Crossover during the crisis

1.2 An exemplary credit crisis

As stated before, we recognize some similarities among all crises we have experienced thus far. This is true for the whole spectrum of financial crises. In this section we introduce the prototype of a crisis which provides us with a template for all credit crises we discuss later in this book. It allows us to compare and contrast all historical crisis scenarios. The subprime turmoil exhibits many criteria of a typical credit crisis, for example.

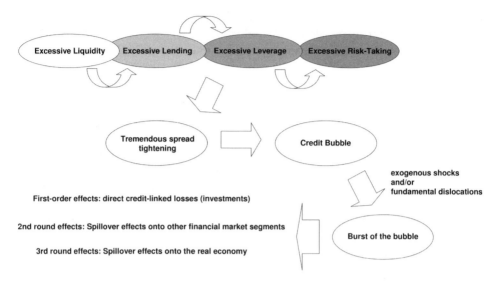

Fig. 1.2: An exemplary credit crisis: the basic template

The starting point of a credit crisis is generally a kind of "Goldilocks scenario", which is characterized by overwhelming liquidity (not only on the investor side but also for companies), by low default (and high recovery) rates, and by subdued risk aversion among credit investors. Everything looks perfect; long carry positions on credit instruments seem to be the only appropriate strategy given the ongoing spread income (even if this is low) accompanied by the positive roll-down (pull-to-par) effect, which is – in general – even more attractive in more leveraged products like CDOs. In such a case, credit spreads tend to undershoot fundamentally fair levels (later on we analyze the credit cycle in more detail), taking longer-term cyclical aspects like the cyclical behavior of default rates into account. This scenario is accompanied by an expansive monetary policy, by excessive lending (e.g., reflected in lending standards of banks), and excessive risk taking (rising leverage in investment books; trend towards lower qualities). Asset price inflation in the form of very tight credit spreads, for example the creation of a credit bubble, are the consequence. Slowly removing the air from the bubble is, unfortunately, wishful thinking (of monetary authorities) rather than a realistic scenario. In many cases an exogenous shock, or simply the occurrence of a fundamental dislocation, triggers a repricing in the market, reflecting the search for a new equilibrium which is based on new fundamentals. This is what bubble theorists define as the burst of the bubble.

The bursting of the bubble does not hit the broad credit market at the same amplitude in many cases but often starts triggering a significant repricing (spread widening) in specific segments. All the losses directly linked to these segments are called first-round or first-order effects, also including all the losses in directly linked derivatives contracts. The more important this specific segment for the real economy is, the higher the risk of so-called second or third-round effects.

While there is no unique definition of these effects in the academic literature, we define spillover effects from a specific segment onto other parts of the financial market as second-round (order) effects, and spillover effects onto the real economy as third-round effects. Such effects occur in any case, although we often do not "feel" them, as they are negligible. The crucial question is not whether these effects appear, but only how severe they are. The markets broadly ignore a decline in consumer spending (third-round effects) of 0.1% following a credit crisis that causes tighter standards of banks in the consumer lending business (second-round effects), while a drop of 1% would be seen as a significant threat for the real economy.

From a purely academic perspective (and we do not ignore the fact that many experts would strongly disagree), the bursting of a bubble is actually only the "special case of an adjustment path towards a new equilibrium in a normal credit cycle". The stronger the deviation from a fundamentally fair value in credit markets, the more pronounced the readjustment towards a new equilibrium. Based on the definition of credit crisis we introduced above, a crisis can be seen as a rather normal phase in a credit cycle. The most important conclusion of this theory is that it will happen again and again, and it will happen in a periodical manner, as credit crises are nothing else but cyclical events.

In the following chronological description of the US subprime crisis, the above-mentioned effects are becoming obvious. This example also highlights that transmission effects from credit markets onto the real economy can be very heterogeneous!

Prologue:
Chronology of a
Crisis

1.3 The chronology of a crisis – The US subprime crisis

1.3.1 What has happened so far? Prelude to the subprime turmoil

Subprime mortgage lending volumes have increased enormously since the 1990s, with the total subprime volume outstanding in 2007 estimated at USD 1.3 tn. Subprime lending became more and more popular, reflected in the fact that the subprime market volumes originated in 2005 and 2006 amounted to 20-25% of the US housing market. In mid-2007, around 6 mn US subprime borrowers could not meet their obligations. Subprime borrowers speculated on significant house price growth, using specific subprime loan features like 2/28 adjustable-rate mortgage (ARM) loans. In 2/28s, the borrowing costs remain fixed for two years at a rather moderate level. After two years the interest payment will be adjusted to a floating rate. The name of the subprime game was simply to purchase a fully-financed house and to sell it within two years at a higher price. Unfortunately, this only works if house prices are rising, although the situation gets uncomfortable if interest rates also rise significantly. From the perspective of the banks, the innovative power of the structured credit and securitization business allowed banks to originate more risk as they would have originated without these new instruments. Simply spoken, Collateralized Debt Obligations (CDOs) and US subprime Residential Mortgage- Backed Securities (RMBS) issues have been used as funding tools. A majority of subprime loans generated by banks have been transferred to non-bank portfolio managers. Hence, the banks acted as an intermediary rather than taking these risks on their own books.

In 2007, some trends in the US housing market materialized that negatively affected particularly the subprime segment and impacted all subprime-linked instruments. The declining housing price growth in the United States was accompanied by rising interest rates, stretched borrower affordability, low underwriting standards, and lax risk-control standards. About 20% of the subprime mortgages originated during 2005 and 2006 are expected to end in foreclosure, while declining housing price growth leads to lower-than-expected recovery for foreclosed properties (higher expected loss given default). US subprime RMBS tranches have been structured into CDOs, which have been purchased by institutions and funds worldwide.

1.3.2 End of 2006: First signs

Following a decade of tremendous prosperity in the US housing market, the market slowed down. In addition, we saw two years of steady increases in the Fed Funds target rate (from 1% to 5.25%) in H2 2006 which increased refinancing cost on the ARM loans. The pressure on the housing market is also reflected in rising delinquency rates on subprime loans, which increases to 13% from 10% seen in 2004 and 2005, leading to a flood of bankruptcies at subprime lenders. Spreads of Collateralized Debt Obligations (repackaged bonds and loans which included subprime mortgage debt) widened significantly in December 2006 and in January 2007. There are initial worries by investors that the problems of some small subprime mortgage originators could spill over to some of the bigger mainstream players. Nevertheless, the 5Y iTraxx Crossover index stands at 219 bp as of December 12, 2006, the tightest level since the inception of the index in June 2004.

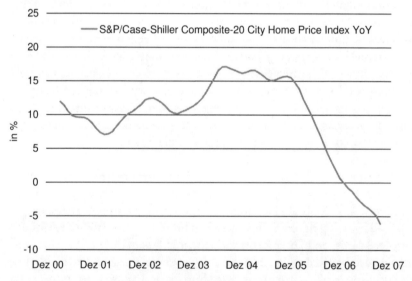

Fig. 1.3: US housing price index – back to the 1980s

1.3.3 February 2007: Microfundamentals get affected

The United States' third largest subprime lender, the California-based New Century Financial Corporation, states that it expects a loss in Q4 2006. HSBC

Prologue:
Chronology of a
Crisis

says that more funds will have to cover bad debts in US subprime lending port-folios, while spreads of sub-investment grade tranches of home equity CDOs widen by more than 200 bp within only two days. On February 27, Chinese stock markets tumble and shares of US securities decline significantly. The least creditworthy borrowers experience trouble repaying their loans due to ris-ing interest rates and falling housing prices. Consequently, the risk inherent in low-rated subprime mortgage bonds jumps to a record high for an eighth consecutive day. At the end of February, the iTraxx Crossover widens towards 210 bp, which is 40 bp wider than the absolute low we saw on February 22, when the index traded down to 170 bp.

A closer look at the underlying markets shows that the worst is not behind us at this time; the opposite is true from a fundamental perspective. US subprime RMBS pools include 75-80% ARM loans, while distressed subprime borrowers most likely fail their credit obligation at the loan reset date (interest shock). Default events are most likely at future reset dates, as the ARM portion is significantly higher in the newest vintages. The chart below points out that ARM resets in the subprime universe will peak in Q1 2008, almost one year after the first significant losses hit subprime-linked instruments.

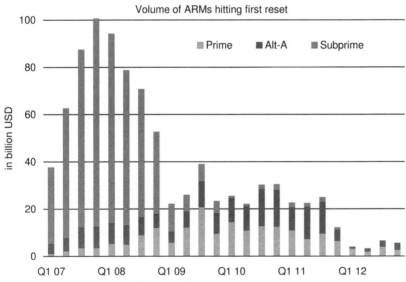

Fig. 1.4: ARM adjustments peak in Q1 2008
Source: Loan Performance; CSFB; Credit Suisse

1.3.4 March 2007: Only a dip?

Wall Street brokerage houses surprise with excellent figures. The companies are strong enough to withstand weak stock markets and subprime woes. Although market participants do not ignore the fact that the US housing market is in real bad shape and a further worsening is in the cards, fears that spillover effects will hurt the real economy through a decline in consumption expenses and a weaker labor market almost dimish. US stock markets recover from their losses in February, while credit markets remain at more elevated levels, as investors' perception of the crisis is that it is merely a credit-related problem. In mid-March, the iTraxx Crossover widenes above 240 bp, while the index ends the month at 227 bp, only 17 bp wider compared to February's closing.

Pressure from subprime woes on financial markets is still rather limited to specific segments, with the famous ABX.HE universe being the best example. ABX.HE denotes a family of synthetic ABS indices of US home equity asset-backed securities launched in January 2006. Five subtypes of the ABX.HE exist, labeled, according to the rating of the underlying assets, ABX.HE.AAA, ABX.HE.AA, ABX.HE.A, ABX.HE.BBB, and ABX.HE.BBB-. Of the total issuance volume in the United States in 2005, almost 30% were related to home equity loans (HEL), the largest sector in the US securitization market. Home equity loans also comprise subprime mortgages, which showed increasing performance problems in the past, such as rising delinquencies and foreclosure rates. In the first two months of 2007, the ABX.HE indices widened significantly, especially the riskiest part of the universe, the ABX.HE.BBB- 06-2, which widened from 380 bp (95 in price-terms) to around 1.500 bp (63 in price terms). (Note that the ABX.HE is quoted in price terms rather than in spread). This trend continues over the whole summer period.

1.3.5 April 2007: The first default

April 2: New Century Financial files for Chapter 11! New Century Financial Corp. is the largest subprime mortgage lender which ever filed for bankruptcy, as it was overwhelmed by rising defaults from borrowers with poor credit records. The company plans to sell most of its assets within forty-five days, according to the Chapter 11 filing in federal court in Wilmington, Delaware. About 3,200 people, more than half the workforce at the Irvine, California-based company, will be let go. The company rode the US housing boom to become the largest independent mortgage lender to subprime borrowers, while it generated about

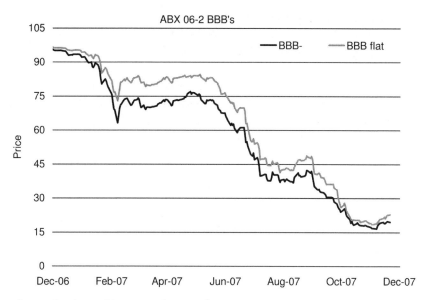

ABX 06-2 BBB's

BBB- · BBB flat

Fig. 1.5: The slump of the ABX market (stated in price terms)

USD 60 bn in loans. Like rival firms, the company lowered its lending standards to keep cash flowing after demand slumped. According to Bloomberg, New Century was founded in 1995 and in the late 1990s survived an industry shakeout that led to the bankruptcy of bigger rivals including United Cos. Since then its growth had surpassed that of all other subprime underwriters. In the past two years, New Century underwrote about USD 120 bn of loans, or more than half the total since its inception. Subprime loans accounted for 86% of all New Century loans in 2006. Since its inception, the company made about 1.4 mn loans totaling more than USD 225 bn. Global credit markets remain relatively unimpressed by the news, and the iTraxx Crossover shows a strong performance over the month, ending up at 204 bp.

1.3.6 May 2007: The impact on the banking sector

At the beginning of May, UBS announces the reintegration of Dillon Read Capital Management (DRCM) Portfolios into the Investment Bank, while outside investor funds will be redeemed. The fund generated significant losses on subprime-related investments. The official press release states:

Zurich/New York, 3 May 2007 – UBS announced today that the proprietary funds currently managed by DRCM within Global Asset Management will transition to the Investment Bank. DRCM's principal finance, credit arbitrage, and commercial real estate businesses will be merged with relevant business lines within the Investment Bank. DRCM's third-party funds will be redeemed. UBS intends to work with DRCM investors to identify alternative investment opportunities for them.

Fig. 1.6: The plummet of New Century shares

This is not the end of the story for UBS, as Peter Wuffli, UBS' CEO at the time, will be ousted only two months later (cf. July 5). European credit spreads grind tighter towards cyclical lows, while the iTraxx universe ends up at 190 bp as of May 31. This translates into a positive spread performance of 14 bp from the already very depressed levels we saw at the end of April.

1.3.7 June 2007: Hedge funds blow up

Two hedge funds managed by Bear Stearns announce losses during April on subprime-related positions. They sell USD 4 bn of assets to cover investor redemptions and potential margin calls. Merrill Lynch sells off assets seized from the funds. In the center of the subprime woes is Bear Stearns' in-house hedge fund, the High-Grade Structured Credit Strategies Enhanced Leverage Fund (what a name!), which had a fund volume of USD 6.6 bn (USD 600 mn in equity and USD 6 bn borrowed money). The fund lost 23% within the first four months of this year, with forced unwinding of some (home equity linked) CDO positions aggravating the situation. The synthetic iTraxx universe cannot withstand this flood of negative news, with the Crossover widening by 40 bp in the course of June, ending the month at 230 bp.

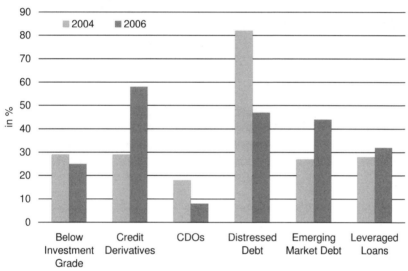

Fig. 1.7: Hedge fund trading volumes as a percentage of sector totals
Source: FitchRatings

Hedge funds have become a major force in credit markets during the last few years. This trend even accelerated recently and is closely coupled with the innovative power of the market. While hedge funds bring additional liquidity to the market, a potential threat emerging from this trend is the focus on similar strategies within the hedge fund arena, increasing the vulnerability of credit markets when tail risk rises. A majority of hedge fund inflows seen during previous years have been allocated to credit-linked hedge funds, including capital structure arbitrage strategies, correlation trading, and leveraged long/short funds (see also section 3.5).

1.3.8 July 2007: A first peak of the crisis!

- On July 5, UBS, the world's largest wealth manager, announces that it is replacing CEO Peter Wuffli with Marcel Rohner, the deputy CEO. "Wuffli, 49, relinquishes all of his functions at UBS," according to an Emailed statement from the Zurich-based bank. The iTraxx Crossover closes at 236 bp, 66 bp wider than its lowest level of 170 bp, which we saw in February.
- July 10: The rating agency Standard & Poor states that it may cut ratings on some USD 12 bn of subprime debt. US companies like Home Depot and D.R. Horton issue warnings about the housing market. The iTraxx Crossover index jumps to 267 bp. Downgrades in the structured credit universe remain a topic over the whole period of the crisis as further downgrades bear the risk that rating-sensitive investors might be forced to sell assets, which would put additional pressure on the segment.
- July 17: Bear Stearns announces that two hedge funds with subprime exposure have "very little value". Later on, Bear Stearns tells hedge fund investors that "there is no value left" in the High-Grade Structured Credit Strategies Enhanced Leverage Fund after the "unprecedented

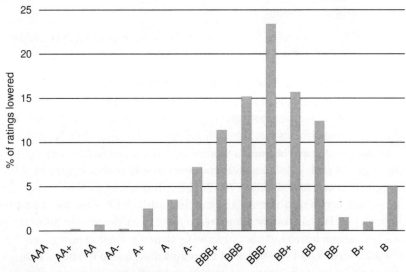

Fig. 1.8: Rating actions in the structured credit arena
Source: Standard & Poor's RatingsDirect

Prologue:
Chronology of a
Crisis

declines" of AAA-rated subprime-linked CDOs! The iTraxx Crossover widens to 287 bp.

- July 20: Following rumors regarding its involvement in US CDOs and substantial spread widening in its bonds and CDS, the German Mittelstandsbank IKB issues a statement saying that only a single-digit million amount of around EUR 5 mn would be affected by the subprime crisis. The iTraxx Crossover continues to remain under pressure, closing at 344 bp.
- July 25: The crisis is spilling over onto the market for leveraged buyouts. LBOs are heavily dependent on credit market conditions given the immense use of debt in such transactions. Arranging banks are forced to postpone the Chrysler and Alliance Boots debt sale, and they will keep the senior loans after failing to find investors to buy them. The banks will sell junior ranking loans of the Alliance Boots deal after increasing the interest rate and using their underwriting fees to discount the price by as much as 5%. Global banks are keeping around USD 350 bn in LBO transactions on their books with the intention to sell these loans to the market. This is also bad news for equity markets, as the record high in LBO transactions in H1 2007 was a major argument for the strong performance of stock markets at this time. The credit universe reacted immediately, and the iTraxx Crossover spread reaches a new high at 363 bp.
- July 30: Our UniCredit financial analyst states in a note to clients:

Within one week, IKB completely destroyed its profile as a conservative capital market participant (built up over recent decades), as it not only suffered severe losses due to bad investments but above all lied about this topic. In a brief statement issued this morning, IKB, in contrast to what it said on July 20 and repeated to market participants last week, said that the operating profit target of EUR 280 mn for FY 2006/07 will be missed substantially. As a result, the CEO has resigned and was replaced by Dr. Günther Bräunig, board member of KfW, Germany's flagship promotional bank and IKB's largest shareholder (38%). KfW said it will protect IKB from any related losses in order to maintain its position as a strong lender for the German Mittelstand.

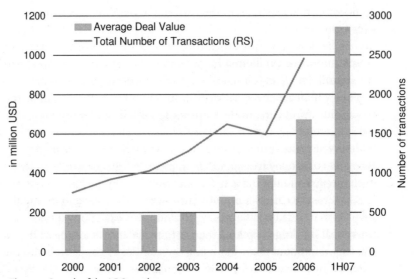

Fig. 1.9: Growth of the LBO market
Source: Standard & Poor's RatingsDirect

Unfortunately, the worst is still to come! (cf. August 9). The Crossover reaches a new all-time high at 505 bp (intraday), while the index ends a very volatile trading session at 461 bp.

- July 31: American Home Mortgage Investment says it may have to liquidate assets, fuelling concerns about a spillover of subprime losses into other areas. Australia's Macquarie Bank warns that retail investors face losses of up to a quarter in two of its high-yield bond funds. The market, however, calms down from previous record wides, while the Crossover ends the month of July at 401 bp.

1.3.9 August 2007: The infection mechanism is getting into full swing

- August 7: The US Federal Reserve leaves interest rates steady at 5.25%, saying economic growth remains moderate despite the current turmoil in credit markets. Inflation risks remain its main concern (cf. August 17). In volatile markets, the iTraxx Crossover ends the trading session somewhat tighter at 375 bp.
- August 9: In reaction to the dry-up in the European money market, the European Central Bank adds EUR 94.8 bn of one-day funds. Concerns

about subprime exposure in the banking industry trigger a surge of the overnight borrowing rate to 4.6%. The move followed news from the French bank BNP Paribas that froze USD 2.2 bn worth of funds referring to subprime problems. Many money market funds are facing the same problem. To increase carry income in their funds, managers continuously increase the share of ABS instruments in the funds. When the liquidity problems in the money market start to negatively affect the ABS market, huge fund withdrawals were the logical consequence. The withdrawals again put pressure on the ABS market but also on the performance of money market funds themselves (see section 3.3). Moreover, the Fed and the Bank of Canada also add liquidity to their banking systems. Germany's Bundesbank sets up a meeting to rescue IKB. The German regulator Bafin says that it was looking into a USD 17.5 bn special funding vehicle of the German state bank SachsenLB, raising concerns about other bank conduits and bank-sponsored structured investment vehicles heavily dependent on easy, short-term financing (cf. August 27). Despite ongoing market worries, the iTraxx Crossover continues its tightening path since the beginning of August, closing at 349 bp.

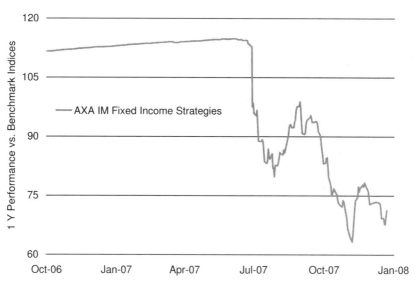

Fig. 1.10: Withdrawals from money market funds after worse performance

- August 13: Coventree, a Canadian financial services company, fails to sell new asset-backed commercial paper (ABCP) to replace maturing debt because of the credit crunch caused by US subprime mortgage losses. In the past, Canadian ABCPs have shown strong demand for leveraged super senior transactions (LSS), instruments which recently came under tremendous pressure. The Crossover ignores potential threats from the ABCP market, closing the day at 345 bp. The outstanding amount of the ABCP market drops during the summer by more than 25%.
- August 16: Countrywide Financial Corp., the biggest US mortgage lender, borrows the entire USD 11.5 bn available in a bank credit. The company turns to the emergency loan provided by a group of 40 banks. Fitch downgrades Countrywide to BBB+ and states that "... when a company draws on its bank lines, it just basically gives off the impression that it has run out of options". "Typically, these bank lines are there but not really meant to be used." The recovery in the Crossover stops, and the index widens to 386 bp.
- August 17: The Fed surprisingly cuts its discount rate for direct loans to banks by 50 bp to 5.75% as downside risks to growth from tighten-

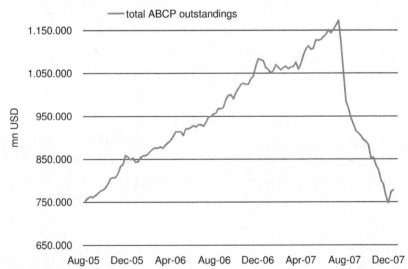

Fig. 1.11: Total ABCPs outstanding – strong drop as a result of subprime woes
Source: Fed

ing credit markets increase appreciably (cf. August 7, 27). World stock markets recover from five-month lows, while SachsenLB states that German savings banks had provided a credit facility of EUR 17.3 bn to secure the liquidity of its Ormond Quay conduit (cf. August 27). Structured Investment Vehicles (SIVs) enter the crisis! SIVs were used by market participants to gain leveraged access to high quality assets. SIVs as well as arbitrage conduits might be forced to sell their assets which usually possess a high quality. The threat in this respect is simply the sheer size of the underlying asset pools of SIVs. Due to the refinancing mechanism of SIV structures (short-term CP refinances long-term debt), liquidity problems might become insurmountable within the next few weeks. Rating agencies estimate the aggregated volume of outstanding SIV, and SIV-lite debt exceeds the USD 350 bn level (Q2 2007). Large parts are invested in structured credit assets. The risk is apparent as the total volume of European AAA rated ABS placed in 2006 was of the same size. Therefore, markets would experience a large shock if they would have to absorb such a volume in a short period. About 60% of the asset pool is related to structured finance (mainly RMBS [23%], CLO/CBO [11%] and CMBS [8%]) and about 98% is rated AAA or AA. The remaining 40% of the portfolio is financial sector (8% AAA, 24% AA, 8% A). In order to guarantee sufficient protection to the senior note holder, the vehicle has to fulfill coverage tests. Such tests and outstanding short-term debt which cannot be rolled forward may force the structure to liquidate assets. The recovery in the Crossover offsets preday losses, ending at 341 bp.

Distribution of SIV Portfolio Assets by Sector

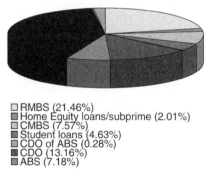

☐ RMBS (21.46%)
☐ Home Equity loans/subprime (2.01%)
☐ CMBS (7.57%)
■ Student loans (4.63%)
☐ CDO of ABS (0.28%)
■ CDO (13.16%)
☐ ABS (7.18%)

Fig. 1.12: SIVs – In the center of the subprime crisis
Source: Standard & Poor's RatingsDirect

- August 21: Britain's Barclays Bank borrows GBP 314 mn from the Bank of England's standing lending facility, the first use of the penalty rate facility since the credit crisis began. Barclays taps the central bank for emergency funds of some GBP 1.6 bn pounds for a second time on August 30, citing a technical hitch in the UK clearing system. The famous first-generation CPDOs (Constant Proportion Debt Obligations, AAA-rated investments which offer a high coupon income by using an aggressive leverage mechanism) issued in Q3 2006 traded down to 55% of their face value. The tightening continues, however, at a moderate pace, and the iTraxx Crossover stands at 335 bp.
- August 27: Finally, Landesbank Baden-Wuerttemberg (LBBW), the largest German state-owned bank, buys SachsenLB in order to avoid an immediate default on EUR 17.3 bn because of investments in US subprime debt (cf. August 9, 17). The iTraxx Crossover still knows only one direction-South-closing the day at 323 bp.
- August 28: London-based hedge fund company Cheyne Capital Management, which manages the special investment vehicle (SIV) Cheyne Finance, reports losses in June and may be forced to sell assets backing a USD 6 bn commercial paper program. The Cheyne Finance SIV publishes a statement saying that it has been selling investments, but there is enough cash to repay CP which will come due in November. Standard & Poor's cuts Cheyne Finance's ratings, citing the deteriorating market value of its assets. Moreover, Rhinebridge Plc, a fund managed by Düsseldorf-based IKB Deutsche Industriebank, says it sold USD 176 mn of assets after it couldn't find buyers for its short-term debt. The iTraxx Crossover experiences some weakness and trades up at 338 bp.
- August 31: US President Bush announces to help people who have fallen behind in their mortgages to keep their homes and to tighten safeguards against predatory lending. Bush admits, "the government's got a role to play, ... but it is not the government's job to bail out speculators or those who made the decision to buy a home they knew they could never afford." The idea is to let the Federal Housing Administration, which insures mortgages for low- and middle-income borrowers, guarantee loans for delinquent borrowers, allowing them to avoid foreclosure and refinance at more favorable rates. The iTraxx Crossover tightens by around 70 bp during August, ending the month at 331 bp.

1.3.10 September 2007: The reaction of central banks

- September 6: The ECB leaves interest rates unchanged at 4%, seen at least as a postponement of the interest rate rise it had appeared to signal in early August. Markets doubt if this is only a temporary reaction to the subprime woes or the beginning of a more dovish monetary policy? In any case, 10Y bond yields have reached their 2007 highs ahead of the subprime turmoil at the beginning of July at 4.68%. Spread volatility remains subdued in the first week of September, while the iTraxx Crossover stands at 332 bp.
- September 7: Disastrous US labor market data triggers rising fears that subprime woes will spill over onto the US economy. The iTraxx Crossover widens to 346 bp.
- September 13: The British mortgage lender Northern Rock seeks emergency financial support from the Bank of England, sparking a run on the bank's deposits by worried savers in the following days. According to a statement of the company, it has agreed with the BoE that it can raise such amounts of liquidity as may be necessary by either borrowing on a secured basis from the BoE or entering into repurchase facilities with it. Such repurchase facilities would include securities that have

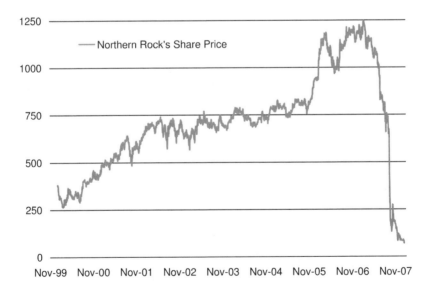

Fig. 1.13: Northern Rock's share price

prime residential mortgage assets as underlying collateral. This additional source of funding will enable Northern Rock to adapt its business model in line with developing market conditions. Despite short-term volatility, the iTraxx Crossover remains unimpressed and ends at 337 bp.

- September 17: British finance minister Alistair Darling says the government will guarantee all deposits at Northern Rock. The iTraxx Crossover stands at 329 bp.
- September 18: The Fed cuts its key Fed Funds target rate and discount rate by 50 bp to 4.75% and 5.25%, respectively. The Fed states that these cuts are a preemptive move to "neutralize the impact of the financial market turmoil on the broader US economy". World equity and credit markets rally. The S&P 500 ends up almost 3% higher, while the iTraxx Crossover reached its tightest level since mid-July, ending the trading session at 308 bp.

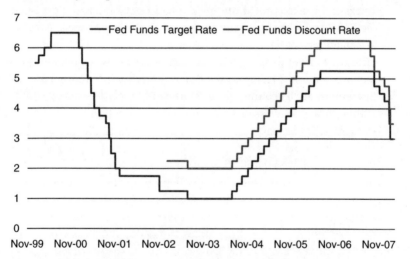

Fig. 1.14: The Fed's emergency cut in September 2007

- September 18-20: US investment banks start reporting third-quarter earnings, with mixed overall results. At first glance Bear Stearns, Goldman Sachs, Lehman Brothers, and Morgan Stanley managed to weather the storm; this is the conclusion one can draw when looking at the results. Bear Stearns had USD 700 mn of write-downs and USD 250 mn of mark-downs on its leveraged loans; Goldman Sachs faced USD 2.40 bn of write-downs and a loss of USD 1.48 bn in credit products; and

Prologue:
Chronology of a
Crisis

Lehman Brothers penciled in a net reduction of USD 700 mn of its revenues in Fixed Income Capital Markets. Morgan Stanley had USD 900 mn of loan mark-downs, which added to losses of USD 480 mn in the quantitative strategies trading group. The figures looked quite different for the four companies reporting their Q3 results. The winner was Goldman Sachs, while the big loser was Bear Stearns. Although the overall figures were mostly in line with the reduced expectations of the past few weeks, question marks still linger. And these are essentially a consequence of the way US investment banks treat their Level 3 assets, or those assets whose prices cannot be found on the market but are inferred by internal models. Given that these assets represent approximately 5-10% of total assets, it is clear how important the amounts at stake are.

- September 19: Liquidity injections remain the only instrument central banks can use to combat the crisis. The Bank of England offers to inject GBP 10 bn of emergency three-month funds into money markets at penalty rates and to accept a wider pool of assets as collateral. The iTraxx Crossover drops below the mystic 300 bp threshold, closing at 277 bp.

- September 20: The iTraxx universe rolls from Series 7 into Series 8. Although many investors fear distortions on the back of activities from structured credit players, the roll is rather smooth. The Series 8 Crossover Index ends in positive terrain, closing the day at 316 bp (S7 at 250 bp). From now on, we are referring to Series 8 levels.

- September 22: This date marks the beginning of second-round effects in the Russian banking sector. According to Bloomberg, the Moscow-based Russian Standard Bank (which has a dominant position in the retail lending market in Russia) has stopped making cash loans to consumers amid soaring refinancing costs due to the worldwide credit squeeze. The bank is also tightening its standards for issuing credit cards and stopping mortgage lending, a small part of its business, until the end of the year. Russian President Vladimir Putin announces that the government will support the liquidity of Russian banks to ensure economic growth amid the rise in global borrowing costs caused by the collapse of the US subprime mortgage market. The iTraxx Crossover continues to tighten to 300 bp.

- September 24: Deutsche Bank is rumored to have record Q3 losses on its loan book of up to EUR 1.7 bn; the bank estimates a 4-6% cut in loan values. The iTraxx Crossover remains stable at 297 bp.
- September 25: The International Monetary Fund's Global Financial Stability report states that problems in the credit and money markets will recur and the tightening of credit will slow the global economy. The Group of Seven's Financial Stability Forum says a "period of adjustment" may take some time. The iTraxx Crossover widens 17 bp to 314 bp on the back of accelerating growth concerns, reflecting that the market is still in a vulnerable mood.
- September 26: The malfunctioning of the European money markets persists, although the ECB allots EUR 50 bn of three-month refinancing at 4.63%. This is the highest liquidity provision since March 2001. The problem in global money markets is not the amount of liquidity but rather the allocation of liquidity, as banks are not willing to lend money to other institutions given the still high uncertainty regarding potential time bombs in the industry. In chart 15, we highlight the problems by plotting the 3M Euribor versus the 3M EONIA Swap. The spread between the funded 3M Euribor and the unfunded 3M EONIA

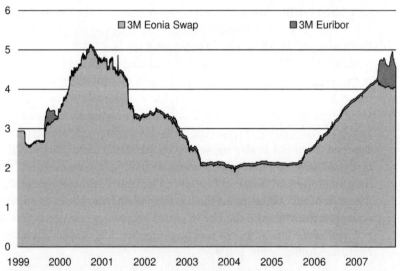

Fig. 1.15: The malfunctioning of the money markets is reflected in the Eonia-Euribor spread

Swap can be interpreted as a premium the banks charge each other for providing liquidity. In October 2007, the spread amounts to 70 bp in Euroland, compared to approximately 6 bp under normal market conditions. This spread can be interpreted as the opportunity costs banks are willing to endure for retaining liquidity on their balance sheets. The situation during the subprime turmoil compares only to the environment prior to the turn of the millennium, when concerns about the stability of banks emerged due to Y2K software problems. At that time, the situation resolved itself after New Year's Eve. Nevertheless, the Crossover grinds tighter to 305 bp.

- September 27: The ECB announces that it lent EUR 3.9 bn at its penalty rate of 5% on Sept 26 but declines to say which bank or banks needed the extra funds. In the aftermath, a flood of denials from almost all big banks in the Eurozone hit the screens. The iTraxx Crossover ends September at 326 bp, the first month of positive performance since May 2007.

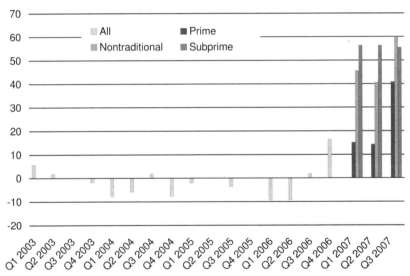

Fig. 1.16: Tighter lending standards in the US housing market
Source: Fed

1.3.11 October 2007: The second subprime wave hits the market

- October 1: The rally in credit markets continues despite resurfacing horror news from the banking industry: UBS announces write-downs of USD 3.4 bn in its fixed-income portfolio and records its first quarterly loss in nine years! Citigroup issues a profit warning and expects a decline of about 60% in third quarter net income! The iTraxx Crossover remains unimpressed and closed at 321 bp.
- October 6: Strong US labor market data trigger a further tightening wave in global credit markets, with the Crossover moving below the 300 bp for the first time since June. Spread levels imply that markets broadly deny any recession risk at that time, despite ongoing bad news from the US housing market, dramatic write-downs in the banking sector, and even the failure of some (although peripheral) banks. Amazingly, the US stock market reaches an all-time high. In order to curb possible spillover effects, major central banks state that banks have already tightened their lending standards (survey provided by the Fed, the ECB, and the BoE). In chart 16, we point out that this move affects primarily the US housing market. However, it affects not only subprime

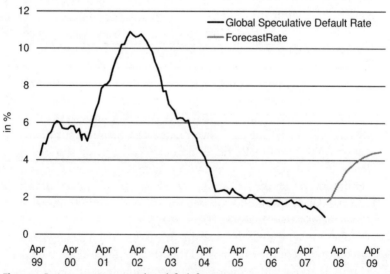

Fig. 1.17: Rating agencies revise their default forecast up
Source: Moody's

borrowers but also prime borrowers. This clearly underpins the fact that the US housing problem is not only a problem in a specific segment but that it will have an impact on the housing market as a whole, which argues for the rising risk of spillover effects onto the real economy. Moreover, the same is true for lending standards in consumer credits and also for company loans. This is not only the case in the US but also in Euroland and in the UK. A major risk factor of tighter lending standards is that companies could face a liquidity squeeze, resulting in major funding problems especially in the universe of lower-rated companies. On the back of this development, rating agencies revise up their default forecasts (please refer to chart 17). Despite the spread tightening, it becomes clear that financial markets still do not function as was the case before the crisis. A rising number of market participants share the view that the longer the malfunctioning in the money market persists, the higher the risk that the so-called liquidity/confidence crisis will be a burden for the nonfinancial segment. This will, inescapably, trigger rising default rates.

- October 15: The next mega headline hits the screens: a group of major banks, led by JP Morgan, Bank of America, and Citigroup, is planning to create an SIV bailout fund (up to USD 80 bn) to buy assets from SIVs to revive the ABCP market. The basic idea behind this move is to bail out some troubled SIVs to avoid forced selling, which would put additional pressure on the structured credit market as a whole. Although no concrete details have been announced, the first market reaction was positive with rather strong Asian markets. But the more critical people argue that as the overall SIV market still amounts to USD 320 bn, the amount of the fund is rather symbolic, and that the more severe problem – credit risk, that is, default risk, instead of only liquidity risk – is not yet solved. However, negative earnings surprises from Citigroup (Q3 profit fell 57% as losses from subprime and leveraged loans amounted to USD 6.5 bn) overshadowed the initially positive sentiment. Bernanke's statement on SIVs will find a place in historical textbooks: "I would like to know what those damn things are worth!" Nevertheless, the Crossover closes at 278 bp.
- October 17: Sentiment turns again, primarily driven by ongoing disappointments in the earnings season, the continuation of the housing slump (markets had to digest the lowest housing start figure in fourteen years), and macro concerns regarding the impact on the US econ-

omy and stronger-then-expected inflation figures (oil prices are trading at all-time highs). The trip below 300 bp did not last too long, and the Crossover ends the day at 302 bp.

- October 18: When investors are asked whether the proposed M-LEC would have a positive impact, 51% answer "Yes" and 49% answer "No". This outcome clearly highlights the current inner conflict of investors, as the former obviously believe in the "liquidity story", while the latter share concerns that the real cause of the crisis is more severe, liquidity allocation problems only being a symptom of this crisis. Arguments for the latter are that, despite central bank interventions, the money market is still distorted, with the Euribor-EONIA spread continuing to trade in distressed terrain, while the US ABCP market remains in free fall (it declined for a tenth straight week, dropping by around 25% within three months, see figure 1.11).
- October 24: Ugly Q3 earnings figures from Merrill Lynch (net loss of USD 2.31 bn) and rumors about write-downs from AIG reflect the on-going nervousness in the market.
- October 31: The Fed delivers another 25 bp rate cut, while the Crossover closes at 338 bp, which translates into a moderate widening of 12 bp on a monthly basis. However, it is around 60 bp wider than the lowest level we have seen during October.

1.3.12 November 2007: The transmission channels of the crisis are getting into full swing

Sentiment at the beginning of November turns to negative again. All efforts by global central banks and bailout plans like the Super-SIV could not yet help markets to restore confidence. Things did not improve, and investors start to doubt whether monetary authorities have the appropriate instruments to combat the real cause of the crisis. The basic transmission mechanisms are still intact and spillover effects are becoming more apparent. The vicious cycle triggered by the subprime meltdown is getting into full swing. This is very well illustrated by the IMF in chart 19, which highlights all the market segments that are involved in the crisis and shows how spillover effects are transferred among the major actors in the subprime show.

- November 1: The positive impulses from the FOMC meeting were short lived. On the contrary, credit and stock markets return to crisis mode again. Citigroup announces a further USD 8-11 bn of subprime-related write-downs and losses. Charles Prince resigns as Chairman and Chief Executive. There are rising fears that the bank has to sell assets, raise capital, or cut its dividend, which causes Citi's stock to fall by about 7%! Moreover, there was also bad news for Credit Suisse, which announced Q3 CHF 1.1 bn of write-downs on structured products. Market sentiment is deteriorating further! The Crossover starts at 317 bp but widens to 337 bp towards the end of the trading session.

- November 5: The next round of the crisis begins, with so-called monoline insurers being in the limelight. *Monoline insurers* are obscure but important players who guarantee the timely repayment of interest and principal on bonds in the event that the issuer defaults. The largest monoliners are MBIA and Ambac. The two were set up in the 1970s as insurers of municipal bonds. The total outstanding amount of paper insured by monoliners reached USD 2.4 tn in 2006. In recent years,

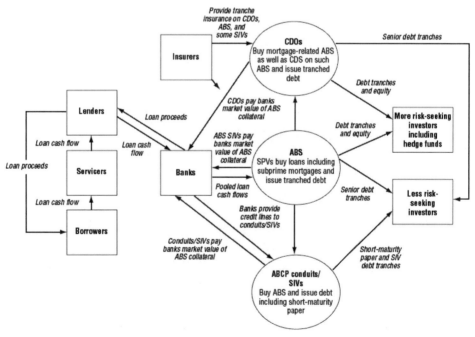

Fig. 1.18: The transmission channel of the subprime turmoil
Source: IMF

much of the monoliners' growth came from structured products, such as asset-backed bonds, and from the now vituperated collateralized debt obligations (CDOs). While the bulk of the financial guarantors' business is insuring securities such as municipal bonds, they have also insured some USD 100 bn of CDOs, most of which are pools of mortgage loans to borrowers with spotty credit histories. Only about 5% of the risky policies on that debt have been ceded to reinsurers. Fitch states that it may downgrade US bond insurers if they fail their renewed capital test. A downgrade will have a severe impact on the business of the financial guarantors, as maintaining an AAA rating is of strategic importance. Moreover, downgrades might trigger another wave of forced selling, as a huge part of investment in high quality paper is driven by these ratings. The risk of another downward spiral is significant. Ac-

Loss Estimates for ABS and ABS CDOs Since February 2007

	Outstanding (Billions of U.S. dollars)	Percent of Total Mortgage Debt	Assumed Default (Percent of Origination)	Assumed Loss Severity (In percent)	Estimated Cash Flow Loss (Billions of U.S. dollars)	Estimated Mark-to-Market Loss (Billions of U.S. dollars)
Subprime total	1,300	15	25	45	–145	
Alt-A total	1,000	11	7	35	~25	
Nonprime Total	2,300				–170	
ABS						~65–70
ABS CDOs						–120–130
Total ABS and ABS CDOs						–200
	AAA	AA/A	BBB/BBB–	Not Rated		
	Mortgage ABS Issuance (Billions of U.S. dollars)					
2004	258	41	9	13		
2005	283	57	13	11		
2006	281	54	14	28		
	Estimated ABX Implied Mark-to-Market Losses of Mortgage ABS Tranches (Percent of outstanding par)					
2004	2–3	5–10	8–10	n.a.		
2005	4–5	10–20	20–22	n.a.		
2006	7–8	20–40	48–50	n.a.		
	ABS CDO Issuance (Billions of U.S. dollars)					
2004	35	3	1	6		
2005	61	8	3	23		
2006	135	15	5	11		
	Estimated Tranched ABX (TABX) Implied Mark-to-Market Losses of CDO Tranches (Percent of outstanding par)					
2004–06	40–70	40–60	40–45	n.a.		

Sources: Lehman Brothers; Merrill Lynch; and IMF staff estimates.
Note: Estimated mark-to-market losses are computed as the total of all estimated losses in the second and fourth sections of the lower panel for the ABS and ABS CDO tranches, respectively. ABS = asset-backed security; ABX = synthetic asset-backed security; CDO = collateralized debt obligation; TABX = tranched asset-backed security.

Fig. 1.19: IMF's loss estimates for ABS and CDOs in the first months of "subprimemania"
Source: IMF

cording to recent financial markets estimations, accumulated subprime losses may reach a few hundred billion USD. In the chart below, we point out the IMF's estimates regarding marked-to-market losses in subprime-linked market segments thus far. The IMF calculates losses to amount to around USD 200 bn. The IMF's figures trigger a flood of publications which include loss estimates from the subprime turmoil up to more than USD 1,000 bn. The explanation for the huge deviations in loss calculation depends on which effects are included. Direct subprime losses only can be calculated very easily. If we know the outstanding volume of subprime loans, we just have to assign a default rate (foreclosures) and a loss-given default (based on an anticipated price decline of the houses that have to be sold after the borrower defaulted). These costs range in the low-triple-digit billion area (USD 250-300 bn). However, the majority of costs in a financial crisis are linked to second- and third-round effects, including mark-to-market losses in other market segments; for example, the securitized credit card business. In the end, a deterioration of the economic environment leads to declining future growth. Global GDP in 2006 was around USD 50,000 bn. A reduction in global growth of 1% can be transferred in an economic loss of around USD 500 bn. The Crossover edges up further and stands at the end of the day at 355 bp.

- November 7: The US dollar slides as traders bet the Fed will continue to opt for further rate cuts if the housing and credit crisis deepens. The euro sets a record high above USD 1.47; sterling reaches a 26-year high above USD 2.1. The Crossover ends the session almost unchanged at 356 bp.
- November 12: Update news on the Super-SIV: According to the NY Times, Bank of America, Citigroup, and JP Morgan Chase reach an agreement on a back-up fund of at least USD 75 bn to help stabilize credit markets. The agreement includes several changes that simplify earlier proposals. According to the newspaper,

> SIVs will no longer have to get the approval of at least 75% of their investors if they want to participate in the back-up fund. And the back-up fund will not distinguish between the assets it buys from each SIV; instead, it will assign the same risk level to all its troubled securities.

A higher fee structure has been proposed, and several crucial tax, legal, and regulatory issues are awaiting approval. The banks will now begin to ask financial institutions to contribute to the fund, which can be raised at the end of the year. The most important feature of the new concept is that not only high-quality assets should be bought by the fund (which was the initial idea). Although the fund can have a positive impact on the structured credit market as it might help ease forced selling pressure from troubled SIVs, the Crossover widens further to 380 bp.

- November 14: Fitch summarizes its recent rating action regarding CDOs on structured finance assets and concludes that 76 formerly AAA-rated tranches were downgraded directly to junk status, affecting a total volume of about USD 14 bn! Fitch stated in a recent report that the weakness of the US housing market is likely to have a broader impact on domestic demand and on the labor market. A weaker economic environment will also translate into rising pressure on other sectors that have so far been immune to the subprime woes. Fitch also expects rising delinquencies in the CMBS market on the back of liquidity constraints as a direct effect of the subprime turmoil. In figure 1.21, we depict the number of downgrades by Fitch since September 2005. The upgrade-

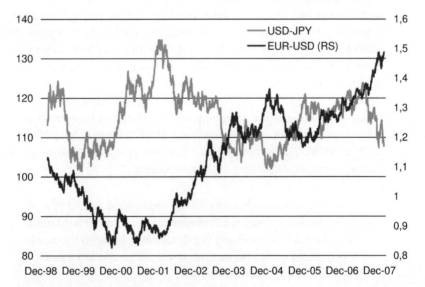

Fig. 1.20: The effect on the USD-EUR exchange rate

downgrade ratio declined from 4.8 in 2006 (full-year) to 0.5 (!) in the first ten months until October 2007. This was driven by the RMBS segment, which is the heavyweight in Fitch's structured credit universe. The ugly news is that things will not get better soon. Fitch also states that the default rates of 2006 RMBS vintages will be almost double the 2005 figures. The worst vintage, however, is H1 2007! The agency has downgraded thus far 11% of the USD 173 bn 2006 RMBS vintage rated by itself. High loan-to-value and debt-to-income ratios combined with low document collateral requirements are a potential threat for all these vintages, while there are not many reasons to believe in a rapid recovery of the US housing market from an economic perspective. Investors expect more to come, as it is hard to believe that the huge subprime exposure disappeared without leaving any significant traces on the balance sheets. The Crossover closes at 358 bp.

- November 15: Barclays writes down a total of GBP 1.3 bn in Q3. However, the market reaction to that is positive, as market participants had expected more. S&P cuts the Bear Stearns Credit Rating on subprime write-downs of USD 1.2 bn, although their share price rises after the news, since fears had been worse. Moreover, the Fed pumps USD 47.25 bn in temporary reserves into the banking system in its biggest combined daily injection of cash funds since shortly after 9/11. The Crossover stands at 370 bp.
- November 19: News from the insurance industry is hitting the screens! Swiss Re has to write down USD 1.07 bn on two transactions backed

RMBS Downgrades: September 2005–September 2007

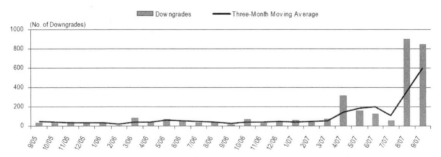

Fig. 1.21: RMBS downgrades in the US in the center of the subprime turmoil
Source: Fitch

by CDOs and other mostly mortgage-related securities. While the stock
drops by 10% on this announcement, Swiss Re's 5Y CDS spreads widen
only moderately. Swiss Re cuts estimates of the value of its CDOs to
zero and the subprime securities to 62% of their original value, bring-
ing the market value of the portfolio to CHF 3.6 billion, the company
says. The second leg of the spread widening is expanding rapidly, with
the iTraxx Crossover approaching the psychologically important 400 bp
level, and this time the situation appears to be even worse, with fears
and concerns rising in almost all areas of financial markets. There
is no segment in the financial industry that has not been hit: investment banks, commercial banks, monoliners, and lately also insurance
companies and the big US mortgage agencies Fannie Mae and Freddie
Mac. Market participants are beginning to realize more and more that
this crisis will not disappear soon, and concerns are rising about whether
central banks have the appropriate tools to fight the crisis. So far, their
actions have provided only temporary relief. The Crossover closing level
is 390 bp.

- November 20: Freddie Mac reports a loss of USD 2 bn (the largest
  ever). Moreover, the company may be forced to cut its dividend and
  raise more capital due to the deterioration of the US housing market.
  Freddie Mac's shares dropped about 30% and its 5Y CDS spread jumped
  to 65 bp from 42 bp. Fannie Mae's stock price is down by 25% and its
  5Y CDS is also trading at 65 bp, increasing from 51 bp the day before
  (please refer to figure 1.22). Moreover, the outlook is bearish, as Fannie Mae says that average home prices could fall by 4%, leading the
  company's loan-loss ratio to double. Northern Rock shares drop almost
  50%, but rebound sharply on speculation that JC Flowers may bid for
  the company. In Euroland, the 3M Euribor spread climbs to almost 60
  bp from 50 bp the week before, signaling that the market may switch to
  a panic mode. The Crossover traded at 385 bp.
- November 22: The situation in credit markets continues to worsen. The
  housing market in the US deteriorates further, with US Treasury Secretary Henry Paulsen repeating that "US home loan defaults will be significantly bigger in 2008 than in 2007" due to lower underwriting standards. The key indicator for the severity of spillover effects, the money
  market, still sends warning signals, with the 2Y Treasury Swap spread
  touching a nineteen-year high at around 105 bp. The structured credit
  universe remains under fire as around USD 40 bn were downgraded by

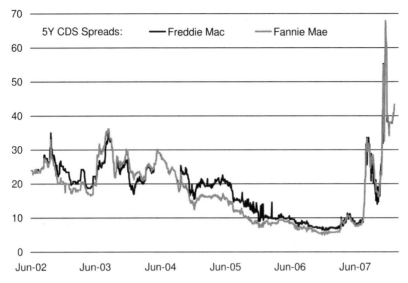

70 ——

5Y CDS Spreads: ——Freddie Mac ——Fannie Mae

60 ——

50 ——

40 ——

30 ——

20 ——

10 ——

0 ——
Jun-02   Jun-03   Jun-04   Jun-05   Jun-06   Jun-07

Fig. 1.22: Fanny Mae and Freddie Mac get hit

Fitch and S&P, while some CPDOs referring to financials only trade at 29% in cash terms! Last but not least, bond insurers remain on center stage, with ACA rumored to be downgraded, which equals the end of its business model, while S&P cuts ratings on two mortgage insurers. The Crossover again exceeds the 400 bp threshold!

- November 23: First CPDO of UBS AG collapses after a drop of its net asset value to 10% forced it to sell its holdings. The Series 103 Financial Basket Tyger Notes, which had a top Aaa rating as recently as September, was downgraded nine levels to C, the lowest ranking, from Ba2, Moody's says. The CPDO, sold by UBS through its Elm BV unit, had a value of EUR 47.5 mn and had been cut twice by Moody's in the past two months. While the CPDO hype emerged in 2006, the construction principle was rather straightforward. The aggressive leverage mechanism ("if you are in trouble – double") characterized these so-called first-generation CPDOs. A CPDO is a leveraged investment in a liquid CDS portfolio (in general index swaps); the leverage will be increased in case the net asset value of the underlying portfolio declines (which means that spreads widen). At first glance, these structures will come under pressure in case the positive carry and roll-down effects will be offset by wider spreads and hence the net asset value of the structure declines. However. back-testing showed that CPDOs even survived 2001/2002 scenarios, as a dramatic widening was offset by the following strong tightening that more than offset the widening as leverage increased. That said, cash-in events of potential CPDO transactions if they would have been issued before 2001/2002 would have taken place within the maturity of the structures. Unfortunately, this proved not to be the case in 2007! The market for CPDOs is rather small; however, there are two very negative impulses for these instruments. First, especially first-time structured credit investors bought this kind of product. These investors are completely losing confidence in the market and will probably stay away for a long period of time. Second, investors have been forced to accept that a AAA-rated structure can default within only a few months, while destroying more than 90% of the initial value of the investment! This triggers an interesting debate about the question "Is a triple-A a triple-A?" Definitely not. And this is something investors fear! The Crossover closes at 381 bp.

- November 26: The recapitalization of the US banking system starts! Citi sells a USD 7.5 bn stake to Abu Dhabi Investment Authority (ADIA). The investment will boost Citi's capital level, which came under pressure due to ongoing subprime losses and write-downs. Citi is selling 4.9% to ADIA, which does not have special rights of ownership or control. In addition, HSBC provides USD 45 bn to support two of its SIVs, initially triggering a statement by Goldman that HSBC will probably have to write down another USD 12 bn. While the latest development in the market clearly shows that we are still in the center of the subprime cyclone, it is also obvious that there is no "muddling through" the subprime swamp. In any case, it is not very encouraging for those who still believe that the Super-SIV is a silver bullet in fighting the crisis. Obviously, HSBC decided to solve the SIV problem on its own, not relying on the effectiveness of the Super-SIV. A rising number of investors are discussing the long-term impact on the securitization market, the reduced earnings generation power of the financial industry, and last but not least, the reduction in growth as the major burdens of the subprime turmoil. The Crossover stays at wide levels at 379 bp.
- November 27: Cheyne Finance, a USD 7 bn SIV, finds a solution for restructuring its debt. Credit investors can either roll their debt into longer maturities, accompanied by a transfer of the assets into a new vehicle, or receive a reduced cash payment. Although the SIV avoids a

fire sale of assets, the solution still causes potentially substantial losses for the involved debt investors. This story fits with the newsflow regarding "solutions" for distressed SIVs. Moreover, losses on structured-finance CDOs (portfolio deals that refer to other structured assets, such as subprime mezz pieces, as underlying) may cause greater losses at the largest US banks than previously anticipated. JP Morgan expects that these losses would double to USD 77 bn, while the whole market will have to digest CDO losses up to USD 260 bn. The Crossover remains unimpressed, trading at 378 bp.

- November 29: LBBW, the largest German Landesbank, reports that its Q3 figures will fall on EUR 800 mn in charges related to the subprime mess. Stress in the money markets increases further, with Euribor spreads now being higher than in August and September. The difference between the 1M Euribor and the 1M Eonia swap jumps from 17 bp to almost 80 bp, as the 1M contract termination rolls into the new year. In the end, the Crossover closes November at 349 bp, some 10 bp wider on a month-to-month basis.

1.3.13 December 2007: "Hope Now"

The subprime crisis is now fully flooding the financial market. In the center of the turmoil is the banking industry, also reflected in the ongoing malfunctioning of the money market. The liquidity squeeze in the banking sector is also reflected in the diverging spread trend between the synthetic universe (iTraxx) and cash bonds. While synthetic indices, which are unfunded and hence do not require liquidity, had traded well below their peak during the summer, cash bond spreads already reached the highest level since the beginning of 2003!

- December 4: Drugmaker GlaxoSmithKline sells a EUR 3.5 bn bond (5Y and 10Y tranche), priced at mid-swaps plus 85 bp and mid-swaps plus 115 bp, respectively. There is high demand (order book about EUR 6 bn), which does not come as a surprise: The 5Y bond is priced at around 45 bp above the respective CDS spread (although 5Y CDs widened about 15-20 bp during the same day)! Buy the bond and buy protection is obviously a screaming no-brainer, while the spread premium in the primary market is another signal for the current liquidity squeeze. Cash credit markets worsened over the last few weeks, whereas in the synthetics universe the situation looks less challenging than was the case in the summer. There is still stress in the system, which is also reflected in the fact that the Federal Home Loan Bank system announces that its outstanding debt rose by USD 32 bn to USD 1.18 tn in November. The debt growth confirms the funding distress in the banking system as it becomes very expensive for financials to borrow outside the system. The Crossover trades at 366 bp, around 140 bp below the spread peak during the summer.

- December 6: US Treasury Secretary Paulson provides more details on the "Hope Now" initiative. The subprime rescue plan includes an interest rate freeze of five years for subprime borrowers, which should help 1.2 mn Americans to keep their homes, according to President Bush. The freeze applies to those mortgage loans that are scheduled to reset between January 2008 and July 2010. Borrowers whose credit scores are below 660 will be given priority. While the freeze will obviously provide some relief stemming from the huge volumes that have to be reset in coming months (and especially as it will be of help for some Americans who are in danger of losing their homes), it is quite clear that this is not a final solution to the subprime problem. First of all, there is criticism regarding the timing (too late) and the amplitude of the rescue plan (up to 2.8 mn mortgage loan foreclosures are expected in 2008 and 2009). Moreover, delinquencies already occur before the reset date takes place, which means that there are some borrowers who are not sensitive to mortgage rates, and hence any relaxation from this side will not help them out. For those borrowers, it is also no relief that 30Y mortgage yields in the United States trade at the lowest level since September 2005. According to Reuters, the Mortgage Bankers Association's chief economist Doug Duncan said that about 994,000 US households are already in the process of foreclosure. Last but not least, the freeze directly affects the terms of securitization deals. Investors of lower qualities might miss interest payments, and IR test failures might be triggered. This could cause a wave of litigation from subordinated tranche holders, which is not very helpful to restore confidence in distressed ABS markets. Moreover, lower-rated tranches might feel additional downgrade pressure. Money markets still trading in systemic shock mode and the ongoing slump in the ABCP market reflect that not everyone is as "hopish" as equity markets are. Moreover, signs that the crisis is impacting also the consumer loan area are fueling concerns that the subprime tentacles are already engulfing the US economy. Delinquencies in the auto loan segment rises to the highest level in years. The 30D delinquency rate for auto loans of the 2006 vintage increased to 4.5% by the end of September from 2.9% the month before. Among the subprime auto loans even 12% were delinquent (the highest level since 2002), up from 11.1% one month before. So the next subprime crisis is already knocking on the door, this time in the auto loan segment, which makes up about 20% of the non-mortgage ABS market. Spread moves are more noise rather than the establishment of a major trend. The Crossover closes at 355 bp.

- December 10: UBS is shocking the markets again. The bank announces that it will need to write down another USD 10 bn due to the subprime crisis. The bank said that it will raise USD 13 bn in capital by selling stakes to investors in Singapore and the Middle East. The bank expects a loss also in the fourth quarter and may even have a full-year loss in 2007. The Crossover trades at 340 bp.

- December 11: As expected, the Fed delivers the next rate cut, a 25 bp decrease of the Fed Funds target rate as well as of the discount rate. However, equity markets immediately start to drop after the announcement, as investors had hoped to see 50 bp (if not in the target rate, then at least in the discount rate). The 50 bp rate cut in September triggered a rally that lasted three weeks, the 25 bp rate in late October triggered a rally that lasted three hours, and this time the Dow Jones plunges by 2.5%. Market participants realize that while the Fed can flood the market with liquidity, it will not hinder the credit crisis from weighing on the real economy. Freddie Mac's CEO says that he expects losses of around USD 10-12 bn on the company's mortgage book. This is due to the gloomy outlook for the housing market, which he expects to decline by as much as 10%. The company's stock fell as much as 10% on this announcement. The Crossover is living its own life, closing the day tighter at 334 bp.

- December 12: The first concerted action by central banks since September 2001 reinsures the market that at least monetary authorities are doing everything necessary to solve the problem and to fight the symptoms of the crisis! The Fed announces that it plans to ease elevated short-term funding pressures by injecting cash to banks through auctions and providing USD 24 billion in currency swap lines to the European and Swiss central banks. The Fed is coordinating the measures with the European Central Bank, Bank of England, Bank of Canada, and Swiss National Bank. In contrast to previous liquidity injections, the two major differences from the current one are that (i) the Fed provides liquidity for a longer period and (ii) the eligibility criteria are rather lax. The Fed will auction term funds to banks against a wide variety of collateral, while stating that all generally sound institutions can participate. By allowing the Federal Reserve to inject term funds through a broader range of counterparties and against a broader range of collateral than open market operations, this facility triggers initially a very positive reaction in the market, while the Crossover remains almost unchanged at 335 bp.

- December 18: Moody's releases a summary of rating actions in the structured finance universe. Since the beginning of December, about USD 174 bn of CDOs related to the US mortgage market were put on review for downgrade. The rating agency downgraded USD 50.9 bn of CDOs made up of structured-finance securities in November, or about 9.4% of the total. Moody's, S&P and Fitch Ratings issued a record 2,007 downgrades on CDOs last month. Moody's also said that it expects more negative rating actions in the coming months. The iTraxx Crossover closed at 349 bp.
- December 19: The re-capitalization of the US banking industry continues. Morgan Stanley announces again a multi-billion dollar write-down (USD 9.4 bn in Q4, USD 5.7 bn above the amount announced at the end of October). China Investment Corp (which already acquired a 9.4% stake in Blackstone for USD 3 bn in May) announces that it will inject USD 5 bn of equity, amounting to 10% of Morgan Stanley's current market cap. CIC becomes the second largest shareholder of Morgan Stanley after State Street Corp. The Crossover closed unchanged at 349 bp.
- December 20: Bear Stearns reports its first-ever loss (USD 854 mn) after write-downs of mortgage holdings and trading losses. Moody's cut the company's credit rating to A2 from A1. Moreover, Merrill Lynch stated that it might receive as much as USD 5 bn in equity from Temasek, Singapore's state-owned fund. With this step, Merrill's new CEO John Thain follows Citigroup, UBS, Morgan Stanley and others who already received cash injections from Asian sovereign wealth funds in order to restore their stressed capital base due to subprime losses. So far, governments from the Middle East and Asia invested about USD 25 bn in Wall Street firms following subprime losses. In addition, the negative newsflow regarding the monoline business continues as MBIA

discloses that it guarantees USD 8.1 bn in risky CDOs. The company's stock drops by 25% and is now down by about 70% from the year-high. Trading activity in the iTraxx Crossover is close to zero, while the index still trades at 349 bp.

- December 28: The effect from the subprime crisis on the LBO market returns into the limelight as Citigroup, Goldman Sachs, Morgan Stanley, and JPMorgan Chase are quoted as offering discounts of as much as 10% on their LBO transactions to clear a USD 231 bn backlog of high-yield bonds and loans. The Crossover closes, after lackluster trading, at 340 bp.

All in all, 2007 was a dramatic year for the global banking sector. According to Bloomberg data, realized write-downs and losses in the banking sector in 2007 amount to USD 97.2 bn, while analysts expect additional write-downs and losses of USD 34 bn, amounting to a total of USD 131.2 bn. So far. The year-end closing level of the iTraxx Crossover was 338 bp.

1.3.14 2008

- January 2: It was a weak start into 2008. Driven by the biggest decline in the ISM manufacturing reading in five years and a record oil price of USD 100 per barrel, global stock markets tumbled and credit spreads widened. The DJIA lost 1.7% on its first trading day and the iTraxx Crossover widened about 15 bp to 352 bp.
- January 8: Ratings for Victoria Finance, a USD 13 bn structured investment vehicle run by Ceres Capital partners, were slashed from AA to B- by S&P. A few days later, S&P cut Victoria Finance's ratings to D as the vehicle failed to pay commercial paper due on January 10. The Crossover widened again, closing the day at 390 bp.
- January 9: Rumors that Citigroup and Merrill Lynch are in talks with foreign governments to get fresh capital are accompanied by headlines that Bear Stearns is closing an ABS hedge fund that held about USD 900 mn in investments linked to mortgages. The fund's value dropped more than 20% in November alone. The Crossover closed above the 400 bp threshold (at 401 bp).
- January 10: Investors expect the Fed to cut rates and Fed Chairman Ben Bernanke pushes in the same direction as he said that more rate cuts "may well be necessary". It is thus no surprise that the futures market implied probability for a 50 bp rate cut at the next FOMC meeting in

late January jumped to 88%. The Crossover ended almost unchanged at 399 bp.

- January 14: Deutsche Bank's CEO Josef Ackermann stated that he expects a "continued collapse in market prices in the months to come" and that the banking industry has "to pay the price for its mistakes". Finally, he mentioned that "if you were to take all the loans back on the balance sheet (instead of securitizing them), you would have to have much more capital to support it, and that would cause a slowdown in lending, which is essential for economic growth". The Crossover widened moderately to 406 bp.

- January 15: Citigroup announced a USD 18 bn write-off. At the same time, however, the bank announced plans to raise capital from private investors (Sandy Weill and Prince Alwaleed bin Talal) and institutional ones (the Singapore and Kuwait governments) and to cut its dividend (by 41%). S&P immediately downgraded Citigroup by one notch to AA- (outlook remains negative). The whole financial segment came under tremendous pressure, and global central banks reacted with additional liquidity injections (Fed, ECB, SNB conducted USD-denominated auctions). Simultaneously, the re-capitalization of the US banking system continues (see table 1.1), with Merrill receiving fresh capital (USD 6.6 bn) from some investors (KIA, Korean Investment Corp, Mizuho). Moreover, the subprime crisis returned to Germany, with Hypo Real Estate announcing a profit slump of 27% on the back of continued weakness in financial markets, as the US subprime crisis requires a revaluation of its CDO investments. HRE shares tumbled 35% and S&P reacted immediately and placed the company outlook to negative. The Crossover remained stable at 407 bp.

Tab. 1.1: Re-capitalization of the US banking system

Company	Infusion in USD mn	Who	Announcement	Instrument	Type of Deal
Citi	14,500		January 15, 2008	Convertible Preferred Securities	Private & Public
(1)	12,500			Convertible Preferred Securities	Private
Of which:	6,880	Government of Singapore Investment Corporation			
	5,620	(a) Capital Research Global Investors (b) Capital World Investors (c) Kuwait Investment Authority (d) New Jersey Division of Investments (e) Prince Al Waleed bin Talal (f) Sanford Weill and The Weill Family Foundation			
(2)	2,000		January 15, 2008	Convertible Preferred Securities	Public
Merrill Lynch	6,600	Institutional Investors	January 15, 2008	Convertible Preferred Stock	Private
Of which:	6,600	Korea Investment Corporation Kuwait Investment Authority Mizuho Corporate Bank			
Morgan Stanley	5,000	China Investment Corporation	December 19, 2007	Equity Units, Mandatory Convers. into Common Stock	Private
Total, US Names	26,100				
UBS	11,930		January 15, 2008	Mandatory Convertible Bonds	Private
(1)	10,095	Government of Singapore Investment Corporation			
(2)	1,835	(Unnamed) Middle East Investor			Private
Total, US & EU	38,030				

The chronology
of a crisis – The
US subprime
crisis

- January 16: Pressure on the biggest bond insurers MBIA and Ambac is rising. Moody's said that it may cut Ambac's AAA rating after the bond insurer reported higher than initially announced write-downs on securities it guarantees of USD 3.5 bn. The company's shares dropped about 40% on the back of the news. In total, the shares are down by almost 90% from the high in May 2007. The 5Y CDS spread trades at 900 bp, but the curve is highly inverse, with the 1Y CDS trading well above 1,000 bp. MBIA is also in deep trouble. 1Y CDS contracts rose to an 18.6% upfront payment. MBIA's shares were down by 16%, with a cumulated loss of 80% since the high in January 2007. S&P said that it will re-assess monoliner ratings, only one month after it affirmed AAA ratings, as losses on subprime mortgages were higher than anticipated by the rating agency. The Crossover widened on the back of the negative news to 420 bp.
- January 17: This is the ugliest trading day since summer 2007, when spreads peaked during the first wave of panic. Markets start to price in a recession in the US. The DJIA dropped almost 3% and credit markets were also hit hard, as the iTraxx Main widened more than 5 bp during the day to around 75 bp and closed at 72 bp. The Crossover jumped above 450 bp and closed only slightly below this level. This means that, since the beginning of the year, the iTraxx Crossover had widened by more than 100 bp and the Main by more than 20 bp. Merrill Lynch's USD 10 bn loss didn't help to stabilize the market, although the immediate reaction was quite modest. 5Y senior spreads widened by 10 bp to the 150 bp area. However, when the Philly Fed index plunged to -20.9, credit markets capitulated. Spreads widened rapidly with no bids around that could stop the blowout. The Crossover closed the day at 445 bp.
- January 22: Following the strongest drop since 9/11, the 75 bp emergency rate cut by the Fed turned around market sentiment and equity markets closed flat, while credit spreads even tightened. All synthetics reached record highs, with the Crossover trading at 530 bp around lunchtime. In the afternoon session, especially synthetics benefited from declining risk aversion on the back of the rate cut. Despite the improving sentiment, negative headlines from the subprime front continued to hit the market. Ambac figures looked incredibly worrisome (loss of USD 33 per share). Nevertheless, there was also good news! Following the shockwaves from the monoline industry, governmental

authorities finally reacted. The New York State Insurance Department announced, "It is continuing to actively monitor the major bond insurance companies and to work with those companies and others to help stabilize the market". The Crossover closed the day at 483 bp.

- January 23: More and more Asian banks announced the magnitude of their involvement in the subprime crisis. The Korean Woori bank said that it would write down another USD 250 mn in subprime-related losses for Q4. The Crossover remained relatively unchanged in a unspectacular trading session, closing at 486 bp.
- January 29: Negative headlines from the micro-fundamental side continue to hit screens. Analysts are continuously revising upward their forecasts for further write-downs in the industry, which does not come as a surprise. Based on the standard procedure to use ABX indices to estimate expected losses in subprime-linked cash instruments, the initial calculation by the IMF in August 2007 (mark-to-market losses during the first wave of the subprime turmoil of USD 200 bn) proved to be far too optimistic from the current perspective. Write-downs and credit losses currently amount to around USD 170-180 bn so far, while there is no doubt that more is yet to come. The Crossover ended up at 439 bp.
- January 30: The Fed cut interest rates by another 50 bp to 3%. With this step, it reduced the Fed funds target rate by 2.25% within five months. However, while the first rate cut triggered a three-week rally, the most recent one added to the bearish sentiment. As expected, the DJIA jumped by 1.5% on the announcement, but gave up all the gains within an hour. Fitch downgraded Financial Guaranty Insurance, the world's fourth-largest bond insurer, by two levels from AAA to AA. Moody's and S&P are reported to also be reevaluating the ratings. This event brings the focus back on the problems of the monoliner industry. Ambac's 5Y CDS spreads are above 1300 bp (in fact, they trade on an upfront basis of around 25%) and MBIA's at 1100 bp. Merrill Lynch announced plans to exit the business of underwriting collateralized debt obligations and other structured credit products after the securities led to a record loss. The company's new CEO John Thain said: "We are not going to be in the CDO and structured-credit types of businesses". Closing levels in the Crossover: 449 bp.
- February 5: The ISM dropped to recession levels, the weakest figure we have seen since 2001. Following the disastrous labor market report the week before, signals are increasing that a recession in the US will be

inevitable. The Crossover closed above the 500 bp threshold for the first time since summer 2007 (at 504 bp).

- February 7: MBIA raised USD 1 bn by selling shares at USD 12.15, which compares to the prior day's closing price of USD 14.20. Although the amount of USD 1 bn appears to be limited in comparison to the losses that were in discussion so far, it shows that bond insurers are fighting an imminent collapse. Apparently, the major threat is for the holding companies, as their existence depends on the approval of insurance regulators to continue to extract dividend payments from the operating insurance entities. Pressure comes from activist investor William Ackman, founder of Pershing Square Capital Management, who recently published a so-called open source model for the monoliner industry (see table 1.2), and who urged Ben Bernanke and Hank Paulson in an open letter to put an end to a bank-led bailout of bond insurers, calling the effort "ill-advised". Such a bailout would obviously hurt his short-selling strategy on the monoliners. The Crossover widened to 524 bp.
- February 8: Rumors regarding the unwinding of correlation books out of France triggered record spread levels in the synthetic universe, with the Main almost touching the magic 100 bp level. Markets are currently experiencing exactly the opposite of the technical bid, which was a major pillar of the credit bubble which emerged in 2004 and lasted until H1 2007. Technical-driven selling pressure is triggering over- and undershooting from what we would call the "fundamental truth". The Crossover remains at elevated levels, ending up at 531 bp.
- February 12: Warren Buffett's announcement to offer to take over the municipal bond business from the monoliners turned around the sentiment and triggered a rally in stock prices and a retightening in credit spreads. The Crossover edged wider to 553 bp.
- February 14: Capital infusion or break-up – these are the two options for the monoliners. Moody's downgraded the insurance rating of the monoliner FGIC by six notches to A3 after the company failed to raise enough capital to compensate for losses on subprime-mortgage guarantees. Moreover, the agency kept the ratings on watch negative. FGIC is now no longer rated AAA by any rating agency. Moreover, the senior unsecured rating on the holding company was lowered to junk status at Moody's (from Aa2 to Ba1). The Crossover closed at 542 bp.

- February 19: Credit markets remain preoccupied with headline risk from banks: Credit Suisse said that it wrote down the value of some asset-backed securities in the first quarter by USD 2.85 bn, just one week after official earnings releases. Net income in the first quarter to date will be reduced by about USD 1 bn, the Zurich-based bank said in an e-mailed statement. The write-downs reflect "significant adverse first quarter 2008 market developments" and are the result of an internal review that is continuing, Credit Suisse said. The bank also "identified mismarkings and pricing errors by a small number of traders" in the structured credit trading business. The Crossover widened to 561 bp.
- February 20: Hedging activities from structured credit desks triggered a further dramatic widening on the back of no significant additional negative newsflow. The Crossover reached an all-time high at 625 bp. The index closed at 594 bp.

Tab. 1.2: Cumulative loss estimates according to the opinion of Pershing Square Capital Management

Insured/Wrapped Product	Underlying Collateral	AMBAC (USD bn)	MBIA (USD bn)
CDO	ABS (RMBS)	6,953	5,738
CDO squared	CDOs	498	-
RMBS	Closed end second liens (CES)	1,884	2,810
RMBS	Home equity lines of credit (HELOCs)	1,002	2,949
RMBS	Subprime mortgages	701	9
RMBS	Alt-A mortgages	567	129
Total		11,606	11,634

The deadline of this book forces us to stop here! Although this means that when this book is published, we will know much more about the medium- to long-term impact on the crisis and further spillover effects, the subprime turmoil in 2007 still provides an almost perfect paradigm for a credit crisis. In addition, we will feel the effects from the subprime shock for a very long time. By showing the vicious cycle in crises times using a real-world example, it allows us to explain the basic mechanism of a credit crisis.

1.3.15 The subprime meltdown is a perfect paradigm for a credit crisis

Why is the subprime shock such a good example for a credit crisis? Quite simply, it includes all ingredients which are necessary for a full-fledged credit crisis. In figure 1.23, we show the complex mechanisms behind the crisis that allow a relatively small segment in financial markets to spill over onto the whole financial system, and, in the end, onto the real economy.

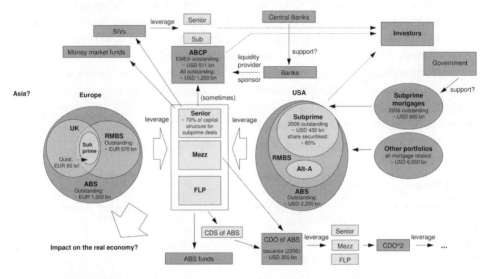

Fig. 1.23: The subprime turmoil as a paradigm for a credit crisis

The whole story started with declining house prices in the United States following two decades of tremendous growth in the US mortgage market. The housing price decline itself did not come as a surprise; it was the logical consequence of the strong growth we have seen before. However, the latest period in the strong-performing US housing market was triggered by the availability of tools which allowed banks to originate mortgage risk without taking the risk on their own balance sheet.

The strong growth of the securitization business and the innovative power in the credit derivatives and structured credit market allowed banks to create more risks than they would have created if they would have taken all risks on their own balance sheets. CDOs as a funding tool to extend the housing boom triggered a deviation of prices from what we would call fair value. In addition, special instruments on the loan side (teaser notes or 2/28 loans) have been used to allow borrowers with low credit scores to participate in and to benefit from the booming US housing market, a symbol for the American Dream. According to the famous "implode-O-Meter" (www.ml-implode.com), the subprime turmoil caused 204 major US lending operations to "implode" at the end of 2007. According to the webpage, "imploded" does not necessarily mean operations are ceased permanently: it can mean bankruptcy filing, temporary but open-ended halting of major operations, or a "fire-sale" acquisition. However, it shows how severe the long-term effects of a "normalization" of housing prices can be.

The excessive use of credit derivatives has also increased leverage in the system, which is (besides excessive liquidity) definitely a major parameter for asset price inflation. The broad use of derivatives at the same time when many specific market segments already showed signs of overheating (e.g., the leveraged loan or LBO business), and a declining quality of the underlying structures to increase the return in an environment where risk premiums traded close to historical lows, made the financial system as a whole very vulnerable to the bursting of the bubble.

Exactly this happened when the US housing market simply stopped growing! However, the involvement of so many different parties that all participated and benefited from the same system was necessary to allow the shockwaves from the mortgage market to spill over onto almost every part of the financial market. And it also triggers the infection of many market participants, causing the crisis to leave the mortgage banking industry and flood the whole financial industry, including monoline insurers, conduits, and money market funds. Hedge funds have so far proved pretty resilient against the shock waves from the subprime crisis, although we estimate that almost 50% of equity pieces generated in the structured credit universe have been bought by the hedge fund industry. However, the broad use of credit derivatives in the industry also triggered some failures of funds, especially those which participated in the capital structure arbitrage business.

Besides the fact that globalization and geographical diversification also means that crises are no longer limited to a specific market (as painfully experienced by Germany's IKB and SachsenLB), we can learn from the subprime crisis that spillover effects are the real problem. The fall of Northern Rock, the end of the SIV market, the significant decline in the leveraged loan business, the spread explosion in leveraged super senior tranches, and the jump of systematic risk premiums in the money market have shown that the question is not whether a credit crisis will have an impact on the real economy, but only at what magnitude.

While we introduced many instruments, financial vehicles, and institutions without explaining them in detail, we will use the examples in the following chapters to explain the players and strategies, as well as instruments and markets. We will elaborate on the similarities of credit crises in general, as well as on specific differences. Also from this perspective, the subprime turmoil serves as a perfect example.

2
Credit Instruments

The last two quarters of 2007 were packed with remarkable headlines like the following one. Moody's and S&P downgraded the tranches of the so-called Carina CDO, a structured- finance CDO, backed by a portfolio of RMBS transactions. Among the downgraded tranches was also the super senior tranche with a volume of about USD 1 bn. On October 30, 2007, Moody's cut its initial Aaa rating for this tranche to B2, five notches below investment grade. One week later, S&P topped that rating action with a downgrade of its AAA rating to CCC-. This is a cut of 18 notches within a ratings scale that has 21 notches in total. From the ratings agencies perspective, this is close to a worst case. This can more or less only be topped by a direct default event of an AAA-rated security (for further insight into the quality of structured finance ratings see also Ref 1,2).

But how could it be that so many market participants, not only ratings agencies but also investors, were blindfolded by glossy product brochures and forgot about all necessary due diligence before putting their funds at stake, terribly underestimating the risks involved in these instruments? Besides lemming-like behavior – one had to be involved in structured finance, the most exciting area of financial markets of recent years – it was the complexity of the underlying risks accompanied by a seemingly high level of liquidity in the underlying structured credit markets that gave investors a false feeling about the manageability of the risk. Most – however not all – investors knew that these products were complicated, but they thought that they could get rid of the risk in case of a downturn. So investors were not only wrong about the pace of the fundamental deterioration in the structured credit arena, but also about the speed of the adaptation of credit markets: spreads blew out and liquidity dried up within a few days. Even managers of smaller exposure had no chance to escape this turmoil once it started, while the large players were obviously lost at sea.

The problem was that the underlying risk – the probability of joint defaults – is conceptually quite complex. Apart from market-implied default correlations, there are no reliable models out there that help portfolio managers to quantify this risk. Hence, investors and rating agencies used historical time series in order to assess the new structures. But recent history did not contain any period

Credit Crises. J. Felsenheimer and P. Gisdakis
Copyright © 2008 WILEY-VCH Verlag GmbH & Co. KGaA, Weinheim
ISBN: 978-3-527-50375-9

with similar exaggerations in terms of leverage in the market. Hence, the whole system was extremely vulnerable to external events. And what investors should never forget about credit risk is that it is an event risk! With a large degree of probability, nothing severe should happen; but if there is an event, the involved losses are huge. Since quantification of these small probabilities for defaults is so difficult, the market's reaction is dramatic with regard to changes in this probability structure. However, uncertainty is not a new concept in financial markets. And that's why risky products pay a premium. But what investors need to understand is how their portfolios perform given certain scenarios. A prerequisite for this is to understand the involved products in detail.

However, our readers also need to understand the characteristics of underlying instruments, as they are key to understanding the developments during the crisis. In the following chapter we introduce the basic risks and instruments in modern credit markets. We highlight the underlying economics of single-name instruments, such as cash bonds and CDS, but we will also characterize the most important properties and features of credit portfolio derivatives, such as CDOs and ABSs. However, in this chapter the focus is on the basic characteristics, while the more complex strategies and risks will be covered in the chapter 4.

2.1 Bonds

The concept of credit risk applies to various products and instruments. However, the first thing that comes to mind when thinking about credit risk will most probably be cash instruments, such as corporate bonds. Here, a borrower receives money from the lender and has to make interest and principal payments on the borrowed amount. The most basic corporate bond example would be a fixed-rate bullet bond, in which the coupon payments are fixed at issue date and the notional of the debt security will be redeemed in one lump sum at maturity. However, debt instruments vary in many different ways. Examples for important characteristics are the seniority level (i.e., senior versus sub), the coupon payment mechanism (i.e., fixed versus floating) and the amortization mechanism. In the following, we elaborate on the most important characteristics of cash instruments.

A quite common classification of cash credit instruments is the coupon payment style. Basically, the instrument can involve fixed-coupon payments, variable-coupon payments, or no coupon payment at all. The latter is usually called a zero-coupon bond. While these instruments are well known from the so-called government bond strips, they recently also arrived in the credit arena in the form of so-called pay-in-kind (PIK) notes. We elaborate a bid more on this instrument, because it highlights the reduced risk aversion of investors ahead of the crisis. In PIK notes, the coupon is not paid in cash but accrues until maturity of the bond, or until the issuer calls the security. They can be seen as an extreme form of negative amortization (which has been an important feature of subprime loans; see section 2.2). Typically, PIK notes are issued on the level of a holding company above the issuer of correspondingly high yield bonds. Hence, PIK notes are usually contractually subordinated to the high-yield issues. The proceeds of the note, in general, are paid out as a special dividend to the private equity (PE) sponsor. These proceeds are often used to bridge-finance his exit. Accordingly, PIK notes have a very short first-call option included, with the call price being near par. This limits the upside potential in terms of price gains. In case of promising exit candidates, the likelihood that the note is called within a very short period is high. Although the PE sponsors have a strong interest in the good performance of the company, as they will receive all excess proceeds from the exit, one may argue that the economic interest decreases, as the sponsors already receive a payment via the dividend. In case of default, the expected recovery rate is close to zero, which corresponds with a rating below existing cash-pay, high-yield bonds. In a default case, however, the investor may receive equity in case the company emerges from bankruptcy. Hence, the involved credit risk for the investor is quite high for this type of security, as the outstanding notional amount and the coupon payments for the whole lending period are at risk. In case the issuer defaults on such a security, the investor not only incurs a loss with respect to all future cash flows, but also with respect to the accrued coupon in the past. Although the risk of such instruments has been apparent, they could be sold easily to a spread-hungry investor base. This indicates how low the risk aversion has been ahead of the crisis.

While for a fixed coupon payment the structure is quite clear – the counterparties agree upon a specified coupon which is then paid on a regular basis – floating rate notes are more complicated, as the coupon is linked to an interest rate index. Very common indices are the Libor (London Interbank Offered Rate, provided by the British Bankers Association, BBA) and Euribor (Euro Interbank Offered Rate) interest indices, which are available on a daily basis covering coupon payment periods from one week up to twelve months. Both indices are derived based on the rate at which banks borrow money in the interbanking market. While the Libor is available in several currencies (including USD, GBP, JPY,

CHF and EUR), the Euribor is the major index for EUR-denominated variable debt. As an example, a variable-rate security denominated in EUR, which pays its coupon quarterly, may be linked to the 3M-Euribor. Following one coupon payment, the rate for the next coupon payment will be reset according to the level of interest rates derived by the interbanking market. Since the Libor and Euribor rates are derived from short-term borrowing rates from bank to bank (remaining time to maturity twelve months and below), they are also called money market rates. Usually, the term structure of the money market rates (i.e., the rates as a function of the remaining time to maturity) is driven by the market's expectation of the future development of the overnight lending rate, or in other words, by the expectation of central bank rates. Before the recent financial crisis, most market participants considered these money market activities more or less risk free. Hence, there was only a very limited and stable spread between the actual lending rate and the underlying risk-free interest rate. This risk-free rate is usually measured by referencing an Eonia-swap contract with the same maturity date. As a swap contract involves only the exchange of coupon payments and no principal exchange, the swap contract is usually considered as credit risk free. However, during the crisis, the cost of borrowing in the interbank market exceeded the risk-free interest rate level significantly and persistently, highlighting the extreme stress in the interbank market. As this stress was expressed in elevated Libor rates, the coupon payments of floating rate notes that refer to these indices were affected. They were up to one percentage point higher than the underlying interest rate level that is driven by the central bank rate.

The major advantage of a floating rate note is that the price sensitivity with respect to the underlying interest rate risk is fairly small, as the coupon payments of the note regularly adapt to the changes of the interest rate level. From a more technical perspective, this limited risk is due to the quite short interest rate duration (about the remaining time to the next coupon payment). In addition, since most of the floaters were viewed as products with a quite high credit quality – floating-rate securities have been issued particularly by banks (bank senior debt) or were used in asset-backed securities – they have been largely considered as (more or less riskless) money market instruments. As a consequence, these instruments have been frequently used by investors who do not want to bear a significant price risk, such as money market funds and liquidity management units from banks.

Besides the floating interest rate index, the coupon payments of a floating rate note usually involve another component, the credit spread, which is fixed at the issue date (and usually kept unchanged until the maturity date). As an example, a floating rate note that is issued at 3M-Euribor plus 20 bp always pays the level of the 3M Euribor plus 0.20%. However, since this spread does not change (ignoring some rarely used instruments with coupon step-up features, where the spread could, for example, be linked to the rating of the issuer), the price of the security will change when the market-implied spread of the issuer changes. As we have seen, spreads for bonds of financial institutions and for asset-backed securities moved significantly higher throughout the crisis, and so did prices. This is due to the fact that, although a floater has a quite short duration with respect to the underling interest rate risk, the duration with respect to spread changes (the so-called spread-duration) is the same as for a comparable fixed-rate bond.

A brief example sheds some light on this topic. We refer to the example above (a floating-rate note which is linked to the 3M Euribor plus 20 bp). Furthermore, we assume that the bond has a remaining time to maturity of 5 years. As a consequence, we approximate the interest rate duration by 0.25 years and the spread duration by 5 years. For a change in the underlying interest rate index of 100 bp (i.e., 1%), the value of the bond will change by 25 bp (i.e., 0.25%). Assuming that the bond was issued at par (i.e., EUR 100), the price gain due to declining interest rates would lead to a value of the bond in the area of EUR 100.25. Note that a decline in interest rates of this magnitude occurred in the US due to the rate cuts made by the Fed in the last three meetings of 2007. However, although the Fed cut the target rate by 100 bp and the discount rate even by 150 bp, the 3M USD Libor declined by only 50 bp. About half of the monetary easing did not affect markets, since the stress in the money markets triggered an explosion in the interbank spread (see section 3.4 for further details). Now, we assume that the market spread for our floater increases by 100 bp (from 20 bp at issue date to 120 bp at valuation date). Although such a spread change appeared to be highly exaggerated before the crisis, several financials – in the US and in Europe – experienced such spread blowouts. A good example is Bear Stearns. Its 5Y credit spreads widened from 20 bp at the beginning of 2007 to almost 200 bp at the end of 2007. A 100 bp spread increase was hence not completely absurd. However, a 100 bp spread widening for our 5Y floater translates into a loss of 5%; the value of the security falls to EUR 95. For a stock investor, that does not appear too dramatic, but just consider how a money market investor feels when he losses 5% on his investment. That is the excess return above Libor he would have earned by holding a 20 bp floater for 25 years. This is a bummer! Hence, although floating-rate notes had been considered as money market securities before the financial crisis, investors discovered that they can involve equity-like volatilities.

Auction-Rate Securities (ARS) also involve variable coupon payments. However, in an ARS the coupon payment is reset on a weekly or monthly basis, via an auction mechanism that involves the potential investor. ARS are quite common in municipal bonds and played an important role in the monoliner crisis (see section 3.6) For the sake of completeness, we should also mention that there are securities that combine several coupon mechanisms. Such a combination is, for example, very common for hybrid bank capital, such as tier 1 bonds. Here, the bond has an initial period of fixed payments (e.g., 10 years) and switches to a floating rate note after this period. Usually, the issuer has the right (but not the obligation) to call the note at the switching date. We will see below that this mechanism is very similar to the 2/28 teaser loans that were frequently used in the subprime mortgage universe.

Another important factor of credit-risky instruments is the difference between bonds and loans. Although these two instruments differ in many ways (structure, investor, accounting rules, etc.), the main difference is the transferability of the claim. While *loans* are usually private transactions, originated by banks and held to maturity, *bonds* are public and tradable securities; they can be acquired and sold without restrictions. Bonds are usually standardized and listed instruments that involve simple coupon mechanisms (either fixed or variable coupons); bullet redemptions (no amortization payments during lifetime), are publicly rated and refer to a standardized documentation (such as a medium-term note program). Although bonds are an important pillar of the capital structure of larger companies, they are usually a more costly type of debt, as they involve fee payments to the arranging banks in addition to the coupon payments to their investors. Moreover, due to the standardized structures and the more complex marketing procedures, bonds are less flexible and it takes more time to raise the funds. There is also a regional difference. While in the United States corporate bonds have existed for a long time, this type of debt was less common for other areas, such as in Europe (and especially in Germany), as loans have been the major source of funding in this area. Nevertheless, companies usually try to diversify their funding sources by borrowing from banks via loans, but also by tapping capital markets via tradable securities. While we will elaborate on mortgage loans in the next section, we will highlight a specific type of loans – the corporate loan (and here in particular the leveraged loan) – at this point to allow its comparison with the corporate bond.

From an issuer's perspective, the big advantage of a loan is its structural flexibility. Since loans are private transactions, the structure of the deal can be designed to meet the specific needs of the borrower; for example, in the way that the borrower can draw and repay the funds. In particular for larger transactions, such as mergers and acquisitions, a loan facility can be perfect bridge financing until the transaction is completed. Afterwards, the bridge loan can be replaced by a standardized bond. But also from the lender's point of view, a loan might involve several advantages. Again due to its contractual flexibility, the loan contract may contain specific covenants; it might be senior to other debt securities or might be secured by a designated pool of assets, giving the lender an additional credit enhancement. However, on the negative side, a loan is a rather illiquid product. Once it is originated, it may be difficult to get rid of the exposure again, at least without resorting to credit derivatives, such as the CDS, the loan-CDS or the collateralized loan obligation (CLO).

However, in some cases, the amount of funding that is required by the borrower is so large that it exceeds the capabilities of a single lender. Moreover, the responsible regulatory body has specific restrictions governing large exposures and loans that exceed certain thresholds. In such a case, banks refer to the *syndicated loan*, which is a loan that is provided by a group of banks (and for which the terms of the loans are the same for all banks). Syndicated loans allow banks to reduce granularity and diversify their portfolios. But they are transferred not only to other banks; other institutional investors, such CLO managers, insurance companies, mutual funds and hedge funds may also be willing to invest in syndicated loans. Due to their structural flexibility, syndicated loans have been a central element in the leveraged buyout (LBO) arena, as these instruments have been used by private equity sponsors in order to leverage their investments. For this reason, syndicated loans that were used in LBO cases are also called leveraged loans.

In figure 2.1, we depict the quarterly issuance volume for US leveraged loans and high-yield bonds since 1999. Growth rates for US leveraged loans have been quite impressive since 2002, while the US high-yield bond universe remained roughly unchanged. In total, the US leveraged loan market featured new issues in 2007 of slightly above USD 1 tn, while the US high-yield bond market involved a primary market activity of only USD 150 bn; seven times lower. Moreover, despite the decline in the last quarters of 2007, the leveraged loan issuance activity grew by USD 350 bn (about 50%) in 2007.

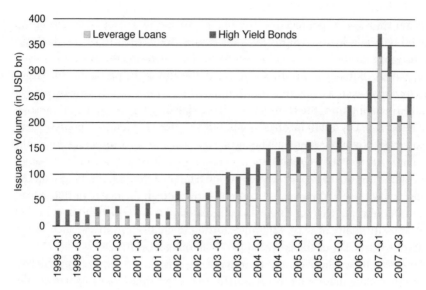

Fig. 2.1: Issuance volume of US leveraged loans and high-yield bonds

2.2 Loans

Loans exist in various different forms and characteristics. They range from consumer loans, over mortgage loans to syndicated loans in the corporate lending business. Banks may offer a large variety – up to a few hundred – of lending products, to their customers. In contrast to a bond, which is intended to be a standardized and tradable security, loans are privately negotiated between the borrower and a bank and are typically considered as a buy and hold investment by the banks. Nevertheless, the intention to make loan exposure tradable is very old, and is the main idea of securitization. Nowadays, credit derivative contracts facilitate the liquidation of mid- and large-scale loan exposures. The availability of such credit derivative contracts and the willingness of investors to take the loan exposure off bank balance sheets motivated banks to change their lending processes. Instead of originating loans for their own books, they just used their balance sheets (or special purpose vehicles) to warehouse loans and to distribute them to investors via securitization. This has, of course, an impact on the credit quality of the originated loans, as banks tend to loosen their underwriting practices in order to increase numbers and volumes. But the deterioration of the credit quality of the originated loans was not only – accidentally – driven by inappropriate underwriting, but also intentionally. Banks focused on subprime loans because there was high demand from the investor base for the corresponding subprime RMBS. Hence, the growth of the subprime loan market was driven, to a large extent, by investor demand for spread products rather than by demand from borrowers.

Although there is no official definition for a subprime credit quality, in the US borrowers with a FICO credit score (a credit score developed by Fair Isaac & Co.) of below 620 are usually considered as subprime (on a scale that ranges from 300 to 850). A subprime borrower may have involved one of the following characteristics. Two or more loan payments paid past 60 days due in the last 12 months, or one or more loan payments paid past 90 days due in the last 36 months; judgment, foreclosure, repossession, or non-payment of a loan in the prior 48 months; bankruptcy in the last 7 years.

The lending business knows only a few central rules in order to keep credit risk for lenders manageable. The most basic rule is that the economic interests of lender and borrower should be aligned. Borrowers should not have any incentives to default on their debt service. In regard to the mortgage business, this is traditionally achieved by a sufficiently large equity stake of the borrower. Typically, mortgage lenders require an initial down-payment of the borrower of at least 20% of the house price. In more technical terms, the loan-to-value (LTV) ratio should be below 80%. Subprime mortgage lenders broke with this central rule. It was not only the case that borrowers have been able to purchase the house 100% by debt, some lenders even provided more than 100% in order to cover the transaction cost, the furniture of the house or even a new car. Such practices did not only occur in the US and are a clear sign of a bubble. In the US, LTVs higher than 80% can lead to the necessity for arranging mortgage insurance. In order to avoid that, subprime mortgage lenders provide so-called piggy-back loans, where the loan balance is split into an 80% mortgage loan and a smaller second-lien loan. In such a mortgage loan package, the LTV of the first-lien loan is misleading as it understates the real exposure. Instead, one should use the so-called combined loan-to-value ratio (CLTV) for the assessment of the default risk of a loan. In fact, the recent history of subprime defaults shows that there is a high correlation between default rates and high CLTV. From a basic economic perspective, this is very clear. First, borrowers who have a high total debt burden are the ones with problems. Second, if the CLTV is greater than one, the borrower may have an incentive to default since it does not make a lot of sense to repay 110% debt for an asset with a value of 100%. This incentive is especially high for so-called non-recourse loans, i.e. loans in which the lender may not have recourse to the borrower after foreclosure in case the realized price from the sale of the mortgaged property is not sufficient to cover the outstanding debt. However, a similar moral hazard may be caused by the application of loss-mitigation techniques, such as special forbearance, deed-in-lieu, partial claims, loan modifications, or pre-foreclosure sales. Although such techniques may mitigate the loss on an individual loan, they may trigger increasing default rates, as they may make the economic consequences for a defaulting borrower less severe. However, one of the most drastic consequences for a borrower when defaulting on his debt is the damage to his credit record. But for a subprime borrower, the track record has most probably already been impaired. Otherwise, he would not have been a subprime borrower.

However, the LTV problem does not only emerge when the acquisition of a house is refinanced. The so-called home equity extraction allows home owners to increase their debt on the house when the value of the house increases. The idea is very simple. When the market value of the house increases by 20%, then the debt volume can also be increased by 20% and the LTV remains the same. However, the LTV will rise when the market value of the house drops. Since a large part of home equity extraction was used for financing consumption, such practices simply led to high gearing of home owners.[3]

However, the requirement for an initial down-payment hinders a large part of the population from buying their own house. The central idea of the subprime mortgage market was to provide appropriate funding tools for those individuals who are otherwise not able to acquire a house. Although we do not doubt that such loan products play an important role in democratic societies, the risks involved with such lending techniques require very strict underwriting standards. This is the second central rule of lending: do not lend to a borrower unless you can verify his ability to service the debt payments. Although this principle is absolutely clear, the financial industry invented a way around it: the so-called "stated income loans" (a.k.a. low-doc or no-doc loans, and sometimes even referred to as NINJA loans, "No income, no job or assets"). Here, the loan is granted without a thorough examination of the borrower's income documentation. There is anecdotal evidence that underwriters not only turned a blind eye to exaggerated income statements, but even encouraged borrowers to do so in order to get the loan approved. Apparently, fraud was an important driver in the subprime crisis, but in fact the principles of subprime lending have been a downright invitation to fraud.

But how did underwriters cope with the burden of mortgage payments that exceed the economic ability of the borrower? Lenders knew that this was the case. Reduce the payments as far as possible using all available techniques and if this isn't enough, allow the borrower to postpone the payments. The reduction of the debt service payments was done by skipping the necessity of amortization payments (the so-called interest-only mortgage loans or "pick a payment" loans, where the borrower can choose whether he will make a full payment, an interest only payment or perhaps even a lower payment) and fixing the coupon period only for a shorter period (the so-called adjustable rate mortgages (ARM)). The latter works, if the yield curve is upward sloping, but it creates the risk of a payment shock for the borrower when interest rates rise (note that the subprime default rates began to skyrocket as interest rates increased and loans were reset to higher rates). A frequently used ARM loan format was the 2/28. In this loan contract, the coupon payment is fixed to a quite low level for the first two years and is then reset to a higher level for the remaining 28 years, including an increase in the credit spread. A large part of the delinquent subprime mortgage loans that triggered the crisis belong to this 2/28 ARM category.

Even if all of this did not lead to a coupon payment that the borrower could afford, there were possibilities for the borrower to get a loan (and the possibility for the loan originator to make his origination fee): negative amortization loans. In a negative amortization loan, the borrower pays only a part of the required interest as a running coupon. The non-paid amount is simply added to the outstanding balance of the loan. It has to be repaid at maturity or at any other point in time. The idea behind all this – 2/28 teaser loans, negative amortization, etc. – is speculation. When the price of the house increases dramatically, the house can be either sold off and the loan can be repaid (incl. the postponed coupon payments) or the loan could be replaced with a prime loan because of the better LTV ratio. Another argument for subprime borrowing was the prospect that the economic condition of the borrower might improve in the future, or simply the hopes that a successful subprime credit record of the borrower (referred to as "credit repair") could qualify for a cheaper prime mortgage loan.

At this point, it is appropriate to mention that the subprime crisis did not only create economic losses for banks and other investors involved in the subprime market. Many families in the US have lost – and will lose their homes – because they were confronted with predatory lending practices. Many borrowers apparently didn't understand the terms and the risks of the contracts which were sold to them by unscrupulous businessmen who did not care about the economic impact on the borrowers and on the whole economy. Most probably, one of the outcomes of the crisis will be a legal trial of the common practices in the subprime business and some legal action in order to prevent such exaggerations in the future. Nevertheless, the subprime crisis highlights the importance of a sound credit process and strict underwriting practices.

2.3 Credit Default Swaps

The credit default swap (CDS) is one of the most important building blocks in modern credit markets. It developed into a highly standardized and liquid tradable security that allows investors to trade the pure credit risk of a reference entity. CDS contracts are frequently used as an underlying of other credit derivatives, such as CDS indices, first-to-default baskets and synthetic CDOs. Due to the highly standardized and easy-to-handle trade format, the contracts were the main driver of the extreme growth in the credit derivatives universe.

In its semi-annual derivatives survey, the International Swaps and Derivatives Association (ISDA) measures the developments in global derivatives markets. In the chart below, we highlight the relative growth rates of interest rate/foreign exchange (IR/FX), equity and credit derivatives. The latter is by far the fastest growing segment, with average annual growth rates of above 100%, while IR/FX and equity derivatives have posted growth rates in the area of 30%. The tremendous growth in credit derivatives brought the aggregated reference notional amount up to USD 45 tn (11.3% of all derivatives). Note that the market cap of the S&P 500 index is in the area of USD 13 tn, while the DJ EuroSTOXX 50 is around USD 4 tn. Moreover, the iBoxx EUR corporates index – i.e., EUR-denominated financials and non-financials corporate bonds of investment grade quality – have an aggregated notional amount of USD 1.2 tn, while the US counterpart is twice as large. This means that the credit derivatives market is larger than the other company-related markets that we know. And the ISDA survey only refers to single-name CDSs and smaller baskets; hence the CDO world is not included (at least not directly, as CDO hedging activity triggers trading activity in the underlying CDS). However, on a purely notional basis, IR/FX derivatives are still the largest derivatives class with an aggregated reference notional amount of USD 350 tn (86.2% of all derivatives), while equity derivatives refer to about USD 10 tn (2.5%).

A *CDS contract* is an over-the-counter transaction between two counterparties to exchange the credit risk of a specific reference entity in exchange for a stream of premium payments. The reference entity of a CDS contract can be a company, a sovereign or a specific defaultable security, such as a mortgage-backed bond. The basic structure of a CDS contract is very similar to a simple insur-

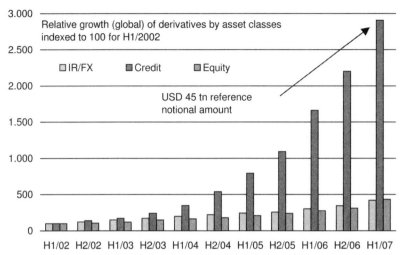

Fig. 2.2: ISDA Derivatives Survey: CDS are the fastest-growing derivatives class.
Source: ISDA

ance contract; for example car insurance. As for car insurance a CDS contract involves two contractual parties, the so-called protection seller (comparable to the insurance company for car insurance) and the so-called protection buyer (comparable to the policy holder). The protection seller assumes the default risk of the reference entity and receives a premium payment in exchange. As for car insurance, it is imperative to specify the reference object of the CDS contract precisely. For car insurance this is apparently done by specifying the type of the car and its license number. For a CDS contract, this is done by specifying a so-called reference obligation, a security that was issued or that refers to the default risk of the reference entity. For example, if a CDS contract referring to General Motors were to be set up, one specifies a certain bond of the company as a reference obligation.

In case the reference entity experiences a default event (this would correspond, for example, to an accident in car insurance), the protection seller (the insurance company) would compensate the involved loss of the protection buyer. This can be done either in terms of a physical delivery (the standard process) or via a cash settlement. In a physical delivery process, the protection buyer delivers a defaulted security to the protection seller and receives the par value of the defaulted security in exchange. This can be viewed as a conditional option of the protection buyer to sell a defaulted security of the reference entity at par

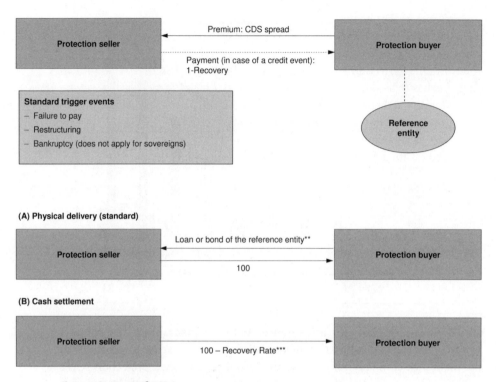

Fig. 2.3: Structure of a CDS contract

to the protection seller. The condition refers to a default event. As the value of a security after a default event is considered the so-called recovery value (Rec), the protection seller realizes the so-called loss-given-default (LGD) with LGD = 1 − Rec. This physical delivery process has an important advantage, as there is no reason for a dispute between both counterparties with respect to the size of the recovery rate. The recovery rate is implicitly exchanged via delivery of a defaulted security. A real valuation is not needed. In a cash settlement, both counterparties have to agree on a mechanism to determine the recovery rate following a default event (e.g., via post-default market prices), and then simply exchange the difference between the par value and the recovery value in one lump sum. This obviously involves a potential dispute, as the default rate cannot be determined objectively – at least at the point when CDS contracts have to be settled. However, there are also some major disadvantages to the physical delivery mechanism. If the protection buyer does not own a defaulted security

– which means that he outright shorted the credit risk of the reference entity –
the protection buyer has to buy a deliverable obligation after the default event.
However, as highlighted by the ISDA survey mentioned above, the outstanding
volume of the CDS contracts is huge. Hence, there is the risk that the volume in
CDS that has to be settled in a defaulted name significantly exceeds the volume
in outstanding debt of the company. Since all (outright short) protection buyers
that agreed upon a physical delivery have to buy such a defaulted bond, the risk
of a short squeeze due to the "crowded in" is significant. In fact, this already
happened for the first time in October 2005 when Delphi defaulted.

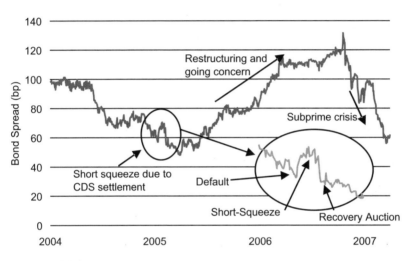

Fig. 2.4: Delphi bond price (DPH 7.125 05/29)

After the company's announcement that it will file for chapter 11 on October
8, 2005, bond prices dropped by only 5 percentage points to a value of 57 cents on
the dollar. By the way, this only marginal drop following a credit event highlights
how efficient liquid credit markets can be, as bond prices fell from about 70%
to 60% in the weeks ahead of the default date. However, after a few days, when
all outright short protection buyers attempted to buy defaulted securities, bond
prices rose to pre-default levels (up to 70% on October 31, 2005), erasing all
previous gains for the protection buyers out of the default event. This poses
a serious problem to the functioning of a CDS contract, as it makes such a
contract useless for traders who do not own defaulted securities. Hence, the
major players in the CDS market stepped in and developed a solution in order
to avoid such an artificial short squeeze following a default event. In this case,

the ISDA will set up a *recovery auction*. This means that all participants in CDS contracts switch their settlement process from physical delivery to cash settlement, and the size of the cash settlement is determined via an auction among all participants. For Delphi this occurred for the first time, and the recovery auction on November 4, 2005 (only four weeks after the default event) revealed a recovery rate of 63.375% (which was also exactly the price of the bond in figure 2.4 at the day of the auction), about 6.5 percentage points below the market value of Delphi's bond after the short squeeze started.

Similar to car insurance, we also have to specify the events that trigger a CDS contract. For car insurance this depends on the type of the insurance contract. In liability insurance, for example, the insurance company assumes liability for any damages to others that are caused by a driver of the insured car. In another type of insurance, the contract may settle any damages regarding the insured car. However, in CDS contracts, market participants usually refer to a standardized set of trigger events: failure-to-pay, restructuring and bankruptcy. The failure-to-pay trigger covers all events in which the reference entity fails to pay a due payment after a grace period. A grace period is applied in order to avoid a technical default. The restructuring event refers to the restructuring of a debt instrument of the reference entity, which affects the contractual relationship between the lender and the borrower, such as reducing the notional amount, changing the coupon structure or deferring payments. However, in case there are clauses in the bond documentation that allow such a change (prepayment options or hybrid bonds which allow the company to postpone a coupon without triggering a credit event, such as upper tier 2 and tier 1 capital issues by financial institutions), these events do not trigger a CDS contract.

In figure 2.5, we highlight the cash flows that are involved in a CDS contract and compare them with the ones from a straight bond (see figure 2.6). The cash flows are shown from the perspective of a protection seller (CDS) or note holder (cash bond). Both bear the risk of a default event. The protection seller receives the premium payment from the protection buyer until the legal final maturity date, or until the default date in case the CDS contract was triggered. In the case of such a trigger event, the protection seller settles the loss that is involved with the credit event, which means that he faces a large cash outflow (par minus the value of a defaulted security either via exchanging a defaulted security or by paying the difference in one lump sum). In contrast to this, the cash flow diagram of a cash bond looks significantly different (Fig. 2.6). At initiation of the note, the investor has to pay the price for the security (e.g., 100 assuming that the security trades at par). However, a par CDS contract does not involve any initial payment. The initial payment in case of a cash bond changes the underlying cash flow structure significantly. Since there is a real cash outflow at initiation, the cash investor not only receives a premium for the credit risk, but earns in addition the risk-free rate of return on his invested notional. Hence, the payments in CDSs are typically much lower than the ones in a cash bond. Assuming a risk-free yield level of 5% and a credit spread of 50 bp, a cash bond would involve a payment of 5.5%, while a CDS contract with the same underlying risk would pay only 50 bp. That is why market participants usually address selling protection in a CDS contract as an unfunded investment (an initial investment, which needs to be funded, is not necessary), while a bond is usually called a funded investment. The funded nature of the cash bond has an additional impact on the cash flow diagram. The protection seller faces the risk of a large downside payment in the case of the credit event (par minus value of a defaulted security), but a cash bond involves a positive, albeit significantly reduced redemption payment in case of a credit event.

(A) No default event

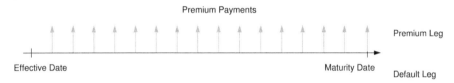

(B) Default event

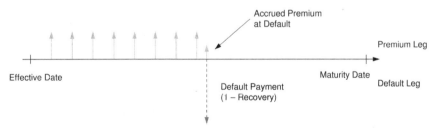

Fig. 2.5: Cash flow for a CDS contract

The central advantage of a CDS contract is that it is highly standardized – in terms of documentation but also in terms of trading usage – which attracts huge liquidity in these instruments. Once an investor has set up the documentation, front/back office and risk management framework, a CDS position can

Credit Default
Swaps

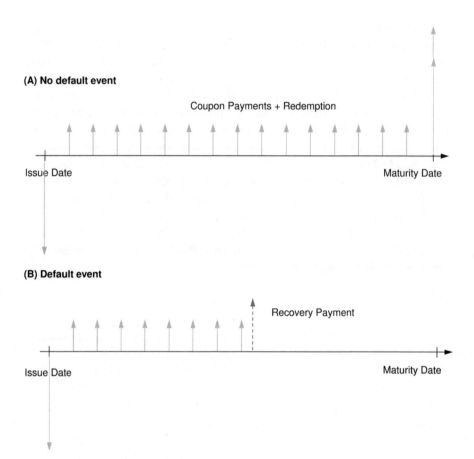

(A) No default event

Coupon Payments + Redemption

Issue Date

Maturity Date

(B) Default event

Recovery Payment

Issue Date

Maturity Date

Fig. 2.6: Cash flow for a defaultable bond

be traded within a minute: he just calls a dealer and requests a price for a certain reference entity, maturity and volume. Nowadays this can even be done without talking to someone, as most market makers also quote on electronic platforms.

In figure 2.7, we show an example screen from Bloomberg with CDS quotes for the EUR-denominated automobiles universe. The screenshot only shows 3Y, 5Y and 7Y quotes, but dealers usually also quote 1Y and 10Y CDS. As can be seen from the example, market makers usually send out so-called two-way quotes, including bid and ask levels. For Daimler (DCX), for example, the 5Y quote is 47/50 bp, which means that the dealer buys protection for 47 bp, while he sells protection for 50 bp. Besides the 3 bp bid/ask spread, there are no further transaction costs involved. These quotes are usually understood for standard ticket sizes of EUR 5-10 mn. On reference entities with a larger balance sheet and more bonds outstanding, such as Daimler or Deutsche Telekom, it is usually also no problem to trade tickets in the range of above EUR 25 mn. The two-way quotes highlight the major advantage of CDS: They allow the investor to short-sell credit risk (i.e., to buy protection). Although such short-selling is theoretically also possible in the cash markets, it is quite expensive due to repo costs, and hence usually unattractive. However, when short-selling is possible (and cheap), investors can set up a larger variety of trading strategies, including long/short strategies, which is not possible from a long-only perspective.

The screen shot in figure 2.7 reveals that not all names and all maturities involve the same bid/ask spreads. CDSs on reference entities which trade at wider spreads, such as the high-yield companies Ford Motor Credit (FMCC) and General Motors Acceptance Corporation (GMAC), involve transaction costs of 20-30 bp. Another advantage of CDS contracts is worth mentioning. The CDS market allows investors to buy and sell protection on a time horizon that is independent from the issuer's bond curve. Valeo, for example, had only one bond outstanding (at the time of the screenshot) with a remaining time to maturity of about 5.5 years (June 2013). Nevertheless, the CDS market allows to trade credit risk on a 1Y, 3Y, 5Y, 7Y and 10Y time horizon, which enables investors to set up relative value plays on the curve, such as curve steepener and flatteners, which would otherwise be impossible.

As already mentioned, CDS contracts enable investors to trade the underlying credit risk, that is, to enter into a position with a very short intended holding period. The trading horizon can be as short as a few trading days, if liquidity and volatility are high enough, which means that price changes cover the transaction costs. Consequently, an investor who opens a 5Y CDS contract does not need to wait five years in order to get out of the position again, but can close the position after a few days. In order to close his position, the investor is not tied to the original counterparty. He can also close it with another market maker, which is called *novation*. This guarantees that the dealers are always quoting in competition. However, one issue is worth noting. A CDS contract is an over-the-counter derivative contract. So far, there are no liquid exchange-listed credit derivative contracts available, although the exchanges are already pressing to enter this segment. This means that CDS contracts bear counterparty risk, as the protection buyer has the risk that the underlying reference entity and his counterparty default at the same time. This is essential if the default risk of the reference entity and the counterparty are highly correlated, for example, when

200<Go> to view in Launchpad
11:22 **AUTOMOTIVE/TRANSPORT** PAGE 1 / 5

Underlying		3 Year					5 Year					7 Year		
		Bid	X	Ask	Time		Bid	X	Ask	Time		Bid	X Ask	Time
BMW	1)	34	X	37	9:17	15)	43	X	46	9:17	29)	50	X 53	9:17
CONTINENTAL	2)	53	X	58	9:17	16)	72	X	77	9:17	30)	77	X 82	9:17
DCX	3)	35	X	38	9:17	17)	47	X	50	9:17	31)	58	X 61	9:17
FMCC	4)	530	X	550	9:17	18)	580	X	600	9:17	32)	600	X620	9:17
GMAC	5)	615	X	625	9:17	19)	630	X	660	9:17	33)	655	X665	9:17
MICHELIN	6)	53	X	57	9:17	20)	65	X	70	9:17	34)	74	X 78	9:17
PEUGOT	7)	52	X	56	9:17	21)	62	X	67	9:17	35)	71	X 75	9:17
PORSCH	8)	55	X	59	9:17	22)	70	X	75	9:17	36)	83	X 87	9:17
RENAULT	9)	52	X	56	9:17	23)	63	X	68	9:17	37)	72	X 76	9:17
SCANIA	10)	32	X	36	9:17	24)	44	X	49	9:17	38)	53	X 57	9:17
VALEO	11)	35	X	40	9:17	25)	73	X	78	9:17	39)	76	X 81	9:17
VOLVO	12)	42	X	46	9:17	26)	57	X	62	9:17	40)	67	X 71	9:17
VW	13)	45	X	48	9:17	27)	59	X	62	9:17	41)	65	X 68	9:17
MAN	14)		X			28)		X			42)		X	

Thomas Kreitmeier / Marco Korn

UniCredit
Markets & Investment Banking

+49 89 378 17600
The indicative quotes above are for credit default
swaps on standard ISDA 2003 documentation.

Australia 61 2 9777 8600 Brazil 5511 3048 4500 Europe 44 20 7330 7500 Germany 49 69 920410 Hong Kong 852 2977 6000
Japan 81 3 3201 8900 Singapore 65 6212 1000 U.S. 1 212 318 2000 Copyright 2007 Bloomberg Finance L.P.
H258-303-0 03-Dec-2007 11:22:39

Fig. 2.7: Bloomberg screen with CDS quotes in the EUR-denominated automobiles universe

one buys protection on a US investment bank from another US investment bank, since the systemic risk is not negligible (any longer). During the crisis, such considerations have become an issue in risk management, as the market-implied default risk for financials – the typical counterparties for a CDS contract – rose significantly. Another issue regarding CDS trading should not be over-looked: OTC derivatives involve a substantial documentation overhead. And if investors really want to enjoy liquidity, they need to implement the documentation framework (this is usually the ISDA derivatives framework) with several counterparties. These problems, together with questions regarding trading systems and risk management procedures, have to be tackled in a timely manner. Implementing CDS capabilities is a project that lasts for months rather than weeks. Hence, the decision to enter the CDS arena when the crisis has already started is simply too late.

However, having CDS trading capabilities up and running was essential during the crisis, as liquidity in the cash markets dried up rapidly. Secondary markets for bonds were simply shut down for months. Hence, cash-only investors had to remain on the sidelines and were forced into the role of bystanders – not a very comfortable position when spreads triple in a few days. The CDS market remained liquid and market participants were able to manage their exposures, although CDS markets involved huge spread swings. One of the reasons for this selective market liquidity was the funding issue. As already mentioned, CDS contracts do not require initial funding, in contrast to the cash markets. However, especially the banking industry, which suffered from a funding squeeze (it was very costly – if at all possible – to tap markets for funding) had no desire to buy into the cash markets. Hence, a lot of players jumped into the unfunded derivatives market for trading credit risk and avoided the cash markets.

Besides the already mentioned advantages of credit default swaps (liquidity, tradable across the curve even if the reference entity does not have a liquid curve outstanding, easy to short, unfunded), there is another very important advantage: the CDS allows an efficient risk transfer between two counterparties without involving the reference entity. For example, a bank can issue a loan for a corporate and synthetically distribute the risk to the market using CDSs. This way, the risk management objectives – for example, the bank does not have any credit lines for the issuer – can be separated from the client relationship. No CFO likes to hear that a bank does not have free credit lines available for his company. However, while this helps to risk manage the portfolio of the bank, it does not mean that pricing the risk on both sides – on the originating side, as well as for transferring the exposure to the market – is independent. Therefore, during a crisis, the bank originator is not necessarily forced to end his client relationship, as not granting a loan to a customer pretty much means losing the customer; but nevertheless, the costs that he has to show to the company might be effectively viewed as "no more loans".

Now we would like to briefly introduce some other single-name credit derivative instruments that can be viewed as slight modifications to the previously outlined CDS framework: the loan-only CDS, the digital default swap (DDS) and the forward CDS. As already mentioned above, the standard CDS framework refers to loans and bonds as deliverable obligations. This means that in case of a default event, the protection buyer can deliver either a loan or a bond. However, while bonds are highly standardized instruments, loans usually involve a high level of structuring with respect to contract details and loan documentation (covenants). Hence, although the standard CDS framework treats both as comparable instruments, they are in fact quite different. Since loans are usually senior to senior-unsecured bonds, their value in case of a default event will be significantly higher than a corresponding bond. Therefore, a protection buyer will hardly be interested in delivering a loan. Even if he has exposure in a loan, he will usually be tempted to buy a senior unsecured bond in the market, which he will deliver to his counterparty (this refers to the so-called cheapest-to-deliver security). Therefore, market participants created another market place, where the so-called loan-only CDS (LCDS) can be traded. However, since loans are not very standardized and involve a significantly higher prepayment risk, the necessary documentation is significantly more complex than the standard CDS documentation. The prepayment risk causes difficulties especially in the leveraged loan arena, where turnover in loans was very high in the past. This is mainly due to the fact that private equity (PE) sponsors choose to refinance their target frequently, either by selling an LBOed company to the next PE fund or by calling the debt and refunding at cheaper levels (which they could do due to the loan and bond documentation). However, for a CDS contract it is a bit of a problem if the underlying risky exposure vanishes every now and then.

Against this background, it is understandable that two different documentation frameworks have evolved: a European one and an American one. While in the European framework, a CDS is usually cancelled if the loan is called or refinanced, the American framework attempts to replace the underlying exposure by a suitable peer. However, such a replacement mechanism involves the risk of a dispute between both counterparties of a CDS. While it is in the interest of the protection buyer to replace the redeemed exposure with a successor that is more risky than the original debt, the perspective of the protection seller is exactly the opposite. Consequently, a non-cancelable documentation is more complex in this respect. However, the impact of both frameworks in the market speaks a clear language. The liquidity in a cancelable (European) framework is negligible, as this framework fits the needs of loan portfolio managers that want to acquire a hedge for their exposures. Obviously from this perspective the cancelable framework is more appealing, as both the underlying risk and the CDS protection disappear in case of prepayment. However, for the other side of the contract, the cancelable feature is not very attractive. Just imagine a risk-taker who accepted transaction costs of 10 bp (in terms of bid/ask spread) for the acquisition of an LCDS, and within a few months the exposure vanished due to the repayment. Moreover, the LCDS has been frequently used for ramping up a synthetic collateralized loan obligation (CLO). But for a CLO manager the prepayment risk is annoying. Hence, the natural buyers of loan risk via the LCDS prefer the non-cancelable format. As a consequence, the market participants reacted and the ISDA published a non-cancelable documentation framework that is now also used in European markets.

Another modification of the CDS mechanism is the *digital default swap* (DDS). The DDS is a CDS contract where the payoff in case of a credit event is fixed in advance. Hence, market participants also refer to this type of contract as a fixed-recovery CDS. A DDS is always cash settled at the pre-specified rate. Moreover, DDS contracts are usually set at a recovery rate of 0% (therefore they are also called zero-recovery CDSs). For an investor such DDSs can be attractive, as the contracts pay a higher premium than the standard floating recovery rate versions. In addition, the regulatory framework was blind with respect to this risk, as it considered a CDS and a DDS as equally risky. But assuming that the average recovery rate is about 50%, a EUR 10 mn position in a DDS pays twice the premium than a normal CDS contract. Hence, blindfolded regulators triggered a business case for investment bankers: regulatory arbitrage. These CDS contracts were especially popular in the high-quality end of the credit curve. A lot of investors sold protection on sovereign risk using the DDS. Furthermore, they were also frequently used as underlyings of digital first-to-default baskets.

However, as the only difference between a CDS and a DDS is the recovery rate in case of a default event, a combination of a CDS (long) and a DDS (short) with a relative notional amount that reflects the different recovery prospects only depends on the recovery rate in case of a default event. Consequently, a package of a CDS and a DDS is called a *recovery default swap* (RDS). Using this product, market participants can trade the anticipated recovery rate in case of a default event.

Last but not least, a CDS can also be traded as a forward contract. In such a forward-start CDS, both counterparties agree to swap the credit risk of a specified underlying against a stream of premium payments at a future point in time. From a contractual perspective, this is very easy, as one only has to specify an effective date in the future. However, as the protection seller is only liable for a default event between the effective date and the maturity date, the contract simply knocks out in case of a default event before the effective date. Hence, these contracts do not bear any immediate default risk but only spread change risk, as the value of the forward CDS changes with the underlying spread curve. Hence, these instruments are used by market participants who want to take a position in the credit spread but do not want to (or are not allowed to) take the outright default risk, because, for example, their credit lines with respect to this specific reference entity are already filled. However, if an outright position in the default risk should be avoided, the investor has to close the position before the contractual effective date, because the forward CDS becomes a normal CDS after the effective date.

2.4 CDS Indices

Although single-name CDS contracts experienced rapid growth in the last few years, the most liquid credit products are the so-called CDS indices, such as the iTraxx in Europe and Asia and the CDX in the US. CDS indices exist for a few underlyings: the corporate credit CDS (iTraxx Europe and Asia indices, as well as CDX North America investment-grade and high-yield indices), the loan CDS (iTraxx LevX and LCDX indices), the sovereign CDS (CDX emerging markets index), but also structured-finance CDS indices, such as the ABX index (referring to US ABS underlyings) and the CMBX index (referring to US CMBS underlyings). Although the ABX was initially designed as a full index family with five sub-indices referring to different structured finance asset classes – the ABX.HE (home equity), the ABX.CC (credit cards), the ABX.SL (student loans), the ABX.AU (auto loans) and the ABX.XX (other loans) – the only actually tradable index is the ABX.HE, which is also know as the subprime index. In this section, we address the basic construction mechanism of CDS indices and demonstrate their usage in credit portfolios based on the iTraxx Europe index. In general, the findings apply to other indices as well.

CDS indices developed into a very central credit portfolio management tool. But before we start with a more detailed description on the characteristics of CDS indices, we would like to stress that although market participants usually address these instruments as CDS "indices", they are in fact not indices. They are tradable instruments and hence are more related to stock index futures rather than stock indices themselves. There is, for example, no official fair-value fixing in CDS indices, in contrast to stock or bond indices. For the DJ EuroStoxx 50 index, for example, there is an official price fixing, which is based on the prices for the underlying stocks and which is calculated by the index provider. In addition to this official price fixing, there is a tradable futures contract. However, the price of the futures contract can deviate from the underlying index value. Only at the settlement date, when the futures are settled with respect to the official index fixing, both the index and the future need to have the same value. In CDS indices that's somehow different, as there is no agent that calculates the fair value of the index. The reason is very simple: we do not need it, as there is no index settlement procedure comparable to the stock index future. In order to understand the difference between stock and CDS index contracts, it helps to know that a CDS index is simply a portfolio of single-name CDSs. Hence, a trader that enters into an iTraxx contract simply enters into a standardized portfolio of single-name CDSs. But in contrast to a portfolio trade, he does not need to do it via 125 single-name CDSs but only via a single index contract.

There is another difference between CDS indices and stock indices. The underlying portfolio of a stock index is usually administered continuously and within the same portfolio. In case one constituent is replaced by another (e.g., due to a merger, an acquisition or a delisting) the underlying portfolio of the future contract changes. For CDS indices this is different. The portfolio underlying is administered regularly, usually every six months, and the changes in the portfolio are organized into series. This means that every six months the index host will announce a new series of the index, which refers to an adjusted underlying portfolio. The already existing series, however, remain completely unchanged. This means that if an investor has exposure, for example, to the iTraxx Europe index series 7, his contract remains unchanged when the index host announces series 8. For stock index futures this is different. When the underlying index changes, the risk of the index future changes as well, as there is only one stock index. It does not come in a series; that is, there is no DJ EuroStoxx 50 index including company XYZ and one where XYZ is replaced by ABC.

However, investors who always want to remain in the newest series of a CDS index – it is called the on-the-run index – have to close their position in the old series and open it in the new series. There is no roll-automatism involved, although some banks sold derivatives based on the indices, which always refer to the newest index, and thus always implement the roll.

For the iTraxx Europe and the CDX North America indices, the index roll occurs on 20 March and 20 September every year (subject to business-day adjustments). The underlying portfolio has a fixed number of constituents and its creation is rule-based. In the iTraxx Europe, the investment grade index contains 125 constituents, which all need to be rated at least BBB- with a stable outlook in order to qualify for a new series. Constituents that are rated BBB- with a negative outlook and below qualify for the so-called Crossover index, which contains 50 names. However, as already mentioned, the underlyings for existing indices are not changed. Hence, an older series can contain CDSs that refer to sub-investment grade companies. Besides the rating criteria, the iTraxx indices should cover the most liquid names of the underlying universe. Ahead of the index roll date, the registered iTraxx market makers agree upon replacements for names that drop out of the index due to rating criteria, mergers, or insufficient liquidity of the CDS contract. Replacements are searched in order to maintain a fixed sector structure within the index (see figure 2.8). This means

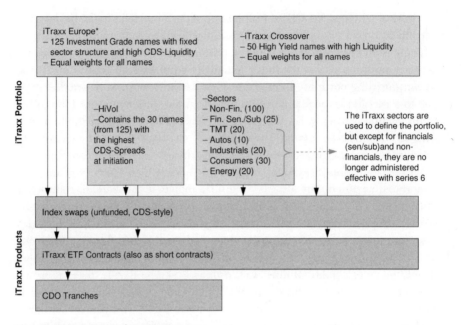

Fig. 2.8: iTraxx Europe index structure

that there always have to be 25 financials among the 125 names in the portfolio, 10 automobiles, 20 TMTs, and so on.

Another difference to stock indices is the fact that the constituents of CDS indices are usually equally weighted. There are a few exceptions to this rule; for example, the CDX.EM (Emerging Markets) index involves different weightings for the constituents. Hence, a CDS index reflects the average credit spread of the underlying portfolio, and it is used exactly for this purpose: Trading the average credit spread of the underlying CDS market, or trading the systematic (beta) risk in credit markets. A portfolio manager who believes in a spread widening across the whole market will choose to buy protection in the iTraxx, just as a stock portfolio manager who fears a decline in stock prices across the board will short-sell stock futures. Sounds quite natural? Well, before the invention of CDS indices, proper trading of the systematic risk of a credit portfolio was almost impossible. Instead, portfolio managers used large-volume corporate bonds, such as the GM 8.375% June 2033 bond as a proxy for a "credit market future". However, as could be seen during the spread blowout of General Motors in May 2005, such an approach involves a decent level of non-systematic risk.

Besides the iTraxx Europe index (note that this is a child with several names: iTraxx Europe, iTraxx Main, iTraxx Benchmark, iTraxx 125 or simply the iTraxx) which covers the 125 most liquid European investment grade names and the iTraxx Crossover, which includes the most liquid European sub-investment grade names, there is also the iTraxx HiVol (the 30 names of the iTraxx Europe index with the highest spread at initiation, also considered the BBBs in the main portfolio) and the iTraxx Financials. The latter can be traded on a senior and on a sub level. Moreover, the iTraxx indices can in general be traded on a 5Y and on a 10Y maturity horizon. For some indices, there are also 3Y and 7Y brackets.

Due to the tremendous success of the CDS indices in the markets, transaction costs narrowed significantly. Under normal market conditions, the 5Y iTraxx Main index can be traded involving a bid/ask spread of 0.25 bp. This means that trading the index contract is much less costly in terms of transaction costs than trading the underlyings. Bid/ask spreads on the Crossover had been as low as 1-2 bp and on the HiVol index in the area of 0.5-1 bp. While these extremely narrow market conditions widened out during the crisis – bid/ask spreads in the Main up to 2-3 bp and in the Crossover up to 3-5 bp – the indices remained tradable also during times of extreme stress, on acceptable liquidity. All other credit market segments had been, at least temporarily, shut down when panic emerged in the market.

Hence, it is no surprise that the most frequently asked question during the crisis was, Where is the iTraxx trading at the moment? The iTraxx turned out to be the fever chart of the crisis. When the heat was on, the iTraxx skyrocketed. In the meantime markets became so liquid that there is even an intraday price chart for the major indices, and intraday spread changes could be easily above 10% in relative terms (i.e., 5 bp spread change for a 50 bp spread level). During the crisis, spreads of the iTraxx main index rose tremendously – from 20 bp to 120 bp – within a few months. Is there any other USD 50 tn market that involves comparable spikes? A fair reply to this question could be that a spread widening of 40 bp for a 5Y CDS contract, which roughly involves a risky duration of 5, translates into a price drop of only 4%, which appears small compared to stock market volatility. However, compared to the upside potential for investing in a credit portfolio which has a carry of 20 bp, this is huge. A 4% drop means that we lost the carry income of 20 years. This is in fact significant, even compared to the stock market.

2.5 Tranches

The central technique used to structure credit portfolio instruments, such as the ABS or the CDO, is *tranching*. The aim of tranching is to create a set of investment products based on a portfolio of assets that have different risk characteristics, ranging from very safe tranches (the so-called super-senior tranches) to very risky tranches (the so-called equity or first-loss pieces). To illustrate how this tranching mechanism works, we refer to a simple example. We assume that the portfolio consists of 100 equally weighted credit exposures. Every exposure has a notional amount of EUR 1 mn. Consequently, the complete portfolio consists of EUR 100 mn. Moreover, for the sake of simplicity, we assume that in case of a credit event at one of the exposures the loss will be EUR 0.5 mn; that is, 50% of the respective notional amount. In other words, the investment recovers 50% of the initial volume in case of a default. When the first credit event occurs in the pool, the investor in the equity piece experiences the first loss in this tranche, hence the name first-loss piece. The loss amount – EUR 0.5 mn – is deducted from the notional amount of the equity tranche. The investors of all other tranches do not experience any loss. Assuming that the equity piece had a volume of EUR 3 mn, which means it has a thickness of 3% of the underlying pool, the equity piece has a remaining volume of EUR 2.5 mn (EUR 3 mn initial volume minus EUR 0.5 mn from the first-loss event). This reveals an interesting property of tranching. While the loss from the single credit event was only 0.5% with respect to the whole portfolio, it amounted to 16.67% with respect to the equity piece, whereas all other tranches did not experience any realized losses at all. Hence via the tranching mechanism the losses for the equity piece were magnified, while the other tranches were protected.

Every time there is a default event, the equity piece absorbs the loss, until it is completely eroded. Referring to our assumptions – EUR 0.5 mn loss per default event – this occurs after exactly six defaults. Hence, with the seventh default the next tranche will be hit. In other words, the investor in the equity tranche does not care whether there were 7, 8 or 20 defaults in the underlying pool. After the sixth default his investment is completed eroded. This property is very similar to the limited liability feature of the equity of a normal company. A stockholder of a company is not liable for losses that exceed the equity of a company. If losses are in fact larger than the equity cushion, the debtholders of the company start to lose their money. The same principle applies to a tranched credit portfolio instrument. However, in contrast to the capital structure of a company, which in its simplest form consists of equity and debt, the capital structure of a tranched portfolio usually involves more than just these two tranches. In general, there are usually three groups of tranches: the equity piece, the mezzanine tranches and the senior tranches. Hence, when the equity piece is gone due to the losses in the portfolio, the mezzanine tranche is next to suffer, and so on. This highlights that it is very important for an investor at which position in the capital structure of the tranche his investment is located. This location is usually defined by the so-called attachment and detachment point. The attachment point states percentage of losses in the portfolio at which a specific tranche starts to get eroded, and the detachment point characterizes the end of the losses. For the equity piece the attachment point is 0%, which means that losses hit the tranche from the first credit event on. The difference between the detachment and the attachment level determines the thickness or volume of a tranche. The higher the attachment point of a tranche, the safer the tranche, as a larger number of defaults are necessary in order to affect the tranche. The attachment level is also addressed as the subordination of a tranche. The higher the attachment point, the higher the subordination, the lower the risk.

The capital structure of a tranched portfolio is thus quite similar to the capital structure of a bank. Besides the shareholders' equity, the capital structure of a bank comprises other equity-like instruments, such as hybrid capital (tier 1), other subordinated bonds (upper tier 2 and lower tier 2), senior bonds and senior secured bonds, such as *Pfandbriefe* or covered bonds. In case of a bank default, the assets would be distributed to the claimholder following the strict priority rule. First, the holder of senior secured debt will receive the collateral assets. Second, the senior unsecured bondholders will receive as many assets from the remainder of the defaulted bank's portfolio until their claim is also satisfied and so on. At a certain stage of this mechanism there will be a seniority class of debt for which not all claims can be completely satisfied, as there is not sufficient volume left over. All debtholders in this seniority class will only recover a certain fraction of their initial investment, while all other claims that are junior to this will simply receive nothing. The individual claims will be satisfied strictly by their seniority. In a tranched portfolio this is also called the *waterfall principle*, as the payments are distributed within the capital structure from the top to the bottom.

However, it is quite obvious that investors in the lower parts of the capital structure would not be very happy to carry a significantly higher risk than investors in more senior tranches without being rewarded for that higher risk. Hence, the returns on the equity piece are significantly higher than the returns on the senior tranches. However, the sum of the interest payments of all tranches together cannot exceed the interest payment that is generated by the underlying assets. Tranching does not affect the size of the cake, but only the way it is sliced.

But how should the risk and the return be allocated to the individual tranches of the portfolio? The risk of a specific tranche depends on the overall risk in the underlying pool of assets, the structure of the tranche (its attachment and detachment points) and another very important factor: the default correlation. An example sheds some light on this issue. We start by assuming the most basic portfolio, namely one with only two constituents, company A and company B, both of which have the same volume. This portfolio can be sliced into two tranches. One that covers the first loss, no matter whether company A or B defaults first (corresponds to the equity tranche) and one that covers the second default (corresponds to the senior piece). Default correlation is merely the answer to the following question: How high is the risk that company B defaults given that company A has defaulted (or vice versa). We'll think about an answer to this question referring to a real example, that of Ford and General Motors. The answer could be: the risk that GM defaults given that Ford defaulted is very low (or very high). However, which risk perception the reader might have will be closely tied to the rationale behind why the first company (Ford) defaulted. If such a credit event occurred because of specific problems at one company (e.g., declining sales due to quality problems), the remaining company might be better off due to reduced competition. The default correlation will be very low. Nevertheless, a negative default correlation does not make a lot of sense (although this example would suggest something like this). The lowest reasonable value for the default correlation would be zero, which means that both default independent of each other. In such a model environment, the default dependency will be given via a direct link between two companies, such as competition in the same market area.

But besides the direct link (we did refer to a case where one company has very specific problems that the other company does not have), there is also an indirect link. Perhaps the first company defaulted because of a significant slowdown in the economy. Then the risk that this slowdown will affect the second company as well will be quite high. This means that the default correlation will also be quite high, hence in a recession, for example, the risk for joint defaults is increasing. But which of the two basic approaches – direct link between two companies or dependency on the overall economic condition – should we use when assessing default correlation? In order to solve this problem, it helps to keep in mind that usually we are not interested in analyzing baskets with just two constituents. In a portfolio of 100 constituents, for example, one would have to analyze almost 10000 pair-wise default dependencies (in fact it would be 100 × 99 = 9900). Moreover, when assessing the default correlation for two companies that have a quite comparable business profile, the analysis of this direct link might be feasible. But what should we answer when referring to Coca Cola and Deutsche Telekom? Most probably it will be a hard task to quantify a direct link between these two companies. The consequence is that we have to use a default dependency approach which refers to an underlying factor that drives the risk for all credit exposures, simply because the pair-wise correlation approach is not feasible.

In contrast to these difficulties, the factor models – the class of approaches, where one or more underlying factors are driving the default correlation – are easy to implement. Moreover, this framework is quite intuitive, as it is quite natural that the risk for joint defaults increases when the economy runs into a recession. Furthermore, the model framework can be easily expanded to incorporate not just a single factor, but a whole range of factors, that cover, for example, industry sectors or the regional distribution. Hence, the factor model approach is used in almost all credit portfolio models throughout the entire industry. Frequently used credit portfolio models that rely on a factor model include the Credit Metrics and the KMV model.

But how does a portfolio model work apart from the default correlation? From a conceptual perspective, this is not very difficult. We refer again to our simple example above, a two-asset portfolio in which both assets have the same exposure. Basically, a credit portfolio model would be a quantitative tool that tells us the probability distribution of the future value of this portfolio with respect to default losses. As we refer to a two-asset portfolio, there are only three different potential default scenarios: no default at all, one default, or two defaults. Moreover, since we refer to the same exposure for both constituents (and due to the fact that one usually assumes the same recovery rate for all constituents for simplicity reasons), it does not matter which credit defaults, given that there is one default. Hence, we only need to model the number of defaults in the portfolio. For the two extreme cases – zero default and two defaults – there is obviously only one scenario per case: either all constituents survive or all default. However, when referring to exactly one default, there are two potential outcomes: either company A could default and company B could survive, or vice versa. From a mathematical perspective, a credit portfolio model is just assigning probability for each potential scenario. If we know the default probability for each constituent (and if we assume uncorrelated defaults), this is not difficult. The probability of zero defaults is just the probability that company A survives times the probability that company B survives. For a two-default event, we do the same for the probabilities that each constituent defaults. For exactly one event, we can derive the probabilities accordingly (note that we have two potential paths here).

For a larger portfolio, we do exactly the same thing: setting up all potential scenarios, assigning probabilities to each scenario by multiplying default and survival probabilities accordingly and aggregating all paths in order to arrive at numbers of default. However, from a pure numeric perspective, this is not very efficient, as the number of potential scenarios grows exponentially with the number of constituents. Just think about the number of scenarios that leads to exactly 5 defaults in a portfolio of 100 constituents. So in a real credit portfolio model, one has to think about efficient number crunching, and about how to lift some assumptions that we have made, namely the so-called homogeneity assumption (same exposure and same recovery rate for all names) and the consideration of the default correlation (recall that we assumed independent defaults). However, this is more of a technical problem for financial engineers, and we refrain from delving deeper into this topic at this point.

However, why is the default correlation such an important issue? A simple example helps to shed some light on this. We refer to a portfolio that consists of 30 constituents. Furthermore, we assume that the individual (uncorrelated) default probability is 25% for all constituents. To remain clear at this stage of the analysis, the assumption that all constituents share the same default probability does not mean that all constituents default at the same time; it simply means that all constituents are comparably risky. In other words, they would share the same rating category. This so-called homogeneity assumption is quite common. The individual default probabilities are replaced by an average one. However, when the underlying portfolio is not very homogeneous, this may be an inappropriate assumption. Although a default probability of 25% might appear quite high this is a level one would usually assign to a so-called junk credit. But one should bear in mind that this figure is the cumulated default probability over a longer time horizon. Referring to a time horizon of five years, this translates roughly into an annualized default probability of 5% p.a. Moreover, when a credit defaults, it usually does not involve a 100% loss of the exposure at risk. It is a quite common – and reasonable – assumption that a creditor can recover about 50% of his investment exposure. Hence, a default probability of 5% p.a. and a so-called recovery rate of 50% translate into an expected loss of 2.5% p.a. This expected loss is the quantity that credit portfolio managers are usually focusing

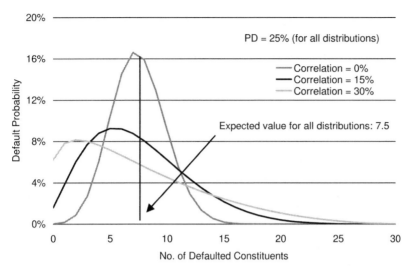

Fig. 2.9: Portfolio default probabilities for various default correlations

on. It can be compared to the credit spread. However, in the course of the crisis, a credit spread level of 250 bp was not unheard of. Our example is thus a reasonable one. The reason why we chose a more elevated level is simply to make the impact of the default correlation more visible in the chart.

In figure 2.9, we show the portfolio default distribution for this example. This chart shows the probability (y axis) of a certain number default (x axis) in this portfolio, for three different levels of the default correlation. This chart can be read in the following way. Under the assumption of 0% default dependency – and the average default probability of 25%, the probability of 10 defaults is about 9.1%. Before we go into the default correlation aspects, we want to highlight some important features about this distribution. First of all, it is quite clear that at the end of the day there has to be either no default or any number of defaults up to 30, the amount of constituents in the portfolio. Consequently, all probabilities for 0, 1, 2, 3, ... 30 defaults have to sum up to 100%. However, it is a natural thing that the probabilities of all possible outcomes of a random experiment have to add up to 100%. The probability that you toss either heads or tails when you flip a coin is 100% – excluding the negligible probability that the coin lands on its side.

The second property of the portfolio default probability distribution is the average number of defaults in this portfolio. It can be derived by multiplying the number of default events with its assigned probability and summing up all possible outcomes. The interesting feature about these distributions is that no matter which level of default correlation we use, the average number of defaults in the portfolio doesn't change. In our example, it remains at 7.5, which equals exactly the number of constituents times the average default probability of 25%. This is a very important issue that we should keep in mind. The default correlation does not change the overall default probability at all; It simply changes the shape of the distribution curve, without affecting the average default risk.

Moreover, another point is worth mentioning. Just take a look at the left end of the chart in figure 2.9. It marks the probability of zero defaults in our model portfolio. For a default correlation level of 0%, the respective probability is almost zero (in fact it is 0.02%). This means that if all constituents in our model portfolio default completely uncorrelated, the probability that we experience not a single default can be safely considered to be zero. However, when the default correlation rises, the probability that we suffer no default event at all also rises. For a default correlation level of 15%, the probability of no defaults is 1.6%, and for a default correlation level of 30% it is even 6.3%.

What is going on here? Intuitively, we would have said that default correlation is something bad. Now it turns out that increasing default correlation also increases the chance of having no default event at all! But an increasing default correlation changes more than just the probability of zero defaults; it changes the whole shape of the portfolio default distribution. At the other end of the chart – the one where we have a large number of default events – the default correlation does exactly what we would naturally expect from a rising default correlation: It increases the risk of having a large number of defaults.

Is there a plausible explanation for this strange behavior of default correlation, or do we need to have a PhD in mathematics and economics in order to understand it? Not at all. The heart of the problem is very easy. We only get confused by the fact that a higher default correlation simply means a rising risk of joint defaults. It does not mean that the overall default probability changes. In general terms, the default correlation only affects the way the probabilities are distributed over the number of defaults. The average default risk has to remain constant. Consequently, when a higher default correlation increases the probability for a larger number of defaults, the probability function has to decrease somewhere as a compensation.

A slightly off-topic example may help to understand this feature better. We suppose that a parachutist was instructed to jump out of an airplane over either one of two areas. Both areas have exactly the same size. Moreover, intelligence identified that there is exactly the same number of mines in both areas. Hence, from a generalized perspective both areas appear to be equally risky for the parachutist. However, we suppose that intelligence additionally discovered the distribution of the mines. As can be seen in figure 2.10, in area A all mines are widespread across the terrain, while in area B the mines are located very close to each other around one spot. The survive-or-not-survive question for the parachutist is: where to jump – into area A or into area B?

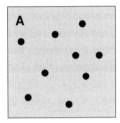 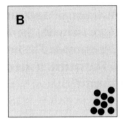

Fig. 2.10: Chart with mine fields

However, for this question the answer appears to be very easy: the parachutist apparently wants to jump into area B, as in this case his chance of surviving is much higher than for jumping into area A. When jumping into area B, the parachutist obviously risks triggering several mines at the same time, and he does not care whether he triggers only one or all mines. A human parachutist obviously has only one life. However, the chance that he does not trigger a single mine at all is higher than it is in area A. This is exactly the risk profile for a single default in a portfolio of credits. The higher the correlation, the lower the risk. Moreover, in this example we find the same feature as in credit portfolios. The overall risk – the number of mines per area – is not affected by the correlation.

Now we stretch this example a little further. The attentive reader might have already noted that we placed exactly nine mines in our minefield. This was intentional. Now we assume that our parachutist is not a human being but a cat. Without going into detail whether a cat has seven or nine lives, we assume that the amount of mines in the minefield will be sufficient to take all of them when triggered at the same time. Which decision will be made by the cat? Obviously its risk profile is significantly different from that of the human parachutist. The cat would most probably prefer area A. Here, it has a higher risk of triggering one or two mines, but the risk of triggering a large number at the same time is limited. We hope that we did not offend any animal lovers among our readers, and we would like to stress that this is only a thought experiment. (Do not try this at home).

Nevertheless, there is another analogy between the minefield, the parachutist and a credit portfolio. The larger the number of mines in the minefield, the higher the risk of triggering one - for the human parachutist, as well as for the cat. For our credit portfolio this means that the higher the individual default probability, the less likely are zero defaults, and the more likely is a high number of defaults. In figure 2.11, we depict several portfolio default probability curves with different underlying default probabilities and with a default correlation of 0%. Although the impact of an increasing individual default probability on the shape of the distribution is a little more complex, the basic movement follows the same intuition as our parachuting example: The higher the probability, the less likely a low number of defaults. The center of the distribution is shifted to a higher number of defaulted constituents.

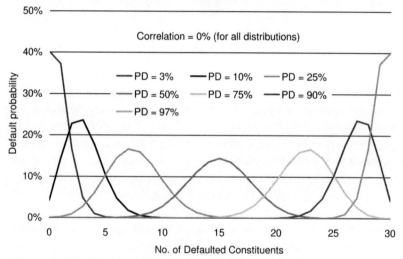

Fig. 2.11: Portfolio default probabilities for various single-name default probabilities

Finally, we would like to highlight another property of default correlation: the impact of a 100% default correlation on the portfolio default probability. We refer to the same portfolio example as shown above – 30 constituents with an individual default probability of 25% – together with default correlation figures of 0% and 100% (see figure 2.12). The impact on the shape of the distribution is significant, but also quite intuitive. In a portfolio with credits that default with a correlation of 100%, there is either no default at all, or all constituents default at the same time. As we used a default probability of 25%, the probability of

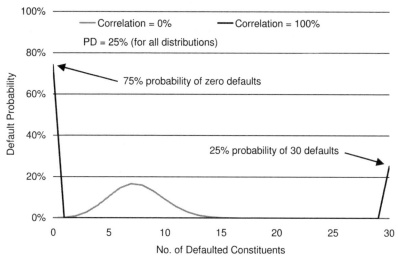

Fig. 2.12: Portfolio default probabilities for extreme default correlations (0% and 100%)

exactly zero defaults is 75%, while the probability that all constituents default is 25%. As either none or all constituents default, the probability for 1 to 29 defaults is exactly zero.

However, this is not rocket science. An average skilled financial analyst should be able to do such an analysis in an Excel sheet within a few minutes. Remember that we have chosen the simplest possible example: a homogeneous portfolio – therefore, we can use a binomial distribution – with a single factor that drives the default correlation and a Gaussian copula for modeling the default dependency. Although these models are quite simple from a mathematical point of view, they can be quite complicated to use in practice owing to the lack of economic intuition the results may involve. Just take one example. In figure 2.9 (correlation 0%, 15%, 30%) we found that an increasing default correlation increases the probability of zero defaults (left end of the chart), while it also increases the risk for a large number of defaults at the same time (right end of the chart). Just follow the order of the lines at both ends: with increasing default correlation the lines move higher. However, is this strictly increasing order valid for all possible numbers of defaults? No! Just look at the probability of exactly 4 defaults. For a default correlation of 0%, the probability is about 6%. For a default correlation of 15%, it is 8.8%, and for a default correlation of 30% it is not higher than 8.8%, but again lower, namely 7.7%. This means that for 4 defaults we cannot say that the probability increases (or decreases) with increasing default correlation; it goes up and then down again. It is quite obvious that such a behavior makes an intuitive feeling for the dynamics of the risk quite difficult.

However, there is another important problem that we did not discuss at all; namely, how to find a reasonable estimate for the default correlation. For the default probability this appears to be manageable, as we can simply use historical default probabilities (or market-implied default probabilities). But is this a reasonable measure for default correlation? No, it is not. The reason is the lack of historical data in order to find a reasonable value for the default correlation. In simple terms, we (fortunately) did not have enough cumulated default events in order to generate a reasonable statistical analysis for the default correlation (or at least, we did not have this before the crisis). Market participants have been quite innovative at this task and have developed a full range of model suggestions in order to derive a suitable default correlation figure. The suggested approaches range from a fundamental analysis (not feasible, as discussed above), to default correlations implied from the corresponding stock price correlations, to the correlation of credit spreads. However, what should we do if we do not have any of this data? Make a bold call. And that's exactly what market participants did in the subprime swamp – with terrible consequences.

But how can these findings be employed in regard to tranches? For this purpose, we only have to transfer our portfolio default probability distributions (recall that on the x-axis we had numbers of defaulted portfolio constituents) into a portfolio loss probability distribution (here the x-axis would be a specific loss ratio, such as 10% of the portfolio volume). For this purpose, market participants usually refer to another homogeneity assumption, namely a common loss-given-default (LGD). For an LGD of 60%, for example, we simply have to multiply the x-axis with 60% in order to arrive at a portfolio loss distribution (assuming also the same reference notional for all constituents in the portfolio). Then we have to derive the expected loss for a specific tranche using this probability distribution. For a 3-6% tranche, for example, all portfolio losses below 3% lead to a full repayment of the tranche notional, while all losses that exceed 6% lead to a complete loss of the tranche notional for the investor. Between 3% and 6% portfolio loss, the tranche loses its notional linearly. Hence, the probability of a full repayment of the tranche notional is given by the probability of a portfolio loss below 3%, while the risk of a 100% loss in the tranche investment is given by the cumulated probability of a portfolio loss between 6% and 100%. Between 3% and 6%, one has to weigh the linear payoff of the tranche with the respective probability.

2.6 Securitization

The securitization market developed rapidly in the past few years. Issuers and investment banks created various types of different instruments, transaction volumes grew rapidly and the rising liquidity attracted a large investor base across different types of financial institutions. Securitization is a structured finance technique in which financial assets, such as bonds, loans and receivables, are pooled together and used as collateral for investors. The funds from the notes that are purchased by the investor are used to refinance the asset pool. The securitization process defines how cash flows from the underlying assets are distributed to the note investors. The pool can involve a wide range of assets, which are typically rather illiquid. They can range from mortgage loans, credit card loans, or car loans to trade receivables or cash flows from leasing contracts. In this respect, the central idea of a securitization process is to convert illiquid assets into liquid financial securities. The purpose of a securitization process can be manifold, but in principle, the motivation is either to transfer the risk involved with the underlying assets or to refinance the assets, or both. However, the securitization market is an Eldorado for shortcuts and buzzwords and market participants tend to use them inconsistently. The term *asset-backed securities* (ABS) is sometimes used as an umbrella term for securitization (which is motivated by the fact that the securitized notes are backed by assets) or as a specific term that describes notes that are securitized by assets other than mortgages. Fewer market participants use *collateralized debt obligations* (CDO) as the respective umbrella term (which is also understandable, since the securitized notes are mostly collateralized by debt instruments). However, in the last few years, the term CDO was more frequently used for instruments that involve pools of more liquid assets, such as bonds, loans or even credit default swaps. But now one describes these instruments more precisely as *collateralized bond obligations* (CBOs), *collateralized loan obligations* (CLOs) or *collateralized swap obligations* (CSOs). The confusion about the different terms and instruments may also arise because there is one basic technique common to most of the securitization processes: tranching. It is the central credit enhancement mechanism. Credit enhancement is an important feature of securitization because it allows one to convert assets of various credit qualities into notes that meet the requirements of different investor types, and it also allows one to decouple the rating of the notes from the corresponding issuer or sponsor of the transaction.[4,5] An easy way to understand the complex and somewhat opaque securitization market is to highlight some of the important characteristics of the transactions. They can be classified in the following way:

- **By the underlying asset classes**: The largest area of the securitization market is the one for mortgage-backed securities (MBS). Here, mortgage loans are used as collateral assets. These transactions are usually further split into residential (RMBS) and commercial (CMBS) mortgage-backed securities. Non-mortgage-related securities are typically subsumed under asset-backed securities (ABS). The most important underlyings in this category are consumer loans, such as credit card or auto loans, but also home equity loans and student loans. As already mentioned above, structures that are related to commercial loans or bonds (such as leveraged loans, syndicated loans or high-yield bonds) are typically considered as CLOs or CBOs. In addition, short-term assets, such as trade receivables, can be securitized, which is typically done in so-called conduits. These instruments typically refinance the assets via issuing asset-backed commercial paper (ABCP). However, the securitization process can even refer to other structured finance assets, such as MBS- or ABS-tranches. These structures are usually addressed as structured finance CDOs (SF-CDO).

- **By the nature of the credit enhancements**: As already mentioned, the most important credit enhancement technique is tranching. The credit enhancement is achieved by creating notes with different subordination levels. A higher-level tranche is protected by a lower level one, as the latter absorbs potential losses in the collateral pool until the corresponding notional is completely eroded. Moreover, the running cash flows from the underlying assets are distributed across the different classes of notes according to a so-called waterfall principle. First, payments of higher tranches are satisfied before payments of lower tranches. However, the tranching mechanism involves a quite complicated risk, that of joint or correlated defaults. As introduced in section 2.5, modeling default correlation risk is quite complex. For securitized transactions that refer to large numbers of underlying assets (such as RMBS and consumer loan ABS), market participants captured the risk of joint defaults only very marginally. This was related to the hope that the large number of assets may lead to a high diversification and therefore to a limited risk of correlated defaults, where losses may eat into higher tranches. A lot of investors might have tearfully regretted such an inappropriate analysis, as the risk of mortgage loans, especially in the subprime area, is closely related to the state of the economy (interest rate levels, business cycle, unemployment rate, etc.) and imposes therefore a non-negligible level of default correlation. The second important credit enhancement technique was the involvement of a *monoline insurer*, which guarantees a specific tranche of a transaction. However, when involving a third-party guarantee, investors have to assess the counterparty risk with respect to the guarantor. In the CDS market, it is a central rule not to buy protection from a counterparty that has a high default dependency on the insured reference entity (for example, you do not buy protection on the Federal Republic of Germany from a German bank, as the risk that the latter will default, given a credit event in the former is quite high). This correlation risk was a huge problem during the subprime crisis, since the monoliner industry was heavily impacted by subprime losses. This is bad news, as the guarantee of the monoliners is especially needed in times of stress like during the subprime crisis. This raises the question whether the credit enhancement stemming from a monoliner is more than just a sedative for investor risk officers. What good is a guarantor if he defaults when we need him? In this respect, the name *monoliner* nicely highlights this default correlation problem. In more positive terms, monoliners insure investors against the risk of isolated events. The risk that they cannot survive a severe economic crisis in which they are especially needed unscathed is very high, as they are not sufficiently diversified. Other credit enhancement techniques are, for example, back-up servicers, letters of credit (both have a similar role as a monoliner but usually come from the banking industry), reserve accounts that collect a potential excess spread and provide additional collateral for the note investor, or turbo-paydown (or acceleration) features, which trigger the early redemption of a higher note when certain triggers are breached. An example sheds some light on the last two mechanisms. The cash flows of the underlying assets are distributed to the holders of the different tranches according to predefined rules. In a waterfall principle, all claims of senior noteholders are satisfied first, followed by mezzanine noteholders, and so forth. The residual cash flow is then distributed to the investors of the equity piece. In a reserve account mechanism, a part of this residual (or excess) cash flow is not directly paid out to the equity investors but accumulated in the reserve account. Only if specific conditions are fulfilled (e.g., when all senior notes have been repaid) will the structure distribute the cash in the reserve account to equity investors. Hence, the reserve account serves as additional collateral for senior investors. Moreover, under certain circumstances (e.g., when specific triggers, such as a certain loss amount, occurred), the cash account and future cash flows for subordinated investors can be used to redeem the senior notes earlier than initially contracted. This is called a *turbo-paydown feature*. Usually a transaction does not involve only a single credit enhancement feature but a combination of various different types. This combination is set up in order to optimize the transaction with respect to the investor's requirements and the issuer's needs. The large number of potential combinations and features explains the high number of different structures. Moreover, more recent portfolio credit derivatives also make use of credit enhancement techniques. A good example is the CPDO, which involves a reserve account. However, the different features have advantages and disadvantages. The disadvantage of a reserve account is, for example, that it needs to be filled in order to provide a decent level of additional security. Hence, it does not help against an early deterioration of the underlying assets. That was exactly the problem that hit the CPDO arena.

- **By the purpose of the deal from the issuer's perspective**: Issuers, as well as investors, may have various different reasons for entering the securitization market. An issuer may, for example, want to offload assets that he already has on his balance sheet to an outside investor. Alternatively, he could also purchase assets only for the purpose of securitization. The former is called a *balance sheet transaction* and the latter is typically addressed as an *arbitrage transaction*. While balance sheet transactions are typically triggered from the issuer's perspective (he wants to offload certain assets), arbitrage transactions are more driven by the investor who wants to obtain exposure to a specific risk profile (however, this leads more to the bespoke CDO arena, which is typically not subsumed under securitization). Furthermore, the purpose of a balance sheet transaction can be also classified as to whether the deal is motivated by risk reduction or refinancing needs. In the former, an issuer might be interested in (or forced, due to regulatory rules, such as Basel II) reducing exposure against a part of assets in his portfolio. As a consequence, the issuer may only want to sell the most risky tranche, the equity piece, to an outside investor in order to get some capital relief. On the other hand, the issuer could also simply want to fund the acquisition of the assets on his balance sheet. Here he would be more focused on selling the large senior part of the tranched portfolio and could even retain the equity piece. In the Anglo-Saxon world, this type of bulk-refinancing of illiquid bank assets, such as mortgage or consumer loans, is more common. ABS and MBS were frequently used to refinance the operating bank business. In other areas, such as in Germany, a different technique, the covered bond (*Pfandbrief*), was used for this purpose. Although there are similarities in the purpose of covered bonds and MBS/ABS, there are some important differences. The most important difference is that the MBS/ABS technique involves a bankruptcy-remote special purpose vehicle (SPV), while a covered bond is issued directly by a bank. The economic difference is that in the SPV-type transaction the investor has only a claim against the SPV, which is backed by the assets; in the covered bond, he has a claim against the whole bank, and only if the bank is in default is he additionally backed by the cover pool. In other words, ABS/MBS allow the direct, unmitigated exposure against the underlying assets, while covered bonds involve a double-default scenario. The investor suffers losses from defaults only if the bank is in default and if the cover pool is not sufficient to satisfy all claims. However, covered bonds are in addition highly overcollateralized. These differences explain why the covered bond market was not hit very hard during the crisis (spreads widened a few basis points during the crisis), while the ABS/MBS market was almost completely shut down. As a consequence, many first-time issuers tapped the covered bond market instead of their traditional funding source, the ABS/MBS market.

- **By the method how the assets are transferred into the transaction**: In a true sale transaction, the assets are completely transferred to the SPV that issues the securitized notes, while in a synthetic transaction the cash flows stemming from the targeted assets are only transferred synthetically. The variant of choice depends on various factors, such as how easily the assets can be transferred (i.e., whether the issuer is entitled and willing to legally transfer the assets), the involved costs and the timeframe for the transaction. In case the legal transfer of the ownership rights to the SPV is difficult (e.g., residential mortgage loans where the loan contract entitles the originator to do so), one can use credit derivatives technology (such as CDS) instead to transfer the economic risk to the SPV. However, the disadvantage of a synthetic transfer is how to insulate the SPV from the sponsor in terms of bankruptcy remoteness. The assets of the SPV should not be consolidated with those of the sponsor given the sponsor's default. Rating agencies typically require bankruptcy remoteness in order to assign a higher rating to the transaction compared to the sponsor. But true sale transactions are legally more complex and typically more time-consuming than the synthetic transfer. Hence, synthetic transactions are preferably used by banks with a strong rating, while true sale transactions are more attractive to an issuer with a weaker credit profile.

- **Whether the underlying pool of assets is dynamic (managed) or static (unmanaged)**: ABS and MBS are typically static, that is, unmanaged structures as the manager's possibility to intervene in the portfolio of illiquid assets is rather limited. The involvement of portfolio managers is more common in CDOs, which typically refer to liquid assets. The manager can therefore buy new attractive assets, sell assets that violate certain investment conditions and change the characteristics of the underlying portfolio on behalf of the CDO investors. However, CDO managers are typically restricted in their management abilities, as they have to follow predefined investment guidelines, such as minimum ratings, sector limitations and duration restrictions. The legal overhead for managed transactions is higher compared to unmanaged ones, and obviously the portfolio manager demands a management fee, which involves extra costs for the investor (either paid directly or taken from the investment return). Moreover, structures that invest in short-term assets, such as conduits and SIVs, also require the interaction of portfolio management since maturing assets have to be replaced by new ones.

- **By the nature of the underlying risk**: Traditional cash flow transactions focus on the default risk of the underlying assets, while market value structures (such as market value CDOs, SIVs, CPDOs, etc.) are more sensitive to the market (spread) risk of the underlying assets. In a cash flow transaction, the cash flows of the underlying assets are distributed to the note investors according to specific rules (waterfall principle, excess spread to reserve account, etc.) However, a realized loss for a specific tranche (from the equity tranche up to the super-senior tranche) can only occur if the there is default in an underlying asset (i.e., a non-payment of a scheduled payment). In contrast, in a market value transaction, the payments to the tranche investors are related to the market prices of the underlying assets. An investor may realize a loss in a tranche only because the market value of the assets in the collateral pool decline, even if there is no default event. A typical example involves credit-linked notes that refer to a certain reference index and that are triggered if this reference index hits a certain loss barrier, such as leveraged super senior and CPDOs. Fitch recently published an exposure draft[6] dealing with the risks in such market value transactions. The rating agency distinguishes between traditional market value securities that are related to management interaction given specific conditions in the market (e.g., market-value CDOs and senior notes and commercial paper from conduits and SIVs) and so-called knock-out structures where a loss is involved if a certain trigger level is breached (e.g., LSS, CPDOs, and capital notes from SIVs).

However, there are other possible characteristics that might help to distinguish different transactions, such as the redemption structure (bullet or amortization), the coupon type (variable or fixed), or whether the transaction is a single- or a multi-issuer structure, where the assets have been either originated by a single issuer or by various different issuers.

Moreover, there are various other topics that have to be addressed when structuring and analyzing such transactions, such as weighted average life (WAL) and the prepayment risk, that is, the risk that the underlying assets amortize faster than initially anticipated (ironically, this was considered the major risk in MBS transactions), overcollateralization (O/C) tests that serve as trigger events for further risk mitigation and credit enhancement measures, and the average credit quality of the underlying pool of assets, which may, for example, be measured by the weighted average rating factor (WARF), etc. The above-mentioned properties and characteristics of individual securitization transactions can only provide a brief overview and do not claim completeness in any sense, as we cannot go into the details of structured finance analysis. In the following, we want to focus on the major characteristics of the securitization market in order to provide an understanding of the impact that this universe has on the whole economy during a crisis.

In chart 2.13, we show the growth in the outstanding amount of global ABS bonds (referring to the above-mentioned definition of securitization with respect to non-mortgage-related illiquid assets). The market grew from below USD 500 bn in the mid-90s to USD 2,500 bn in 2007. Major drivers of growth have been home equity loans and other ABS, while growth in the traditional ABS segments, such as auto loan and credit card ABS, stagnated in recent years. In 2007, home equity loans made up 25% (USD 600 bn) of the whole ABS mar-

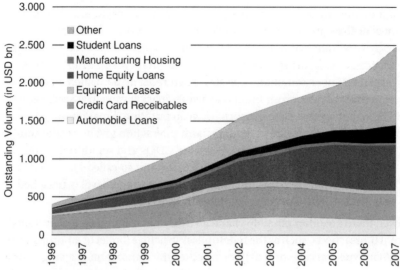

Fig. 2.13: Outstanding Asset-Backed Securities
Source: IFMA

ket, while other ABS even amounted to 40% (USD 1,000 bn). In the mid-90s, credit card ABS have been by far the largest segment (almost 45%), while home equity loans and other ABS made up 12.5% each.

Mortgage-related issuance activity (see chart 2.14) amounted to almost USD 2,000 bn only in 2007 (note that here we refer to issuance volume while the previous statistic referred to the amount outstanding). About 2/3 of the issuance activity is agency-related debt (i.e., backed by one of the government-sponsored enterprises Fannie Mae or Freddie Mac) while the rest was issued by other financial institutions. However, the market share of non-agency-related mortgage debt increased sharply over the last few years. In 2006, the market share of commercial mortgage lenders was only 6%. The peak of issuance activity was in 2003, with more than USD 3,000 bn in new debt.

The strong growth in market share of home equity loans and the non-agency-related mortgage debt highlights the run-up to the crisis, as both have been the major catalyst for the financial market turmoil. In the aftermath of the bursting of the tech bubble and the overwhelming liquidity that flowed into the market by the Fed in order to combat the post 9/11 crisis and Enronian economics, investors recognized the return potential of mortgage-related debt market in particular in the US, and expanded their franchise heavily. However, the focus was more on the "attractive" high-margin segments (subprime and home equity loans) rather than on typical agency mortgage loans. The consequence of this investor-driven expansion was a housing boom and declining credit quality of the originated and securitized mortgage loans as the leverage employed in the housing market increased. Many investors simply bet on a continuing housing boom, ignoring all warning signs of a slowdown in the housing market that had been already apparent in 2005 (cf. Alan Greenspan's paper on the housing market in Ref. 7).

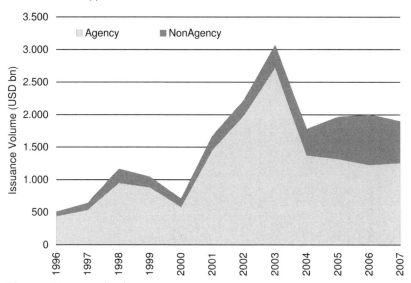

Fig. 2.14: Mortgage-related issuance
Source: SIFMA

One consequence of the strong growth of low-quality mortgage debt was an embarrassing performance of the different mortgage-related structured finance asset classes during the subprime crisis. From an initial amount of securities of about USD 3,000 bn (see table 2.1, which summarizes the rating actions from S&P with respect to Q1 2005 to Q3 2007 vintages until December 28, 2007), about 5% were downgraded during the crisis (2% of which from investment grade to sub-investment grade), 0.1% defaulted, about 2% received a credit watch negative and 0.6% were downgraded and placed on credit watch negative. On a relative basis, the worst-performing segments have been the closed-end, second-lien RMBS (RMBS CES: 35% downgraded with 22% from IG to SG,

Tab. 2.1: Original issuance-based cumulative performance and creditwatch until December 28, 2007: US RMBS, CDOs of ABS, and SIV-lites for Q1 2005 to Q3 2007 vintages (in USD bn) Source: Standard & Poor's

Subsector	Original Issuance	Downgraded	IG to SG	Defaulted	CW negative	Downgraded CW negative
US CDO cash flow CDO of ABS	233.49	6.82	1.59	0	18.4	3.47
US CDO hybrid (mainly CDO of ABS)	158.11	29.84	14.11	0.49	20.41	13.2
Global CDO market value/SIV lites	34.03	1.96	1.96	1.44	0.53	0.52
US synthetic CDO of ABS	52.12	5.54	0.89	0	0.09	0.09
Total	477.74	44.15	18.55	1.92	39.43	17.28
US RMBS Alt-A	991.72	11.21	3.99	0.02	0.91	0.01
US RMBS CES	80.12	28.32	18.03	1.57	11.06	0.01
US RMBS NIMS	26.06	8.5	7.64	0	1.06	0.18
US RMBS prime	397.95	0.18	0.17	0.17	0.01	0
US RMBS subprime	1,055.89	49.01	21.23	0.12	5.46	0.02
Total	2,551.73	97.22	51.05	1.88	18.51	0.22
ALL	3,029.48	141.37	69.6	3.8	57.94	17.49
ALL (%)		4.67	2.3	0.13	1.91	0.58

2% defaulting and 13% on credit watch negative). The second-worst performer was the net interest margin RMBS (RMBS NIMS: 32% downgrades and 30% directly to junk), which is essentially an interest-only strip from the net interest proceeds of an underlying transaction. However, the performance of structured finance CDOs – almost 10% downgrades with 4% directly to junk, in an almost USD 500 bn asset class – is also non-negligible.

In total, S&P downgraded almost USD 150 bn of structured finance assets and almost USD 70 bn of debt to junk status. However, the rather limited amount of defaults can be understood by the fact that a single tranche usually does not default; it absorbs losses until its reference notional is completely eroded. Typically, rating agencies downgrade tranches that are hit by losses to the C-rating area.

3
Credit Players

3.1 Banks

The US mortgage business experienced significant structural changes in recent years, when investment banks shifted their focus to this market. Traditionally, mortgage loans are given to borrowers with good credit quality, which is measured by the so-called FICO score. The market for mid-size, good-quality mortgage loans is traditionally dominated by the mortgage agencies Fannie Mae and Freddie Mac, two government-sponsored enterprises. Between 1996 and 2003, the percentage of non-agency debt origination in the US mortgage markets was below 15% on average. From 2004 on, the market share of non-agency institutions rose steadily and peaked with almost 40% in 2006 (see chart 2.14 in the introduction of securitization). However, the majority of non-agency mortgage origination was related to subrime loans. The tremendous growth of this segment stems from, to a large extent, the way in which mortgage loans are traditionally refinanced in the Anglo-Saxon world, namely via mortgage-backed securities (MBS).

In an MBS, the mortgage loans are pooled in a bankruptcy-remote special purpose vehicle (SPV), which issues debt in the form of tranches in order to refinance the loans. The tranches are then sold to investors. However, the bank sponsoring the MBS transaction typically does not guarantee the loans in the pool. An investor who purchases such tranches runs, depending on the seniority of the tranche, a direct default risk. Moreover, if the sponsoring bank can sell all tranches to the market and does not retain a part of the so-called equity piece, then it does not have any default risk. In order to provide investors with securities with a decent credit quality, or at least with a rating that signals a decent credit quality, MBS transactions involved several different credit enhancement mechanisms, such as subordination or a guarantee from a bond insurer (a monoliner). In Europe, for example, mortgage debt is traditionally refinanced by covered bonds (e.g., the German *Pfandbrief*, the French *obligation fonciére* or the Spanish *cèdulas hipotecarias*). The central feature of these instruments is that they are directly issued by a bank and are additionally backed by the assets in the cover pool. Hence the credit risk of covered bonds involves a so-called

Credit Crises. J. Felsenheimer and P. Gisdakis
Copyright © 2008 WILEY-VCH Verlag GmbH & Co. KGaA, Weinheim
ISBN: 978-3-527-50375-9

double default scenario. Default losses only occur for a covered bond investor in the case of a credit event at the issuing bank and if the assets in the cover pool are not sufficient to repay the claims of the covered bond investor. In the long history of German *Pfandbriefe*, for example, this has never occurred. Besides the safety from a double-default scenario, this mechanism has another advantage for the investor: it prevents a moral hazard at the issuing institution. If losses in the underlying pool mount, the issuing bank goes bust before covered bond investors face losses.

However, in the subprime mortgage loan market a new concept of mortgage lending developed, which was specifically designed to fit into the processes of investment banks and brokerage firms and which became very popular also in other areas of the world. Instead of the traditional process of originating loans that remain on the balance sheet of the financial institution ("originate to hold"), the investment banking style became fashionable. "Originate to sell" was the corresponding buzzword. Loans should no longer be managed and refinanced directly on the balance sheets of the banks but should be transferred to the capital market in the form of structured credit products. This would allow the balance sheet of the banks to be kept smaller and therefore also their required risk capital. Moreover, using the securitization market banks would be better able to diversify their risk, because they could offload their risks to the market and could acquire other assets instead. Regional banks, for example, would benefit, as they have a regional cluster risk; their borrowers are all from the same region.

In the new lending process (see also section 4.6 for a detailed analysis), the traditional one was broken down into several pieces. Instead of a single bank that originates loans to retail clients at its branches, performs the servicing in its data center, and manages them on its balance sheet, the ideal new process would involve several independent institutions that each focus on one part of the business process. In this process, a *sales bank* originates the loans that are directly transferred to a *warehouse*, which refinances the loans for a short period of time until the exposure can be added to an RMBS and sold to the market. This warehouse and the structuring process are typically managed by an investment bank. However, since an investment bank does not have the ability to manage the loan servicing, they also build up *loan factories*, which manage the cash flows, detect delinquencies, answer borrower questions at call centers, etc. For delinquencies, another specialized group gets involved and takes care of the work-out of the loan. The underlying idea behind this new lending process is quite clear: applying industrial manufacturing principles to the lending business, outsourcing personnel-intensive processes to streamlined organizations and adapting it in a way that it can be controlled by investment banks.

As a consequence, companies like Daniel Sadek's Quick Loan Funding and New Century Financial emerged at the beginning of the new century. The purpose of these mortgage lenders was to originate (subprime) loans that could be structured and sold to the clients of investment banks. Quick Loan Funding, for example, a mortgage lender that was founded in 2002, focused almost completely on the subprime market. Ninety-five percent of the loans originated were made to subprime borrowers. The average FICO score of Quick Loan Funding was 465 out of a maximum score of 850. The median score in the US is 720. With the backing of Citigroup, which provided a short-term credit line of USD 400 mn, Quick Loan Funding pioneered lending to borrowers with credit scores below 450.[8–12] Citigroup used these loans to structure subprime RMBS in its Citigroup Mortgage Loan Trust Inc (CMLTI) subsidiary. For example, the CMLTI 2007-SHL1 transaction, a 2007 vintage RMBS backed by first and second lien residential mortgage loans with an initial balance of USD 575 mn, has an average credit score of 572. About 25% of the mortgage loans were originated in California, where Quick Loan Funding is located. By the end of 2007, the 90+ delinquency rate (the percentage of borrowers with a 90-day delinquency plus foreclosures and real estate owned loans (REO), i.e., loans where the lender bought back the house at an auction) was over 30% and the foreclosure rate was above 10%. Furthermore, the portion of borrowers that provided full documentation was only about 50%.

However, Citigroup was not the only bank involved in such lending practices. Other investment banks had even acquired mortgage lenders in order to push subprime origination. Merrill Lynch, for example, acquired the subprime lender First Franklin Corp at the end of 2006 for USD 1.3 bn from National City Corp (see table 3.2 for more acquisitions). Subprime RMBS were issued under the First Franklin Mortgage Loan Trust. A 2007 vintage bond was issued, for example, with an initial balance of USD 2.6 bn, an average credit score of 654 and a weighted average loan-to-value ratio of almost 93%. By the end of 2007, the 90+ delinquency rate was 13.2% and the foreclosure rate was 9.2%.

The cooperation between people like Daniel Sadek and investment banks with a broad investor base and a strong placing power, in conjunction with a year-long rally in the US housing market, helped to triple the subprime loan market in only four years from 2002 to 2006. Daniel Sadek was a new type of mortgage lender. The press characterized him as follows: "With his shoulder-

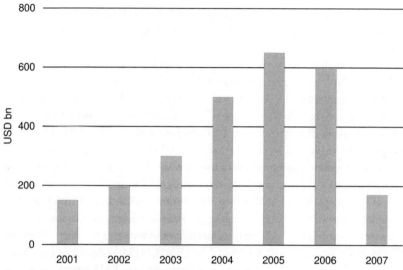

Fig. 3.1: Total subprime mortgage origination (in USD bn)
Source: Home Mortgage Disclosure Act data

length hair and beard, torn jeans and T-shirts with slogans such as 'Where is God?' Sadek looked more like a guitarist for Guns N' Roses than a mortgage banker."[9] Sadek, who had pumped gas and sold cars before creating Quick Loan Funding, brought a car-selling mentality to the traditionally very conservative mortgage lending business.[9] Selling subprime mortgages not only provided investors with the desired high-yielding assets, but also originators with high fees.

However, originating mortgage loans and selling them to clients in the form of structured products was not the end of the story. In order to allow for a proper risk management of the subprime securities, market participants – investors as well as originators – required appropriate derivatives contracts. CDS on ABS was the appropriate tool for this purpose, which allowed investors to buy and sell the risks involved in specific subprime RMBS tranches in an unfunded manner. The major investment banks involved in the subprime market had even set up an index on the most liquid home equity ABS deals, the so-called ABX.HE. These derivatives instruments have been an important building block in the securitization chain of subprime risks. Besides being based on the central "originate to sell" process, another important idea lay behind them. By putting certain aspects of the capital structure of subprime RMBS into other structured

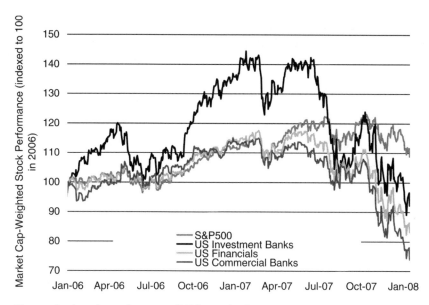

Fig. 3.2: Stock market performance of US financial industry

products – e.g., CDOs on RMBS or SIVs – the subprime players designed investment tools that were also attractive for their own investment books. Credit derivatives helped to manage those positions. Furthermore, in the course of the lending process, originated subprime debt had to be parked in the so-called warehouses for a few weeks or months to allow for an accumulation of a sufficient volume that could be sold to investors via RMBS. However, the managers of these warehouses also needed hedging tools. The ABX.HE appeared to be an attractive instrument for this purpose. As the ABX.HE comprised a portfolio of the most important home equity RMBS for each vintage, it did not allow to hedge against the default risk in a specific tranche unless this tranche was part of the ABX.HE portfolio. But managers wanted to immunize their portfolios against a systematic decline in market value. Moreover, the ABX.HE was even enhanced by structuring the TABX, an index that allows trading of the default correlation of specific tranches of a CDO on RMBS that refer to the BBB tranches of the ABX portfolio. However, despite some celebrated hedge funds and Goldman Sachs, most of the central players "got it wrong" (Stan O'Neal).

US banks – investment banks and commercial banks – were among the first and the most heavily impacted victims of the subprime crisis. In 2007, from the stock market highs before the crisis to the end of the year, the five largest US investment banks (Goldman Sachs, Morgan Stanley, Merrill Lynch, Lehman and Bear Stearns) lost almost USD 150 bn of their market capitalization, which is more than 40%. However, the S&P 500 declined in the same period by only 11%. Moreover, as can be seen from chart 3.2, the first sharp drop from the high in mid-June 2007 to the low in mid-August 2007 took only nine weeks, in which a third of their market value was wiped out. These dramatic moves reminded of the bursting of the tech bubble at the beginning of the century; ahead of the crisis almost nobody in the investment industry would have believed that such large drops could be possible for companies which are usually considered to be the brightest addresses on Wall Street. On an individual basis, the maximum mark-to-market losses (based on our calculations of the difference between the highest and the lowest price during the crisis in chart 3.3) for Goldman Sachs was about USD 34 bn, (34%), for Morgan Stanley it was USD 45 bn (48%), for Merrill Lynch about USD 40 bn (49%), for Lehman USD 16 bn (37%) and for Bear Stearns USD 12 bn (54%). The aggregation of the individual losses leads to the above-mentioned correction of about USD 150 bn. During the period from 2000 to 2002, with the bursting of the tech bubble, the collapse of Enron and 9/11, these five banks lost 60% of their market cap. But this decline took about two years. The market value of Morgan Stanley, Merrill Lynch and Bear Sterns traded at the end of 2007 about the same as it was after the Enron crisis.

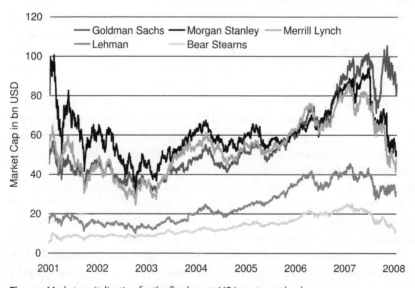

Fig. 3.3: Market capitalization for the five largest US investment banks

Tab. 3.1: Banks losses in the subprime crisis reported until February 22, 2008 (All figures are in USD bn and are net of financial hedges the firms used to mitigate their losses.)[13]

Firm	Writedown	Credit Loss	Total
Merrill Lynch	24.5		24.5
Citigroup	19.6	2.5	22.1
UBS	18.1		18.1
HSBC	0.9	9.8	10.7
Morgan Stanley	9.4		9.4
Bank of America	7	0.9	7.9
Washington Mutual	0.3	6.2	6.5
Credit Agricole	5		5
Credit Suisse	4.8		4.8
Wachovia	2.7	2	4.7
Societe Generale	3.6		3.6
Barclays	3.2		3.2
JPMorgan Chase	1.6	1.6	3.2
Canadian Imperial (CIBC)	3.2		3.2
Mizuho Financial Group	3.2		3.2
Bayerische Landesbank	2.8		2.8
Bear Stearns	2.6		2.6
Dresdner	2.6		2.6
Royal Bank of Scotland	2.5		2.5
Deutsche Bank	2.3		2.3
Natixis	1.8		1.8
Fortis	1.8		1.8 *
Wells Fargo	0.3	1.4	1.7
Lehman Brothers	1.5		1.5
National City	0.4	1	1.4
BNP Paribas	0.9	0.3	1.2
Nomura Holdings	1		1
Gulf International	1		1
Asian banks (excl. Mizuho, Nomura)	3.2	0.6	3.8
Canadian banks (excl. CIBC)	1.8	0.1	1.9
European banks not listed above	2.7		2.7
Total **	136.3	26.4	162.7

* Estimate based on the profit guidance provided by company.
** Totals reflect figures before rounding.

On a relative basis, the five largest commercial banks (Bank of America, Citigroup, JP Morgan Chase, Wells Fargo, and Wachovia) were slightly less impacted (35%), but the absolute figure in the same period is impressive: a loss in market capitalization of USD 320 bn. Citigroup's stock contributed USD 135 bn to this loss. During the crisis, the formerly largest bank in the world halved its market capitalization and is now only number three in the US behind Bank of America and JP Morgan in terms of market value. Citigroup's stock market crash does not come as a surprise given its huge subprime losses. Including the USD 18 bn write-down in Q4 2007, Citigroup incurred subprime losses of as much as USD 34 bn, followed by Merrill Lynch with USD 25 bn. Number three in term of subprime losses is UBS, with USD 14 bn. All three banks ousted their senior management during the course of the crisis. Vikram Pandit followed Chuck Prince at Citigroup, John Thain replaced Stan O'Neal at Merrill Lynch and Marcel Rohner succeeded Peter Wuffli at UBS. It appears that the new CEOs were trying to clean up the mess as quickly as possible. In total, banks reported more than USD 130 bn of subprime-related losses. Although the sheer size of this figure is already breathtaking – recall that the first loss estimate by Ben Bernanke in the summer of 2007 was USD 50-100 bn – it is clear that there is more yet to come.

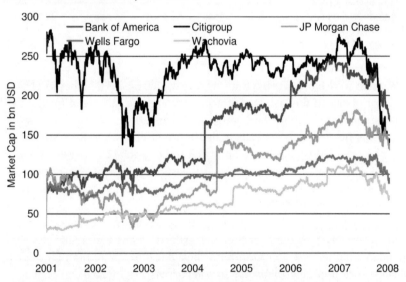

Fig. 3.4: Market capitalization of the five largest US commercial banks

However, the drop in the market value is only one issue figuring into the recent trouble of the banking industry. The prices of their debt securities were affected even more adversely. For some US investment banks, credit spreads were signaling an existential threat. Until a few days ahead of the subprime storm, 5Y CDS spreads for Goldman Sachs, Morgan Stanley, Merrill Lynch, Lehman and Bear Stearns traded at around 20 bp (see figure 3.6). Within only a

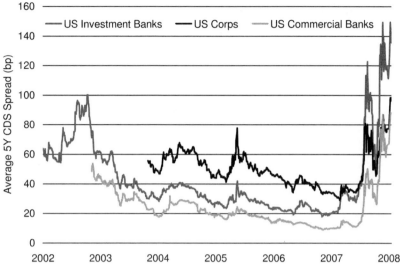

Fig. 3.5: 5Y CDS spreads for US investment and commercial banks (both senior) and for US corporates

few days they were blown out by almost 100 bp, which means that they increased by a factor of six. In the last days of 2007, the average 5Y spread for the five investment banks even traded up to 160 bp. During the hottest days in August, Lehman and Bear Stearns' spreads traded above 170 bp, while Bear Sterns' 5Y spreads reached levels above 200 bp in December 2007. The tightest level of the iTraxx Crossover – a CDS index that measures the credit risk of the fifty most important junk bond issuers in Europe – traded below 170 bp just a few weeks before the crisis had started. There is even another analogy between Bear Stearns, Lehman and companies with junk ratings. Their credit curve became inverse in the course of the crisis, which means that a CDS investor demanded a higher risk premium for a short-dated exposure than for a long-dated exposure. Typically an inverse spread curve is a sign that a company is in financial distress. The General Motors CDS curve, for example, became inverse in 2005 when investors were speculating that it would default. A credit spread of 200 bp translates into a market-implied cumulated default probability of 15% over the next five years, while one of 30 bp implies a default probability of only 2.5%. These figures were estimated using the standard market assumption for the recovery rate of 40% in the case of a default event.

Tab. 3.2: Subprime victims – businesses sold[14]
Source: Bloomberg

Businesses Sold	Parent	Buyer	Price (USD mn)	Date[*]
Centex Home Equity	Centex	Fortress	554[c]	Mar-06
Chapel Funding	–	Deutsche Bank	N/D	May-06
Aames Investment	–	Accredited Home	301	May-06
EHomeCredit	–	Shearson Fin'l	5	Jun-06
HomEq	Wachovia	Barclays	469	Jun-06
MortgageIT	–	Deutsche Bank	430	Jul-06
Allstate Home Loans	–	Shearson Fin'l	5	Jul-06
Saxon	–	Morgan Stanley	706	Aug-06
First Franklin	National City	Merrill Lynch	1,300	Sep-06
Encore Credit **	ECC Capital	Bear Stearns	26	Oct-06
Irwin Mortgage **	Irwin Financial	Four buyers	261	Oct-06
Irwin Mortgage **	Irwin Financial	New Century	N/D	Nov-06
Champion	KeyCorp	HSBC, Fortress	N/D	Dec-06
Millennium Funding Grp	–	Roark Capital	N/D	Dec-06
EquiFirst	Regions Fin'l	Barclays	76	Jan-07
ABN Amro Mortgage	ABN Amro	Citigroup	N/D	Jan-07
New York Mortgage[a]	NY Mort. Trust	IndyMac	14	Feb-07
New York Mortgage[b]	NY Mort. Trust	Franklin Credit	N/D	Feb-07
All Fund Mortgage	–	CMXL Corp.	N/D	Mar-07
Senderra Funding ****	–	Goldman Sachs	N/D	Mar-07
ResMae Mortgage	–	Citadel	180	Mar-07
SB Financial	–	W.J. Bradley	N/D	Mar-07
MortgageTree Lending	–	W.J. Bradley	N/D	Apr-07
Fremont[d]	Fremont General	Ellington	–	Apr-07
Lime Financial Services	–	Credit Suisse	N/D	Apr-07
New Century servicing	–	Carrington Cap.	184	Apr-07

Tab. 3.2: Continued

Businesses Sold	Parent	Buyer	Price (USD mn)	Date [*]
Opteum Fin'l retail	Opteum	Prospect Mortgage	1.5	May-07
Pinnacle Financial	–	Impac Mortgage	N/D	May-07
Dollar Mortgage Corp.	–	Shearson Fin'l	1	Jun-07
Green Tree Servicing	Fortress/Cerberus	Centerbridge	N/D	Jun-07
First NLC Financial	Friedman Billings	Sun Capital	60	Jul-07
Winstar Mortgage [**]	–	Am. Sterling Bank	N/D	Aug-07
ACC Capital assets [***]	ACC Capital Hld.	Citigroup	N/D	Aug-07
Fair Home Lending Fin'l	–	Principal Mtg.	0.8	Oct-07
Accredited Home	–	Lone Star Funds	296	Oct-07
Litton Loan Servicing	C-Bass	Goldman Sachs	–	Dec-07

a) Retail assets.
b) Wholesale assets.
c) Actual price before taxes, per 10-Q filing. Centex's release cited after-tax proceeds of about USD 540 mn.
d) Residential subprime unit.
e) Shutdown of subprime lending and mortgage banker finance warehouse lending units announced in December 2007.
f) Purchased in July 2007 for USD 188 mn.
g) Not applicable.
h) Units served mortgage brokers and bought home loans from mortgage bankers, thrifts, builders and credit unions.
i) Formally known as Mortgage Investment Lending Associates.
j) Confirmed by company e-mail on July 5, 2007.
k) Owners included Cerberus Capital Management LP. Retail lending halted in June, wholesale lending in August.

Companies listed may have engaged in conventional, Alternative A or subprime mortgage lending. Status of deals, prices and terms reflect date of entry and are subject to later adjustment.
N/D Not disclosed or not available.

[*] Announced date, first known disclosure or effective date if disclosed after completion. Some announced closings have not yet been completed.

[**] Asset sale.

[***] Citigroup obtained an option to buy ACC Capital's wholesale mortgage origination and servicing businesses.

[****] Per Goldman Chief Financial Officer David Viniar 6/14/07 in conversation with reporters. Web site lists company name as Avelo Mortgage LLC d/b/a Senderra Funding.

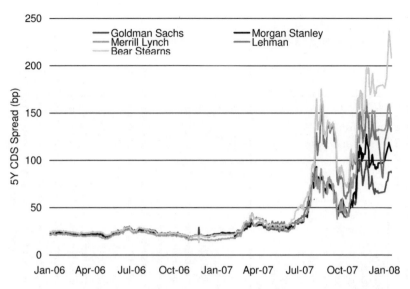

250 ―
    ―Goldman Sachs   ―Morgan Stanley
    ―Merrill Lynch   ―Lehman
    ―Bear Stearns
200 ―

5Y CDS Spread (bp)

150 ―

100 ―

50 ―

0 ―
    Jan-06 Apr-06 Jul-06 Oct-06 Jan-07 Apr-07 Jul-07 Oct-07 Jan-08

Fig. 3.6: 5Y CDS spreads for the five largest US investment banks

In the same period, the 5Y spreads for the five largest US commercial banks widened from 12 bp to 95 bp. Although this performance is already quite ugly, the real challenge for the banks is that the non-financials trade at lower credit spread levels. The average spread for the CDX.NA.IG CDS index – an index of the 125 most liquidly traded CDS contracts on North American investment-grade companies – widened from 34 bp to 100 bp. As shown in figure 3.5, the cost of debt protection on the investment banks is higher than the cost on the broad corporates index. In turn this means that the investment banks would have to pay more for the debt than they can charge their clients on average. This is obviously not a sustainable situation. Either the spreads for the banks have to decline, or the ones for the non-financials have to go up, with the latter being much more likely.

3.2 Fannie Mae and Freddy Mac

In mid-October, Fannie Mae and Freddie Mac – the two largest US mortgage players – have arrived in the subprime swamp. Shares of both companies have lost almost 60% from their 2007 highs. In November, 5Y CDS spreads for Fannie Mae – the largest player in the US mortgage loan market, which owns

Tab. 3.3: Subprime victims – businesses cut, closed or bankrupt[14]
(Companies listed may have engaged in conventional, Alternative
A or subprime mortgage lending. Status of deals, prices and terms
reflect date of entry and are subject to later adjustment.)
Source: Bloomberg

Cuts/Closed/Bankrupt	Parent	Status	Date[*]
Acoustic Home Loans	–	Halted applications	Apr-06
Ameriquest Mortgage	ACC Capital Hld.	Shut retail branches	May-06
Meritage Mortgage	NetBank	Closed	Nov-06
Summit Mortgage	Summit Financial	Closed	Nov-06
Sebring Capital	–	Closed	Dec-06
Ownit Mortgage Solutions	–	Bankruptcy	Dec-06
Harbourton Mortgage	Harbourton Capital	Closed	Dec-06
Alliance Home Funding	Alliance Bankshrs.	Closed	Dec-06
Millennium Bankshares	–	Closed mortgage unit	Dec-06
Popular Financial	Popular	Closed subprime unit	Jan-07
Bay Capital	Clear Choice Fin'l	Closed	Jan-07
EquiBanc Mortgage	Wachovia	Closed	Jan-07
Funding America LLC	Ocwen Financial	Closed	Jan-07
DeepGreen Financial	Lightyear Capital	Closed	Jan-07
Eagle First Mortgage	–	Closed	Jan-07
Mortgage Lenders Network	–	Bankruptcy	Feb-07
Lenders Direct Capital	–	Halted wholesale loans	Feb-07
ResMae Mortgage		Bankruptcy, loan halt	Feb-07
Central Pacific Mortgage	–	Closed	Mar-07
FMF Capital LLC	FMF Capital Group	Closed	Mar-07
Silver State Mortgage	–	License revoked	Feb-07
Ameritrust Mortgage	–	Shut subprime unit	Mar-07
Master Financial	–	Halted originations	Mar-07
Investaid Corp.	–	Suspended	Mar-07
People's Choice	–	Bankruptcy	Mar-07
LoanCity	–	Closed	Mar-07
New Century Financial	–	Bankruptcy	Apr-07
SouthStar Funding	–	Bankruptcy	Apr-07
Peoples Mortgage	Webster Financial	Closed	Apr-07
WarehouseUSA	NovaStar	Closed	Apr-07
Copperfield Investments	–	Bankruptcy	Apr-07
First Horizon National	–	Halted subprime loans	Apr-07
Opteum Fin'l wholesale	Opteum	Closed unit [h]	Apr-07
H&R Block Mortgage	H&R Block	Closed	Apr-07
MILA [i]	–	Bankruptcy	Apr-07
Texas Capital Bank	Texas Cap. Banc.	Closed mortgage unit	Apr-07

Tab. 3.3: Continued

Cuts/Closed/Bankrupt	Parent	Status	Date[*]
Millennium Funding Grp	Roark Capital	Halted originations	Apr-07
Columbia Home Loans	OceanFirst	Closed	May-07
Lancaster Mortgage	–	Halted wholesale loans	Jun-07
Oak Street Mortgage	–	Bankruptcy	Jun-07
Starpointe Mortgage	–	Closed	Jun-07
Heartwell Mortgage[j]	–	Halted retail/wholesale	Jun-07
Wells Fargo	–	Shut correspondent unit	Jun-07
Wells Fargo	–	Shut subprime wholesale	Jul-07
Premier Mortgage Funding	–	Bankruptcy	Jul-07
Alliance Mtg Investments	–	Bankruptcy	Jul-07
Entrust Mortgage	–	Halted loans	Jul-07
Alternative Financing	–	Halted wholesale loans	Aug-07
Trump Mortgage	–	Closed	Aug-07
American Home Mortgage	–	Bankruptcy	Aug-07
MLSG Home Loans	–	Halted loans	Aug-07
Fieldstone[f]	C-Bass	Bankruptcy, closed	Aug-07
HomeBanc Mortgage	HomeBanc Corp.	Bankruptcy	Aug-07
Aegis Mortgage	Cerberus[k]	Bankruptcy	Aug-07
Regions	Regions Fin'l	Shut warehouse unit	Aug-07
Express Capital Lending	–	Halted acceptances	Aug-07
Bay Finance	Commerce Group	Halted loans	Aug-07
First Indiana	–	Shut wholesale unit	Aug-07
Guardian Loan	–	Closed	Aug-07
Unlimited Loan Resources	–	Halted loans	Aug-07
Pacific American Mtg.	Golden Empire	Halted wholesale loans	Aug-07
Thornburg Mortgage	–	Suspended applications	Aug-07
National Home Equity	National City	Halted loans, merged	Aug-07
NovaStar Financial	–	Halted wholesale loans	Aug-07
GreenPoint Mortgage	Capital One	Shut wholesale unit	Aug-07
First Magnus Financial	–	Bankruptcy	Aug-07
First Nat'l Arizona	1st Nat'l Hld	Halted wholesale loans	Aug-07
Quality Home Loans	–	Bankrupt, sale reported	Aug-07
Amstar Mortgage	Amstar Financial	Closing	Aug-07
BNC Mortgage	Lehman Brothers	Closed	Aug-07
Transnational	–	Halted wholesale loans	Aug-07
CIT home lending	CIT Group	Closed	Aug-07
Ameriquest Mortgage	ACC Capital	Halted applications	Aug-07
Group One Mortgage	Northwest Mortgage	Shut (wholesale lender)	Aug-07
WarehouseOne	–	Halted warehouse loans	Sep-07

Tab. 3.3: Continued

Cuts/Closed/Bankrupt	Parent	Status	Date *
First Collateral	Citigroup	Halted new clients	Sep-07
BrokerSource	BSM Financial	Halted wholesale loans	Sep-07
Washington Mutual	–	Shuts various units [e]	Sep-07
CapitalSix	–	Suspended operations	Sep-07
E* Trade	–	Closed wholesale unit	Sep-07
Impac Mortgage	–	Suspended most loans	Sep-07
Decision One	HSBC	Closed	Sep-07
NationStar Mortgage	Fortress	Halted wholesale loans	Sep-07
NetBank	–	Bankruptcy	Sep-07
Morgan Stanley	–	Merges three units	Oct-07
Miami Valley Bank	–	Failed	Oct-07
Summit Mortgage	–	Closed	Oct-07
UBS Home Finance	UBS AG	Closed wholesale unit	Nov-07
Tribeca Lending	Franklin Credit	Suspended operations	Nov-07
Option One Mortgage	H&R Block	Closed	Dec-07
Delta Financial	–	Bankruptcy	Dec-07
Webster Bank	Webster Financial	Halted wholesale loans	Dec-07
WMC Mortgage	General Electric	Halted subprime lending	Dec-07
National City	–	Halted wholesale loans	Jan. 08
ComUnity Lending Inc.	–	Bankruptcy	Jan. 08

N/D Not disclosed or not available.

* Announced date, first known disclosure or effective date if disclosed after completion. Some announced closings have not yet been completed.

** Asset sale.

*** Citigroup obtained an option to buy ACC Capital's wholesale mortgage origination and servicing businesses.

**** Per Goldman Chief Financial Officer David Viniar 6/14/07 in conversation with reporters. Web site lists company name as Avelo Mortgage LLC d/b/a Senderra Funding.

a) Retail assets.

b) Wholesale assets.

c) Actual price before taxes, per 10-Q filing. Centex's release cited after-tax proceeds of about USD 540 mn.

d) Residential subprime unit.

e) Shutdown of subprime lending and mortgage banker finance warehouse lending units announced in December 2007.

f) Purchased in July 2007 for USD 188 mn.

g) Not applicable.

h) Units served mortgage brokers and bought home loans from mortgage bankers, thrifts, builders and credit unions.

i) Formally known as Mortgage Investment Lending Associates.

j) Confirmed by company e-mail on July 5, 2007.

k) Owners included Cerberus Capital Management LP. Retail lending halted in June, wholesale lending in August.

or guarantees about 20% of the USD 11.5 tn US home loan market – blew out to 67 bp. Freddy Mac's CDS spreads have been impacted comparably. Earlier in 2007, their credit spreads traded around 5 bp.

The huge volatility in credit spreads and market volatility of Fannie Mae and Freddie Mac, however, has to do with very low numbers. Fannie Mae recently reported that their credit loss ratio in the first nine months of 2007 is about 4 bp. This figure measures the losses involved with Fannie Mae's loan investments based on its total exposure. A ratio of 4 bp appears to be very low and it is in line with the target credit loss ratio. However, the subtle point that makes this figure sobering is that it is based on an adjusted methodology, which they used in order to make the figure "more transparent." Without this correction, the credit loss rate would have been around 7.5 bp, according to an article in *Fortune* magazine, which triggered the sell-off in November 2007. As mentioned above, Fannie Mae and Freddie Mac have already been involved in an accounting scandal; hence, bad memories have resurfaced ("It's Enron all over again"). But what was the change in methodology? Formerly, Fannie Mae included so-called SOP 03-3 losses, which state the difference of the face value plus accrued interest on a loan that the company guaranteed minus the current market value. Fannie Mae said that it can safely exclude these losses from the credit loss ratio, as there is historical evidence that it can recover a large fraction of these valuation losses. In Q3, however, these losses were up to USD 670 mn from USD 37 mn one year ago. The central question is: Is this sharp increase due to the drop in market value of existing claims or to the fact that the company has to buy back an increasing volume of bad loans? Especially the latter sparks investor concerns that, because of rising delinquency rates and declining house prices, Fannie Mae's and Freddie Mac's involvement in the crisis is mounting. Moreover, the argument that losses from mark-to-market valuation could be safely ignored is an old and extremely dangerous one: it simply claims that markets are wrong.

In the US home financing business, the major players are the so-called government-sponsored enterprises (GSE) Federal National Mortgage Association and Federal Home Loan Mortgage Corporation are more commonly known as Fannie Mae and Freddy Mac and the twelve regional Federal Home Loan banks (FHL Bank System). Originally founded as a government agency in 1938 to provide liquidity to the mortgage market, Fannie Mae was transformed into a publicly traded and shareholder-owned company in 1968. Until 1970, Fannie Mae held a de facto monopoly on the secondary mortgage market in the US. Therefore, the US Congress chartered Freddie Mac in 1970 to establish competition in this market. Similar to Fannie Mae, Freddie Mac is authorized to

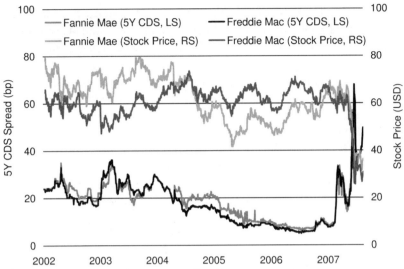

Fig. 3.7: The performance of Fannie Mae and Freddie Mac in capital markets

make loans and loan guarantees. In principle, the business model of both firms is to buy home loans from banks and other lenders and to sell the mortgage portfolios as securitized bonds (MBS) in the capital market. The GSEs earn a spread because they guarantee repayment of the MBS. Today, Fannie Mae is the largest US buyer of home mortgages, whereas its competitor Freddie Mac ranks as the second-largest buyer. The combined portfolios of both firms have grown more than tenfold in terms of volume during the last decade. Today, the GSEs also have substantial investment books with assets that are not mortgage loans at all. Furthermore, Fannie Mae and Freddie Mac are entitled to use interest rate and certain credit derivatives to hedge their business activities.

Despite its huge loan (guarantee) books, Freddie Mac and Fannie Mae are not banks. Their regulators are the US Department of Housing and Urban Development and, in particular, the Office of Federal Housing Enterprise Oversight (OFHEO). However, since the US House of Representatives passed the Federal Housing Finance Reform Act of 2007, that may change in the future. Presently, the activities of Fannie Mae and Freddy Mac are less restricted by regulatory burdens than normal financial institutions are. In particular, the capital requirements for MBS transactions are distinctively below the corresponding requirements for other financial institutions. This fact is, of course, a competitive advantage that amounts indirectly to a government subsidization of the firms. Contrary to a widespread misperception, bonds of Fannie Mae and Freddie Mac are, by law, not guaranteed by the US government. However, both firms receive the best possible issuer ratings for senior unsecured debt.

In recent years, both companies have attracted public attention due to severe accounting scandals. Weak regulation, weaker-than-usual capital requirements and accounting irregularities call for an improved supervision of the GSEs to ensure that Fannie Mae and Freddie Mac pose fewer risks to the US financial system. From a political point of view, subsidization of the firms is directly connected to a charge – namely, that their commercial activities must provide important social benefits. This may contradict the present situation, in which only approximately half of the assets of the GSEs are home loans.

A US *conforming loan* is a mortgage loan that conforms to the guidelines agreed to by Fannie Mae and Freddie Mac. The two firms have developed uniform mortgage documents since the 1970s. Apart from debt-to-income ratio limits and documentation requirements, which are adjusted on an annual basis, there is a maximum loan amount that depends on the object that is funded.

Fannie Mae and Freddie Mac only buy conforming loans to repackage them in MBS transactions. Mortgage loans not meeting the criteria for conforming

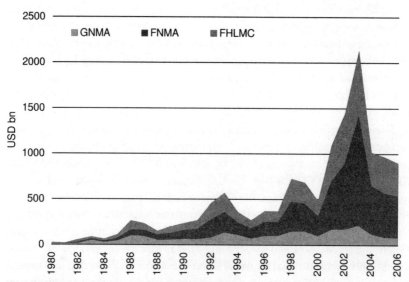

Fig. 3.8: Issuance of agency Mortgage-Backed Securities
Source: SIFMA

loans are referred to as *jumbo loans*. Due to the business activities of the GSEs, the market for conforming loans provides greater liquidity compared to jumbo loans. This factor has immediate cost advantages for customers who request loans that meet the conforming loan criteria.

More than 8,000 community financial institutions from all fifty US states are members of the FHL Bank System. The members are shareholders and may become so by purchasing equity. However, equity is not traded publicly. The purpose of the FHL Banks is to provide low-cost funding to American financial institutions that are members, primarily for home mortgages, economic development lending and community credit. Within the US, the FHL Banks and their member institutions are the largest providers of home mortgages and community credit, which emphasizes their importance in the present context.

The majority of current FHL Bank members are small neighborhood banks, or thrifts, known as Community Financial Institutions. Others are federally insured depository institutions, and even commercial banks and credit unions (cooperative financial institutions).

The FHL Banks' mission is to serve a public purpose – namely, to increase access to housing for all Americans and to extend credit to member financial institutions, thereby supporting local communities. Therefore, FHL Banks enjoy certain tax privileges. Established in 1932 during the Great Depression, the FHL Banks have been regulated by the Federal Housing Finance Board since 1989. They are privately capitalized and do not have express governmental assistance in case of financial distress. Nonetheless, they are regarded as sovereign agencies due to the implicit involvement of the federal government, and their credit ratings clearly benefit from this status (AAA ratings). The latter is also supported by the fact that the liabilities of each FHL Bank are guaranteed by all of the other FHL Banks. FHL Banks are mainly funded by bond issuance in the capital market.

3.3 Money Market Funds

When the subprime turmoil started, some money market funds were among the first victims. In the years before the crisis, a new kind of money market funds emerged, the *enhanced money market* (or *money market plus*) *funds*. Some of these funds were invested up to 95% in ABS and RMBS assets. The investment rationale was simple: Most of the ABS and RMBS bonds are floating rate notes and hence do not involve significant interest rate risk. Furthermore, the instruments pay a spread above Libor and are therefore a perfect investment for those funds that have to provide an excess return over Libor. The only concern was the liquidity in secondary markets for these instruments. Since money market funds are usually used in order to park liquidity for a short period of time, the portfolio manager needs to be able to liquidate assets quite rapidly when an investor calls back his funds. But liquidity was constantly rising over years, and especially the AAA-rated tranches could be traded in good amounts in the secondary markets. These developments gave portfolio managers increasing comfort to extend their positions in ABS and RMBS. However, the liquidity in the secondary markets has never really been stress tested.

When the financial market turmoil started in mid-July, investors who were invested in such money market funds wanted to pull out, as they didn't know how large the fund's exposures was with respect to subprime paper. This activity triggered a fund run. As everybody wanted to pull out of these investment funds, the fund managers were forced to liquidate all assets at any price. Large-scale bid lists (a.k.a. *BWIC-lists,* which stands for "bids wanted in competition") started to circulate in the market. These are lists that fund managers put bonds they wanted to sell on – and most probably they put all assets they had on them – and distribute them to the brokers. The latter can choose which bonds they want to bid on. The broker with the best price will buy it. It is like in an auction. You show all your inventories, and potential buyers bid for them. However, if nobody wants to buy the assets, then prices plunge. And that is what happened in July 2007.

The fund run triggered an unseen performance of money market funds. Usually a money market fund is expected to constantly increase its value. Its performance should come from the carry on the investments. A mark-to-market volatility has to be avoided. As shown in chart 3.9, there are money market funds that lost up to 40% of the fund value in the crisis. This collapse was triggered by the sharp drop in total assets.

3.4 Central Banks

Entire books have been written on central bank action in order to combat a crisis. And much has been said about the responsibility of the Fed for the subprime crisis, as it blew the housing bubble by flooding markets with liquidity in order to fight the impacts of 9/11 and the Enron crisis. In this book, we do not want to participate in this admittedly interesting and important discussion.

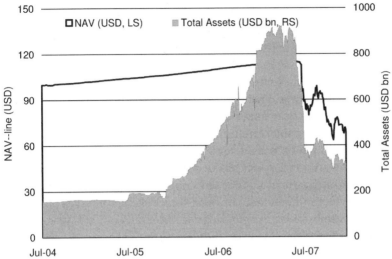

Fig. 3.9: Performance of money market funds (an example from a US Libor Plus Fund)

We just want to raise the question whether a central bank has the proper tools in order to fight a credit crisis. Just think about the measures that are available to the Fed, for example. It can try to calm down markets with speeches. It can inject cash in the money markets via tender offers. It can increase accessibility of these funds for banks by allowing a wider range of assets as collateral for its money market operations. It can even allow banks to downstream liquidity that was acquired from the central bank to some subsidiaries. Furthermore, it can cut the target rate, or it can open the so-called discount window wider by cutting the discount rate (i.e., by lowering the difference between target rate and discount rate). It can even provide an inter-meeting rate cut. All this was done by the Fed during the first seven months of the crisis, and it did help to stop it.

One of the most important outcomes of the subprime crisis is that it shows how the ability of a central bank to bail the market out of a full-blown credit crisis is limited. That does not mean that the Fed's efforts were not needed, but that it can only fight the symptoms. One of the symptoms was the malfunctioning money market. A few days after the crisis had started, money market spreads started to widen dramatically. The interbank market was no longer working properly. In December 2007, the difference between the 3M-Euribor and the 3M-Eonia swap contract had reached almost 100 bp, compared to a normal level of about 5-6 bp (see figure 1.15). Such levels haven't been seen before, even in the aftermath of 9/11. Investors use this yield difference in order to asses the cost of liquidity. The 3M-Euribor refers to the rate that is charged among banks when lending money for a period of three months. The 3M-Eonia swap, in contrast, is a derivatives contract that swaps the average Eonia rate (i.e., an overnight lending rate) against a payment that is fixed in advance, the so-called swap rate in the 3M-Eonia swap. This swap rates expresses the expectation of the development of the short-term interest rate. The risk-neutral value for this swap rate is the 3M interest rate. However, this swap contract does not involve the exchange of principle payments. Consequently, there is no premium for exchanging liquidity. The above-mentioned difference between the 3M-Euribor and the 3M-Eonia swap measures therefore this liquidity premium. In the United States, investors often refer to the difference between the Fed Funds Target Rate and the 3M-USD Libor (a.k.a., the TED spread), which was also blown out tremendously.

The dramatic increase in money market spreads happened because banks were not willing to lend cash in the interbank market. But why did banks not lend cash among each other? This was not so much driven by fear that the counterparty might default over the next three months, but by the fact that banks accumulated all cash they could get in order to finance their operating business. In this sense, the money market spread is really a liquidity premium and not so much a credit spread. Since the credit crisis triggered an almost complete shutdown of structured finance and bond markets, banks had problems to get funding for their lending business. As some examples showed, banks could indeed issue bonds, but at extremely high spread levels. However, tapping the market with a five-year bond and paying 70 bp means that the bank locks in the "pain" of 70 bp premium over the next five years. But banks were expecting that primary markets would reopen over the next couple of months. Hence, they were accepting higher money market spreads that they would only have to pay for a few months, hoping that funding would become more attractive further down the road.

Although this is a rationale strategy, the resulting shortage of cash in the interbank market creates the risk of a systemic crisis if weaker banks urgently needing cash are no longer able to fund. Northern Rock was an example for such a shortfall. However, such a systemic crisis is an issue for central banks. Consequently, they were flooding the market with cash (on one day in December, for example, the ECB injected USD 500 bn), hoping that it will arrive at banks where it was urgently needed. These activities triggered the joke of the Fed flying around with helicopters and dropping bundles of cash. Market participants should not confuse these important and highly welcome activities to stabilize money markets that were devoted to prevent a systemic banking shock with measures to fight the credit crisis. While the former can and has to be done by a central bank – and the joint action of several central banks in December was successful – the consequences of a credit crisis have to be dealt with by investors. The only successful strategy for this problem is to deleverage investments that were employing a far-too-high leverage, simply by taking the loss. Hoping for a central bank bailout is not a rational strategy, irrespective of the moral problems that arise when gains should be for investors, but losses covered by taxpayers.

3.5 Hedge Funds

In line with the strong growth of the credit derivatives universe, credit-oriented hedge funds became a major player, especially in the structured credit and the credit derivatives markets. The participation of hedge funds in the credit market was driven by the innovative power of the market, the OTC character which offers some arbitrage opportunities, and the low correlation of some credit-related strategies with other established trading strategies, like M&A arbitrage. During recent years, credit hedge funds grew at a faster pace than all other segments in the hedge fund industry. Their impact on the market is greater than the market share that corresponds to their net asset value, as hedge funds implement a relatively large leverage within their trading strategies.

Hedge Funds Participation in the Credit Markets

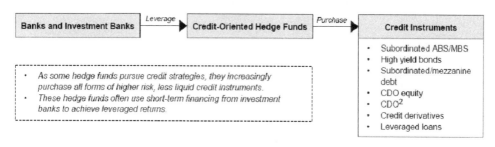

ABS/MBS – Asset-backed securities/mortgage-backed securities. CDO – Collateralized debt obligation. CDO² – CDO squared.

Fig. 3.10: The role of hedge funds in the global credit market[15]
Source: Fitch

The role of hedge funds in the global credit market is illustrated in figure 3.10. Within their prime brokerage business, banks and investment banks provide leverage for credit-oriented hedge funds, which invest in credit-risky instruments.

Hedge funds are a major provider of liquidity in the credit market, as they have a significant share of trading volumes in specific segments, which is related to the leverage implied in their positions. The dominant role of hedge funds was also caused by the low interest rate environment in the aftermath of the global meltdown on the back of the credit crunch in 2001-2002 and easy credit. Banks discovered hedge funds as profitable clients for their prime brokerage business.

The hedge fund industry grew from approximately USD 1 tn in 2005 to USD 2 tn in 2007, while financial leverage on average is expected to amount to 2-3 tn, leaving the industry with an asset volume of USD 4-6 tn. The industry is becoming global, with hedge funds located all over the world, playing a major role in almost all market segments, but increasingly in markets which offer

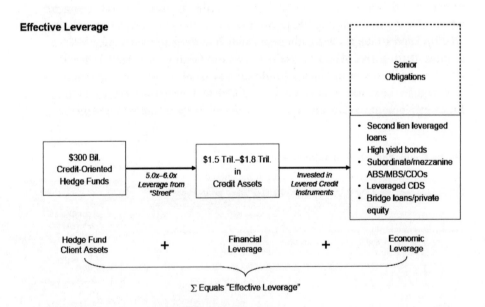

ABS – Asset-backed securities. MBS – Mortgage-backed securities. CDOs – Collateralized debt obligations. CDS – Credit default swap.

Fig. 3.11: Financial leverage & economic leverage[16]
Source: Fitch

the opportunity to leverage further via the unfunded nature of the instruments, namely the availability of derivatives. Most of the funds are called *multi-strategy funds*, which means they are opportunistically looking for investment strategies in many different segments, including cross-asset strategies (e.g., capital structure arbitrage). Although there is a lack of exact data, Fitch estimates that credit-oriented hedge funds had a volume of USD 300 bn under management in 2005, leveraged by five to six times. In figure 3.11, we depict the leverage in the market, which consists of financial leverage (provided by the prime brokers) and economic leverage due to the investment into leveraged instruments, like lower tranches in the CDO universe, etc. This reflects the shift into more speculative investments, which accelerated significantly over the last few years. Hence, the market volume should have been much higher in 2007, especially when we take the rising financial leverage into account, as the rising competition in the prime brokerage business resulted in an increasing maximum allowable leverage for certain strategies. A survey showed that prime brokers have experienced rising pressure during the last few years to provide easy credit.[15,16]

Depending on the strategy, hedge funds vary the leverage of their trades. The higher the economic leverage, the lower the financial leverage, and vice versa. That said, hedge funds keep the overall leverage relatively constant over all strategies. In table 3.4, the average financial leverage of different strategies is indicated. The highest leverage is implemented in CDS carry trades, while distressed debt shows the lowest implied leverage. Moreover, it is interesting to note that the leverage remained relatively constant over time. That said, hedge funds did not adjust their strategies in respect to leverage applied during a period of tremendous spread tightening.

Tab. 3.4: Indicative leverage of specific hedge fund strategies[16]
Source: Fitch

Strategy	2007	2005
Fixed-Income Relative Value	15	12.5
Long/Short Credit	10	12.5
CDS Leveraged Carry	20	20
MBS and ABS Arbitrage	8	7
Long/Short Cash Credit	4.5	5.5
Emerging Market Long/Short	3	3.5
Distressed Debt	1.75	1.75

The share of hedge funds regarding the trading volume amounts to almost 60% in the credit derivatives universe, while it is above 40% in distressed debt and emerging market debt (see figure 3.12). Especially the rising dominance of hedge funds in the credit derivatives is worth mentioning against the backdrop of the strong growth of the outstanding amount of these instruments. In mid-2007, the outstanding volume of CDS amounted to almost USD 50 tn!

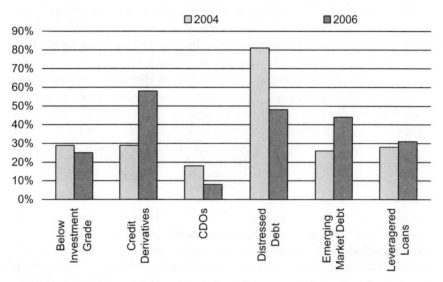

Fig. 3.12: Trading volume in specific market segments[16]
Source: Fitch

The dark side of the dominance of hedge funds in the global credit market is simply that a forced deleveraging of the funds can trigger major market distortions, as there is the risk of synchronic actions by many funds. For example, Amaranth, the hedge fund that became troubled in 2006 on the back of failed commodity bets, reported to have sold RMBS and leveraged loans to cover margin calls. Hence, there is a risk of rising technical pressure on some markets when a tail event occurs anywhere in financial markets.

However, there have been primarily two major arguments of the hedge fund industry explaining why an LTCM event will not happen again. First, not only hedge funds but also prime brokers significantly improved their risk management capacities and tools; at the same time, they are more closely monitoring positions, which allows them to react to potential crisis signals earlier. Second, the number of hedge funds increased significantly since 1998 (when the LTCM crisis occurred). This means that the market is less dependent on the potential

A New Credit Market Paradigm

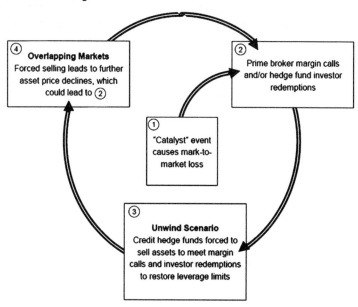

Fig. 3.13: A potential vicious cycle in the hedge funds industry[16]
Source: Fitch

failure of a single fund, as was the case during the LTCM crisis. But despite the more sophisticated risk management systems, we can not ignore the fact that the instruments became more complex too. In addition, there are some markets which proved to be rather illiquid in periods of stress, as was the case during the subprime crisis in the structured credit market. Even if the risk management tools work properly and signal increasing risks, those risks could probably not be reduced, as there is simply no market to sell the corresponding exposure! Regarding the second argument, it is important to know that trading strategies in credit-oriented hedge funds should be rather similar. This is especially true for arbitrage trades in the synthetic CDO market. That said, if a majority of hedge funds within the industry have implemented relatively similar positions, then the correlation of their profits and losses should be rather high. This also means that it does not matter whether there is one hedge fund selling a bunch of assets to the market or whether this is done by many hedge funds! The effect on the market should be pretty much the same.

In case there is a forced unwinding of hedge funds' positions, it is again the leverage which bears systemic risk for the market. For instance, assume a four-times leverage fund, which invests an amount of 100 with a margin requirement of only 20. A mark-to-market loss of 5% will translate into a reduction of the "equity" from 20 to 15. Thus, the leverage rises from 4 to 5.33. To restore a four-times leverage, the invested amount has to be reduced to 75 (60/15 = 4), resulting in a forced selling of 25% of the asset. A margin increase to 25% (restoring leverage to 3) would result in a forced selling of 40% (equity 15; leverage 3 $\Rightarrow$ 3*15 = 45; investment volume = 45+15 = 60). Obviously, the existence of margin requirements poses a systemic risk to the market, especially via leveraged positions.

This forced delivering of some funds can have a significant market impact. However, there might be also second and third-order effects. Second-round effects include a rising volatility especially in lower qualities (high-yield but also in the structured credit universe) and/or declining liquidity in crisis times. Tertiary effects would be a negative impact on the issuance volume of high-yield bonds, as the risk premium the companies have to pay to tap the market might be too high.

The role of hedge funds was a broadly discussed topic when the first wave of the subprime turmoil hit the market. On the one hand, statistics show that hedge funds indicated strong demand for equity pieces, which were in trouble during 2007. On the other hand, the number of hedge funds reporting losses was very subdued. One can argue that there are good ones and bad ones, and in the end it is a zero sum game. However, also in this case, there should have been some failures of hedge funds. One reason why there weren't might be that banks did not trigger margin calls, as highly leveraged hedge funds are simply not able to provide additional liquidity – and finally they would have to deliver collateral, meaning that banks would end up with further distressed investments on their balance sheet. To sum up, the hedge fund industry might be more sophisticated as it was ten years ago, but the leverage component in the industry still argues for accelerating risk when adverse movements hit the market. The hedge fund industry remains a potential Damocles sword for the structured credit market.

3.6 Bond Insurer

When Moody's placed the ratings from Ambac and MBIA, the two heavy-weights in the monoliner industry, on review for a possible downgrade in mid-January 2008, they had to put a warning on their website: "During the week of January 14, 2008, Moody's placed AMBAC and MBIA's financial strength ratings on watch for possible downgrade. Because of the large volume of watchlist changes resulting from these actions, ratings appearing on this website may not yet reflect current information." The sheer amount of rated debt affected by the downgrade was too large for the company keep its website updated in the short term. This is understandable, as more the 380,000 rated bonds were affected. However, that is not the only scary figure. In 2007, the monoliner industry guaranteed about USD 2.4 tn of debt, about two-thirds of which is public debt; the rest are structured finance assets.

One month before, in mid-December 2007, S&P announced rating actions on several US monoliners. The rating agency cut ACA to CCC from single-A; revised its outlook to "negative" from "stable" for Ambac (AAA/AA/A+), MBIA (AAA/AA/-) and XL Capital (AAA/-/-); changed the ratings of FGIC (AAA/AA/-) to "negative" from "stable"; and affirmed ratings and outlooks on Assured Guaranty (AAA/-/- stable), CIFG (AAA/-/- negative), Financials Security Assurance

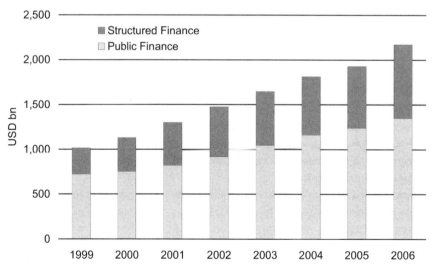

Fig. 3.14: Growth of monoliner-insured debt
Source: AGFI

(AAA/AA/A+ stable), Radian (AA/-/- stable) and PMI Guaranty (AA/-/- negative). In parenthesis we stated the following S&P ratings if they are available: financial strength, financial enhancement/senior unsecured/subordinated. The market's reaction to these announcements was drastic, especially regarding Moody's watch status for Ambac and MBIA. On that day, Ambacs shares were down by 50%, while MBIA's stock priced dropped by 40%. However, since the recent highs in mid-2007, both stocks were already down by 80 to 90%. A few days later Fitch kicked in and cut Ambac's AAA ratings to AA and announced downgrades for more than 130,000 securities, mainly municipal bonds.

For most companies a downgrade from AAA to AA wouldn't be a bummer. Credit spreads would widen and the refinancing costs would increase slightly. For the bond insurer, however, such a step endangers their existence. The business of the bond insurer dates back to the 1970s. They guaranteed bonds issues by US municipals and received a premium for this. As the bond insurer had an AAA rating, the guaranteed bonds were also rated AAA. This helped the bond issuer to reduce funding costs and provided an attractive business case for the bond insurers, because municipals usually do not default. However, the bond insurer did not stick to their business model but wanted to participate in the booming structured finance markets. From the early 1990s to 2006, the percentage of structured finance deals in their business increased sharply to reach more than 30% in 2006. That amounts to about USD 800 bn, and the assets they wrapped are obviously not the ones with the best ratings; otherwise a bond insurer wouldn't be needed. What makes the situation ugly, especially for the two heavyweights Ambac and MBIA, is that they employed huge leverage. Both companies placed guarantees for USD 140 in bonds for every dollar of equity. This is, for example, twice as high as the equity leverage in the SIV-lite Sachsen Funding I, the SachsenLBs vehicle with the highest leverage among all SUV-lites. Under sunny economic conditions, such a leverage is obviously a money machine, but it can turn into a death spiral when the wind blows into the face. Under current economic conditions the equity cushion of the insurance companies can be wiped out rapidly, leaving the investors in wrapped bonds without any guarantee.

And the vicious cycle guarantees that there is no easy way out. Although these could be happy times for a bond insurer – the losses justify significant increases in the risk premiums – the troubled companies will not participate in the party. No investor would like to purchase a guarantee from a tumbling insurance company. Fresh money is the only chance for Ambac and MBIA. Warren Buffet's idea of building a new bond insurer shows how to participate at the party without having to deal with the troubles of the past. However, credit markets already discount an extremely high default probability for bond insurers. MBIA's 5Y CDS spreads (the ones that refer to the holding company), for example, traded up to levels above 1000 bp and the spread curve had been inverse (i.e., spreads at the short end of the curve were higher than those at the long end). Such a situation occurs only if dealers are expecting a default event in the coming weeks.

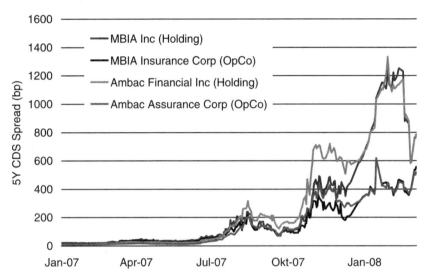

Fig. 3.15: 5Y CDS spreads of selected monoline insurance companies

What will the impact of a downgrade (or a default) of the bond insurers be on the debt they guarantee? Without a guarantee, the rating agencies would simply assign the rating that corresponds to the credit quality of each issue. At first glance this is good news, as a downgrade, or even a default of the insurer, does not lead to a default of the guaranteed debt. However, the fundamental credit rating of the guaranteed debt will most likely be lower than AAA. For a bond that has an AAA rating anyway, it does not make any sense to involve a guarantor; it would just lead to higher costs, without the benefit of a better rating. Hence, for bonds that are not guaranteed, the rating agencies will most probably downgrade the rating. If the monoliner is not in default but only downgraded (as mentioned above, Fitch downgraded Ambac to AA from AAA), then the guaranteed bonds will simply have the better of both ratings – the one from the monoliner or the fundamental one. However, a large part of the buyers of monoliner guaranteed bonds require a very high rating due to their investment guidelines. Money managers that oversee, for example, pension plans could be restricted to invest only in riskless paper, such as US treasuries. However, since the amount of investment funds by far exceeds the amount of available US government bonds, investors move to so-called government substitutes. Until the subprime crisis, monoliner-wrapped bonds belonged to this category. However, nobody wants to imagine the consequences when investors dump USD 2.4 tn of paper onto the already illiquid markets.

Regarding the ratings assigned to monoliners, there might arise some confusion. A closer look at the company structure helps to shed some light on this. In the following, we will refer to the two largest monoliners – MBIA and Ambac. For both companies the stock market listed entity is the holding company, while the operating insurance business is a subsidiary. For Ambac, the holding is AMBAC Financial Group Inc., while the operating subsidiary is Ambac Assurance Corp. For MBIA, the holding is MBIA Inc., while the major insurance subsidiary is MBIA Insurance Corp (MBIA has also other regional operating units). The confusion about ratings arises as agencies assign different ratings to the different entities. Typically, the holding company has a lower rating than the operating subsidiary due to structural subordination. Thus, the AAA ratings under suspicion are the so-called insurance financial strength ratings of Ambac Assurance Corp and MBIA Insurance Corp, while the holding companies have a senior unsecured rating of Aa2 and Aa3. The earnings generated in the operating entity are transferred to the holding via dividend payments. However, the amount of cash which the holding can extract from the operating company level depends on the insured risks and is closely watched by the insurance regulator. The spread blowout in early 2008, which affected particularly the CDS spreads that refer to the holding company, was triggered by concerns that all premium income from guaranteed assets is needed to cover the corresponding losses, which would limit the ability of the operating unit to pay a dividend to the holding company. In such a case, the holding company would suffer.

In February 2008, the monoliner debacle even became a political topic. Due to the fears of downgrades of the monoliners, which would trigger downgrades of wrapped municipal bonds, US municipals experienced a very rapid credit crunch. The major transmission channel have been the so-called Auction-Rate Securities (ARS). In these instruments, the coupon payment is reset regularly – on a weekly or a monthly basis – via an auction mechanism. In these auctions, potential investors place a bid for a share of the outstanding bonds. However, if no bids are submitted, the bonds remain at the previous investors, but coupons are reset to a pre-defined rate level. However, these levels are extremely high. For example, the Port Authority of New York and New Jersey got its bond reset to a coupon of 20% in February 2008, after the respective auction failed. This creates an immediate threat for the borrower, as such a payment shock creates the risk of a self-fulfilling process. Due to the penalty-rate feature ARS are dangerous instruments, as they accelerate the infection mechanism. Concerns among investors create a very immediate deterioration of the borrowers funding situation.

How painful the collapse of a bond insurer may be can be seen in the case of CIBC. The Canadian bank purchased an insurance contract for about USD 3.5 bn of its US subprime investments from ACA Financials. The downgrade of ACA Financials to CCC from A was a disaster for the bank. Its shares dropped by 6% on the announcement, and after that, the bank had to write down USD 3.2 bn on its investments tied to the US subprime market and shored up its balance sheet by selling USD 2.7 bn in stocks.

3.7 Private Equity Sponsors

The private equity business was an important factor in credit markets in the recent years. Private equity funds have been packed with cash, and banks have been willing to provide an extreme additional leverage, so that ever-growing deals could be tackled by KKR and others. However, leveraged buyouts triggered fear and comfort at the same time in credit markets. The fear was devoted to the fact that the announcement of an LBO – or even the rumors of such an event – triggered a spread blowout with the related mark-to-market losses for the respective debt investors. However, the booming private equity activities were also taken as a positive sign. First, investors were happy to provide the loans for the takeovers, although the conditions of these loans were more and more tilted to their disadvantage. Second, credit investors took the willingness of private equity investors to spend their money as a sign of continuing prosperous economic conditions. Moderate equity valuations, low interest rates and easy credit conditions were the perfect ingredients for a private equity rally. These perfect conditions were triggered by the flood of liquidity the central banks provided in order to fight the credit crunch in the aftermath of 9/11 and the Enron crisis. From 2003 on, the deal number and sizes were constantly on the rise.

However, not only the number of LBO deals was rising, but also the willingness of a broader credit investor base to enter the field of leveraged loans. Besides, subprime RMBS and fancy corporate credit CDOs, leveraged loans, and the corresponding credit derivatives technology including CLOs have been the third central topic in credit markets. And not a few market players expected that the exaggerations occurring in the LBO arena will be the trigger for a credit crisis. Although the leveraged loans market wasn't the trigger, it was one of the hot spots once the crisis had started.

Before we analyze the developments in the LBO market and their impact on credit spreads, we want to briefly describe the mechanisms in a leveraged buyout. However, to keep this presentation short, we need to simplify things a bit. In an LBO transaction, an investor buys all shares of a target company. However, in order to implement the takeover, the private equity investor injects only a limited amount of its own funds; it obtains the remaining capital from a bank in the form of a loan. However, the trick in an LBO transaction is that the private equity sponsor does not guarantee for the loan. The lender has no claim against the fund in case of a credit event at the LBO target. The debt that the private equity sponsor uses for taking over the company is simply rolled over into the company itself; it is the target company that repays the loan for its own takeover. An LBO transaction is typically implemented by establishing

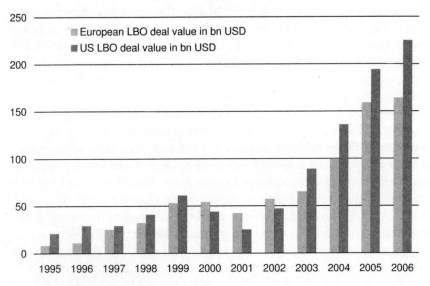

Fig. 3.16: LBO deal sizes in Europe and the US

Credit Players

a new company – the so-called NewCo – whose assets are simply all shares of the target company and which are funded via an equity injection of the private equity sponsor and the debt provided by the banks. After a successful takeover, the debt is typically pushed down to the level of the operating company. The question why a company can be bought with a minimal equity injection simply by releveraging its balance sheet has to be discussed elsewhere; here we just want to interject a few ideas. Most of the takeover targets involve a business problem that the private equity investors attempt to solve. However, one should not confuse private equity sponsor with the so-called vulture funds. In contrast to the latter, which are usually interested in failed companies, a PE sponsor targets operating companies. An interesting company might have, for example, a problem with an inefficient capital structure or a cost-cutting problem. The private equity investors use their expertise to work on the problems. In this respect they are typically not pure financial investors but also have a great deal of industry and management knowledge. It is also quite common that they have close connections to business consulting companies. Other targets might emerge when a larger entity wants to spin off a part of its business. Moreover, PE sponsors use the debt not only for paying the purchase price, but also in order to align their interests with the ones from the management of the takeover target. Due to the huge debt burden, the management has to focus on the business problems; otherwise the company will go bust.

Although the conceptual idea is very simple, the actual implementation can be very difficult. Besides the typical valuation, legal and contractual issues that have to be solved in a takeover, an LBO investor needs to negotiate the funding for the transaction. And since an LBO transaction can be quite large, the funding might have to be arranged by a consortium of banks. Furthermore, the funding of a takeover typically involves not only a simple loan, but a package of different debt instruments, such as a senior loan, mezzanine capital or a subordinated high-yield bond. The structure of the funding package typically needs to be negotiated on a confidential basis, so it cannot be discussed among a wide investor base. Typically a smaller number of banks provides a bridge financing for the takeover, which can then be legally confirmed. After the execution of the deal, the bridge loan has to be replaced by a long-term funding package. And the latter has to be placed in the market. However, this process involves a significant credit risk, since the bridge loans – although typically with a short duration – contain a huge volume. What if the bank is not able to place the debt in the market? The result could be examined during the crisis. The major players in the leverage loan market had to realize large mark-to-market losses, as the bonds and loans could only be placed in the market at a significant discount.

However, prospects for fee generation in the LBO business sparked a tremendous appetite for providing leverage loans. Moreover, by using credit derivatives technology – LCDS and CLOs – banks were able to distribute the risks to an increasingly broader investor base, and PE sponsors found the easy credit conditions they needed to implement transactions. It is therefore no surprise that the prices the PE sponsors were willing to pay increased sharply. In 2003, LBO transactions had on average a purchase price in terms of an EBITDA multiple (including fees) of below seven. Three years later, it climbed to a multiple of almost nine.

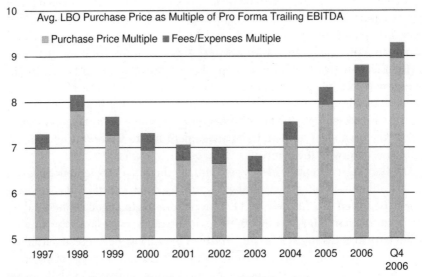

Fig. 3.17: Average LBO LBO purchase price in terms of EBITDA-multiple
Source: Standard & Poor's

This trend not only drove up prices in the stock markets, but also lead to a decreasing credit quality of LBO debt, due to the huge leverage that had been employed. The risk of such a strategy is not only that it might fail and cost individual investors money; it also poses a systemic threat. Highly leveraged companies have only limited financial flexibility in an economic downturn, and the most leveraged ones will fall first. But an increasing default rate leaves its traces on the balance sheets of lenders, which will tighten lending standards and therefore deepen the credit crunch. The risk of such a self-fulfilling process is clearly increased when a large number of companies suffer under a huge debt burden. But the private equity sponsors are already prepared for this case. They already set up distressed debt funds in order to pick up the defaulted bonds and loans they created and to turn them into dollars.

4
Credit Strategies

In 2006 and early 2007, before the subprime bomb exploded, investors had to struggle with a problem that appears slightly exotic from the center of the storm: "how to generate returns in a low-yield, low-spread environment". Investors were flooded with research notes, conferences and product presentations that addressed this problem. No matter how sophisticated and varied the suggested solutions may have been, there was one thing they all had in common: leverage. The citation a few lines above was the subtitle of a conference that one of the authors of this book was invited to as a guest speaker. One of the bullet points under the title nicely highlighted this solution: "how to extract leverage using exotic structured credit instruments and strategies". In this chapter, we want to present the major strategies used by investors to access leveraged exposure to credit assets. While creating leverage is not a difficult task in general, banks and other regulated financial institutions have to implement it in such a way that it does not alarm regulatory bodies. In this respect, the state-of-the-art credit derivatives technology helped a great deal to implement so-called "smart" leverage.

The leverage not only triggered the subprime crisis and the subsequent financial market crisis, however; it also had a huge impact on the markets before and kept large parts of the financial community busy for years. Subprime mortgage loans, for example, allowed the private customers of banks to implement a leveraged bet in the US housing market, one of the major drivers of the US economy for years. The leverage loans business provided private equity sponsors an enormous firepower and was one of the major pillars of booming stock markets. The structured credit arena was one of the shiniest spots in global financial markets; investment banks earned billions by structuring, trading and selling ever-more complicated products, and some of their employees became millionaires. Looking back, it seems like there was a new hot product in the pipelines every day and everybody was busy to jump on the bandwagon. Nevertheless, behind most of the innovations there was again just one theme: leverage.

But how does this "smart" leverage look, especially in the credit world? Leverage strategies in credit risky assets are as old as banks. Banks lend money to

Credit Crises. J. Felsenheimer and P. Gisdakis
Copyright © 2008 WILEY-VCH Verlag GmbH & Co. KGaA, Weinheim
ISBN: 978-3-527-50375-9

their customers and borrow the funds in financial markets or from deposits. However, since originating (illiquid) long-term mortgage loans and refinancing them via short-term debt from savings accounts creates a significant risk, banks are regulated in order to limit the risk for the stability of the financial system that might stem from exposures that are too aggressive. In order to boost returns, financial market players are constantly seeking ways to bypass these limitations. There are generally two solutions:

- Find risks that you can carry on your balance sheet, but which the regulatory framework does not recognize as such;
- Offload risks to vehicles that you don't have to consolidate on your balance sheet.

In this chapter, we introduce examples for both strategies, which were on center stage in the financial markets turmoil in 2007 and which have been one of the key drivers for the run-up to the crisis. Leveraged Super Senior (LSS) tranches and Constant Proportion Debt Obligations (CPDOs) belong to the first category. While in LSSs one refers to AAA-rated assets as underlyings which are then leveraged using credit derivatives technology, in CPDOs the underlying risk is typically a non-AAA-rated investment-grade exposure, which is packaged in a (leveraged) trading strategy that attempts to eliminate the default risk. Examples for the second solution are the Structured Investment Vehicles (SIVs), SIV-lites and arbitrage conduits. The idea behind these strategies is to offload assets to a vehicle outside the balance sheet and to refinance them with cheap funding. The source of cheap funding that these vehicles use is the money market, as it simply refinances long-term assets with short-term debt, without involving interest rate risk.

Besides leverage and credit assets, there is a third point these structures have in common: Their main source of risk is not default risk, but market risk. The great achievement of credit markets is that they have enabled investors to buy and sell credit-risky assets, thus transforming an event risk (i.e., the risk of a default event) into a price risk (i.e., the risk that the value of an asset declines over time). The price expresses the probability that such an event occurs and the anticipated loss that accompanies the event. This transformation process was accompanied by the development of derivatives structures in order to improve the tradability of the underlying risks (we introduced the basic mechanism of the credit derivatives technology in section 2.3). However, as a consequence of the increasing liquidity and the simplicity of trading credit risk using the derivatives, products emerged that allow investors to make leveraged bets not only on the default risk of credit assets, but also on their price risk. In its simplest form this leveraged bet on the price risk is only about refinancing tradable long-term assets with short-term debt. When the price of the assets decline below the outstanding amount of debt at maturity of the debt, then this strategy is in default. A credit event in the assets is not necessary – although it would have a similar effect. This is all but new. The innovation of recent years, however, was simply the amount of leverage that was used to implement these bets and the transformation of this strategy into a derivatives format in which real debt was no longer needed. Instead of acquiring assets with short-term debt, one can simply design a contract which bets that the value of the assets will not decline below a predefined barrier. Such a contract is also not very new; it is essentially a put. However, what was quite new in fact is that these puts have been rated, and not few of them had been given AAA ratings, the same rating as US Treasury bonds.

The problem with assigning a rating to a market value strategy is that assessing price dynamics in financial markets is something fundamentally different than analyzing the credit quality of a borrower.[6] While the ability of a borrower to repay a loan is closely linked with his financial situation, which can be determined via an objective analysis (or at least the amount of subjectivity is quite limited), price changes are frequently driven by factors that do not have much to do with the credit quality of a specific issuer. The spreads of most European investment-grade companies widened by a factor of 5 through the crisis. Does this change reflect the risk that the default risk of these borrowers increased by a factor of 5? If the answer would be Yes, than rating agencies should have been busy with slashing the ratings of US investment banks deep into the junk territory, as market-implied default probabilities for Bear Stearns and their competitors had been as high as single-B-rated companies before the crisis.

In the current chapter, we introduce the central strategies which have been implemented in credit markets and which have lead to the turmoil in financial markets. LSSs and CPDOs were mainly focused on the corporate credit universe, while structured-finance CDOs and SIVs were largely invested in RMBS assets. As already outlined above, a common theme of all these strategies was that the aim was to leverage exposure in order to boost returns in a "low-yield, low-spread environment". However, as we will show in the last section, the interrelation of these vehicles and the excessive leverage employed for each of the vehicles caused a spillover of the subprime crisis into money markets, as a chain of structured credit products linked subprime mortgage loans with the asset-backed commercial paper market.

4.1 Leverage

As already mentioned, the appropriate answer to the low-yield, low-spread investment dilemma appeared to be: leverage. The investment rationale was very simple: if the risk premium is low, then the risk has to be low. And if the risk premium provides only a quarter of the required return, then just invest four times as much. This strategy was supported by financial markets, since in a low-yield, low-spread environment the cost of capital is also low.

Let us begin with a simple example. We assume an investor with a risk budget of EUR 10 mn. If he invests this amount in a security that provides a return of 10% pa, he earns EUR 1 mn on his investment per year. However, if he requires a higher return, then he can invest in a leveraged manner using borrowed money. Let us assume that the investor borrows an additional EUR 90 mn and can therefore invest EUR 100 mn in the risky asset. For a 10% return on the risky asset, his upside is EUR 10 mn minus the cost of the leverage, or a return of almost 100%. The lower the cost of leverage, the more attractive such a strategy might appear. In order to keep the increased risks of a leveraged investment strategy under control, portfolio managers use quantitative risk management techniques, such as the value-at-risk, to guide the investment decision. However, in a low-yield, low-spread environment, the volatility of risky assets is very low (in fact, the more common argument is the other way around: risk premiums (i.e., spreads) are low because volatility is low). As a consequence, VaR measures will also signal low risk, which provides a further argument to increase the leverage. However, as can be shown by our example, the leveraged strategy has a different return profile. While for the unleveraged investment a decline of 10% in the risky asset results in a loss of 10% (i.e., EUR 1 mn), a 10% decline in the leveraged investment wipes out all of our initial investment volume (and the cost for the leverage adds to this loss).

In this example, we referred to an arbitrary risky asset. This can be a single stock or a portfolio of stocks, but it can also be a credit investment. As already introduced in the CDS section, leveraging a credit investment using CDS is quite easy. The investor could sell protection on EUR 10 mn – his initial amount – or on a higher volume, say EUR 100 mn. Since the CDS is an unfunded investment, borrowing costs – at least the explicit ones – are zero. There will be implicit costs of leverage, as the counterparty of the CDS contract will demand some collateral for the leveraged investment. In the (unfunded) CDS world, the leverage is easily accessible. The investor just buys a government bond for his EUR 10 mn investment amount and asks his counterparties how much leverage they will provide on a specific name for EUR 10 mn collateral. The amount of leverage will obviously depend on the risk of the underlying asset. For a CDS on a safe-haven sovereign, such as a Western European country, the leverage can be up to 20 (which means that EUR 10 mn in collateral translates into EUR 200 mn in a risky investment); while for a sub-investment grade risk the allowed leverage might be only one (i.e., no further leverage). However, an investment in a high-yield asset, such as a high-yield bond or a leveraged loan, already has a certain level of leverage by itself.

In general, there are two different ways of leveraging investments: financial leverage and economic leverage. The investment strategy outlined above, borrowing additional funds for the leveraged acquisition of a risky exposure, is an example of a financial leverage. Here the leverage is directly employed (and managed) by the investor and is external to the risky assets. In an economic leverage, the gearing is directly related to the risky asset; for example, a high-yield bond issued by an LBO target. Sometimes it is difficult to distinguish between financial and economic leverage, as both concepts are either tied together or blurred by a difficult derivative structure. The example of a leveraged buyout highlights how financial and economic leverage can often go together. In this case, the investor in the high-yield bond has an exposure to an economically leveraged risk, but at the same time he provides the financial leverage for the private equity sponsor.

Other examples for a leverage effect are CDO investments. The equity tranche of a CDO is economically leveraged, such as a high-yield bond, as the gearing is already part of the risky exposure. However, the other end of the capital structure of a CDO, the senior and super-senior tranches, have different risk characteristics. Investing there is less risky (keeping highly correlated defaults aside) but the return for an investor might be too meager. Hence, he might employ an external leverage and acquire a senior CDO tranche using borrowed funds. So here are again two strategies: investing without external leverage in the lower part of the capital structure (economic leverage) or investing with external leverage in the upper part of a capital structure (financial leverage). Nevertheless, at the end of the day, both strategies are built on the same groundwork: leverage. What is the difference between the equity piece of a CDO and a leveraged position to the underlying assets? Nothing! Hence, acquiring a senior tranche of a CDO using borrowed money is nothing else than the equity piece of another CDO for which the underlying asset is the senior tranche of the original CDO. The borderline between economic and financial leverage can be even more blurred than in these examples. Just think about a mezzanine tranche in a CDO. Is this economic leverage or financial leverage, or something in between?

There were in fact two main leverage strategies at center stage in the structured credit arena before the subprime crisis.

- In Strategy A investors compiled assets with poor credit quality (i.e., with a high economic leverage) in a portfolio and mitigated the risk by buying a high-level tranche (i.e., by reducing the financial leverage externally).
- In strategy B investors compiled a set of high-quality assets (i.e., ones with a low economic leverage) in a portfolio and bought a low-level tranche (i.e., applied financial leverage externally).

But since there have been squared and cubed structured credit products (structured credit products that invest in other structured credit assets), things became a little more opaque. As we will see below, there have been structured credit products that acquired senior tranches of subprime RMBSs (i.e., strategy A) and refinanced this portfolio again via tranches. Hence, acquiring an equity piece of such a structure is like applying strategy B to a portfolio of assets that was compiled via strategy A. And obviously there have been also products where the portfolio was built the other way around, such as senior tranches of CDOs and ABSs that acquired mezzanine tranches of the primary subprime RMBS. In the following sections, we elaborate a little more on these strategies.

4.2 Leveraged Super Senior Tranches

At first glance, the leveraged super senior (LSS) tranches appear to be a classical example of the above-mentioned strategy B: investing into high-quality assets and enhancing spread income by employing an external (financial) leverage. Such an investment approach was also the initial idea of LSS, as this type of transaction gained in importance in 2005 following the correlation crisis, as CDO dealers intended to hedge their senior exposures. However, a closer look at more recent transactions reveals that LSS developed more into a combination of strategy A and strategy B, since for a large fraction of the implemented deals the underlying portfolio of the super senior tranches consisted of assets with lower credit quality in order to boost returns.

In an LSS transaction, the investor sells protection in a very high-level tranche (above a AAA-rated senior tranche, hence the name super senior tranche), either on an index portfolio, (such as the iTraxx or the CDX), or on a bespoke portfolio. However, in contrast to lower tranches (equity or mezz), in which the leverage is provided by the tranche subordination internally, in leveraged super senior tranches, leverage is implemented externally. This means that the arranger employs the leverage by selling protection with respect to a higher volume in the tranche than the note's notional amount. A typical example would be a note with a volume of EUR 10 mn and a leverage factor of 10. This would translate into an exposure to the super senior tranche of EUR 100 mn. However, this structure involves a gap risk for the arranger, in case losses on the leveraged investment exceed the collateral provided by the investor in form of the notes notional. In order to mitigate this gap risk, the LSS transactions usually involve features that trigger the unwinding of the leveraged position before the losses exceed the notional amount of the note. These trigger events are linked to the market value of the underlying exposure; hence, investing in a LSS transaction bears mark-to-market risk rather than actual default risk. In other words, since unwinding the note simply means that the investor is forced to realize the mark-to-market loss, such products convert the market risk into event risk. Moreover, the transaction also involves a structuring fee for the arranger. That is why an LSS deal usually pays less than the spread of the underlying super senior tranche times the leverage factor. If the underlying super senior tranche is a liquidly traded tranche (e.g., an iTraxx or CDX tranche), the fee structure is quite transparent. However, most of the LSS transactions are based on bespoke portfolios where already the spread of the underlying super senior tranche is not completely transparent. It was quite obvious that the fees on such deals have been substantial.

Besides the above-mentioned structure, where the investor simply has a leveraged exposure to a specific tranche, such as 10 times a 10-20% tranche on a specific portfolio, early transactions were slightly different. In such a transaction, the underlying tranche was a 10-100% tranche, that is, one that covered the whole super senior part of a portfolio. However, the investor only provided collateral for 10% of the whole exposure, that is, he just covers roughly the 10-20% tranche with his notional amount. In this structure, the leverage is created via the ratio between the volume of the note and the volume of the tranche. This version of a LSS transaction is especially interesting for the purpose of hedger of a specific portfolio. Consider a CDO manager who already sold the equity and some mezzanine tranches of a portfolio to the market. Now he still has an open exposure to the super senior tranche. Via this type of structure, this exposure can be easily hedged. However, as the LSS market developed, bespoke LSS structures hit the screen. This type of transaction is not driven by hedging needs of a specific portfolio manager, but is an investment product that is tailor-made to the needs of an investor. Here it is easier to refer to a specific tranche, say the 10-20% tranche. The arranger of the LSS transaction will not sell protection on the corresponding 10-100% tranche, but will simply create the leverage by selling protection in the 10-20% tranche on a notional amount that amounts to 10 times the notional of the note.

But why did investors enter into such transactions? From the brief introduction above it is quite clear that the replication of the economic risk of an LSS transaction is very easy – just buy 10 times as much volume – and saves the transaction fee? The answer is as usual: regulatory arbitrage. From a notional perspective, the investor only has the unleveraged note volume at risk, although the economic risk refers to the leveraged amount. If the investor would be forced to show this leveraged market risk also on the regulatory level, an LSS transaction would appear almost like a linear super senior exposure with the leveraged notional amount with an embedded stop-loss trigger (the trigger event). A real LSS transaction just gives an additional protection for the gap risk beyond the trigger structure (i.e., that the accumulated losses exceed the note's notional amount faster than the triggers are breached). In the following, we show how these products work and also investigate main risk drivers, as well as the sensitivity of the upper part of the tranche capital structure towards spread changes in the underlying pool.

In general, there are four different types of LSS transactions, depending on the trigger structure. Of these four different types, only three (the first three in the list below) were actually used on a broader scale.[17,18]

- **A pure loss trigger**: Here the LSS is unwound, after the underlying portfolio accumulated a certain default loss amount. This is usually not static, but evolves with time. For example, in the first year of a 10Y deal one would have 5% loss trigger, in the second 5.5%, etc. This increase reflects the declining risk of a large number of joint defaults with declining remaining time to maturity. Although these products are very attractive from an investor's point of view (no mark-to-market trigger, no mark-to-market problem), they are very difficult to hedge from an arranger's point of view. Hence, not many investment banks offered these products.

- **A combination of loss and spread trigger:** Here one has a trigger matrix, which is a function of default losses and remaining time to maturity. The spread trigger refers to the weighted average spread (WAS) in the underlying portfolio and not to the spread of the super senior itself (see last bullet point). As an example, an LSS with 10Y remaining time to maturity and 0% accumulated default loss might be triggered if the average portfolio spread is in the area of 3 times compared to the initial portfolio spread. These triggers depend on changes in the accumulated losses and remaining time to maturity. A large fraction of outstanding LSS transactions was structured this way. However, during the credit crisis, these products proved to be quite dangerous, as – depending on the underlying portfolio – they bear the risk of being triggered even without any actual defaults. There are several market segments, such as the iTraxx, the CDX and the iTraxx financials, which even more than tripled their spread levels in the course of the crisis. Ironically, there is one issue which might prevent a larger amount of trigger events: Usually investors in bespoke LSS used a basket with a lower average (investment trade) credit quality. LSS structures with a large fraction of financials have been limited, since super senior tranches on portfolios that involved a high exposure to financials offered only tiny spreads due to the overall tight spreads. And since the deals referred to quite high tranche levels, investors felt comfortable, for example, with corporate credit in the BBB area. This feature, by the way, is what we referred to when we mentioned at the beginning of the LSS discussion that LSS is more a combination of strategies A and B: one compiles a portfolio of assets with lower credit quality (in the BBB area) and structures a high-level (i.e., super senior) tranche, which, in turn, is geared up by a factor of up to 10 times and more. In addition to the weighted average spread, some transactions also implement triggers on individual spread changes. Furthermore, when referring to spread triggers one has to define the maturity bracket of the reference. This can be done by either referring to the maturity date of the LSS deal (however, this means that one has to interpolate on the market curve) or by referring to a constant maturity bracket (i.e., 5Y). Usually one refers to the latter mechanism as it is easier to implement.

- **A WARF (weighted average rating factor) trigger**. This trigger structure is used when the underlying portfolio refers to other structured finance assets, such as RMBSs, ABSs or CDOs. Here, the deal is triggered when the weighted average rating factor of the underlying portfolio hits a predefined level. This version is similar to the spread trigger LSS transaction. The only difference is that the trigger matrix refers to the WARF instead of the weighted average spread (WAS) of the underlying portfolio. Given the large number of downgrades in the structured finance universe, deals that use such trigger events bear a significant risk of being unwound, depending on the assets they involve.
- **A mark-to-market trigger in the tranche**. In this LSS structure, the contract is triggered when the tranche to which the LSS refers hits a certain loss barrier (not the average spread in the underlying portfolio as in the previous case). Although this variant would be the most attractive one from an arranger's point of view, due to the unforeseeable risks (also the risk of a dispute between arranger and investor regarding the valuation of the underlying tranche) this variant was not frequently used. Given the huge spread blowout, not only in the average spreads of the underlying portfolios but in particular in those of senior and super senior tranches, the risk that LSS with mark-to-market triggers will be triggered is extremely high during a credit crisis.

In addition to the unwinding mechanism, where the underlying tranche exposure is closed and the investor realizes the mark-to-market loss, there is another mechanism for managing the gap risk available: deleveraging the LSS transaction. This mechanism works as follows: In case the trigger events are breached, the investor has the choice whether the note will be completely unwound or whether he injects additional cash. For our example of a EUR 10 mn note with an initial leverage factor of 10, this could mean that the investor has to inject an additional EUR 10 mn to the transaction. The notional of the note would now be EUR 20 mn and the leverage factor would reduce to 5, since the absolute amount of spread payment of the note would remain the same. This mechanism can be implemented until the initial leverage is completely taken out, that is, until the volume of the note equals the volume of the underlying tranche exposure (EUR 100 mn). The definitions of the trigger events for this kind of transaction are similar to the one where the note is completely unwound. The difference is that we need to define a cascade of deleveraging triggers; that is, the investor has to inject an additional notional for the first time when the underlying spread reaches a level of X bp, a further injection is required when the spread reaches an even higher level of Y bp, and so on. However, in order to keep the analysis simple, we will focus on the pure unwinding mechanism in the following.

How does marketing, structuring and pricing in the LSS arena work? Basically, the LSS structures have four variables that can be adjusted to investors' (and arrangers') needs:

- the structure of the underlying portfolio,
- the tranche's detachment and attachment points,
- the leverage and
- the trigger structure.

We highlight this process based on the most common version: the combination of loss and spread trigger (the second trigger structure in the list above). Here, the risk for the arranger is that the tranche value (and hence his gap risk between tranche value and collateral value) is not only affected by defaults and the average spread of the underlying portfolio, but also by the implied correlation of the tranche. So he will set the trigger matrix in a way that he is protected against gap risk in a (correlation) stress scenario. Hence, these trigger matrices are the crucial point for pricing LSS derivatives. This means that an investor usually decides on the underlying portfolio (if it is a bespoke deal), the level of the tranche (i.e., 10% to 20% detachment and attachment level), the leverage, and demands a minimum spread. The arranger then quotes a trigger matrix.

How big can mark-to-market losses in super senior tranches be? To illustrate the magnitude of potential spread swings in the super senior area, we refer to the spread time series of the iTraxx Main index and the corresponding 12-22% tranche (for series 7 and 8). In chart 4.1, we derive that due to the financial market crisis, the 12-22% tranche traded above the spread levels of the underlying iTraxx in early 2007. During its peak in November 2007, tranche spreads were even twice as high as the iTraxx Main all-time low in May, while in February 2008 they have been blown out to levels above 150 bp, compared to 2 bp before the crisis. Such levels indicate extreme stress, as they reflect a probability above 10% that there will be more than 25% defaults in the investment grade universe in Europe over the next 5 years. Furthermore, the super senior tranche spreads do not move in a linear dependency with the underlying spreads, as can be seen in chart 4.2. The dependency is more of an exponential nature: when underlying iTraxx spreads tripled, the tranche spreads moved out by a factor of 10. This highlights the tremendous problems in the super senior area. Assuming a risky duration of roughly 5 for a 5Y tranche, a spread widening of 40 bp trans-

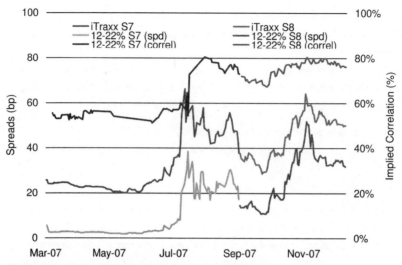

Fig. 4.1: Market spreads in the iTraxx Main index and in the 12-22% tranche (for Series 7 and 8) as time series

lates into a mark-to-market loss of 2% in the tranche. If this was leveraged by a factor of 10, then the note lost roughly 20% in value, which is substantial for a AAA-rated buy-and-hold security. Moreover, such instruments have been used as assets in arbitrage conduits and SIVs, which means that there was another layer of leverage.

What we have learned so far is that "super senior" does not necessarily equate "super risk-less". When the subprime crisis recently turned into a "leveraged super sickness", investors painfully experienced that there are in fact serious risks involved in these products, although, from an isolated default-risk perspective – as well as from a rating agency perspective – these super senior tranches appeared to be almost risk free. (However, this changed as rating agencies stopped assigning AAA ratings to LSS transactions in the meantime.) The spread widening during the credit crisis, which hit especially the super senior part of the capital structures, caused tremendous mark-to-market losses, leaving several investors and investment vehicles in deep trouble. But how did the subprime crisis – which deals with assets of poor credit quality – turn into a crisis of the most secure part of the tranche capital structure, which was considered to be of almost "risk-free nature"? In the following we shed some light on this infection channel, which triggered unknown spread volatility in super senior tranches.

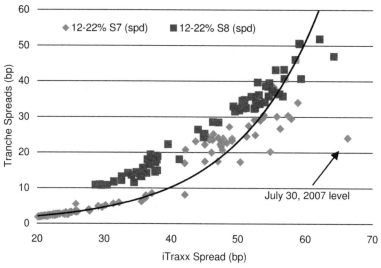

Fig. 4.2: Market spreads in the iTraxx Main index and in the 12-22% tranche (for Series 7 and 8) as a scatter plot showing the tranche-underlying dependency

The easiest and most apparent infection channel that triggered a spillover from the subprime crisis onto the super senior universe is increasing risk aversion accompanied by global repricing of risk. In this argumentation, there is no need for a direct fundamental link between two asset classes. It is sufficient that the boom in both markets ahead of the crisis was driven by excessive leverage. When investors realize that one bubble is bursting, they obviously look for other potential bubbles and initiate a sell-off in the identified asset classes. However, while there is some logic behind this argumentation, there was also a more fundamental infection channel in place. LSS investors were caught in the same trap as other high-quality structured credit investors in SIV, ABCP and other "enhanced" money market investments.

As can be seen in charts 4.1 and 4.2, the super senior tranches suffered not only from spread widening in the underlying credit portfolio, but also because of an increasing implied default correlation, that is, an issue that is specific to this level in the capital structure. There are two explanations for this rising default correlation. The fundamental one is that a full-fledged credit crisis poses a systematic if not even a systemic risk. However, in a systemic crisis the risk for joint defaults rises, and correlation desks translate this into a rising implied default correlation, in particular in the upper part of the capital structure.

But there were also some technical factors that pushed implied default correlation higher. Due to the blowout in subprime RMBS (which occurred across the whole capital structure of these deals), also non subprime-related ABS suffered as no one was willing to invest in these products. This buyers' strike hit even the safest part, the AAA-rated tranches. However, such bonds were frequently used in asset pools of conduits and structured investment vehicles (SIVs). One of the goals of these vehicles was to provide leveraged access (again the buzzword *leverage*) to safe havens, implemented by spread term structure transformation (refinance long-term assets with short-term debt). As these conduits came under suspicion, also the super senior assets came into the focus of investors. This was not necessarily due to concerns regarding the credit quality of the high-quality assets, but simply due to the risk of fire sales from forced unwinding of troubled conduits and SIVs. As such fire sales hit an already illiquidly structured credit market, spreads of these products were pushed out further. Moreover, some conduits – especially in Canada – invested directly in leveraged super senior tranches, which involve spread triggers. This however, becomes a risk of a self-fulfilling crisis: spreads in super-senior tranches blow out, which increases the risk that LSS transactions are triggered. This increasing trigger risk causes an additional sell-off in the super senior and leveraged super senior, as commercial paper (CP) investors try to escape by refusing to roll their positions forward and force conduits and SIVs to liquidate positions.

Another technical problem for super senior tranches stems from correlation desks that structure bespoke tranches. Usually, the correlation hedgers leave the most senior part of the capital structure unhedged in order to enhance their spread income, although the costs for the hedges have been quite low. However, as correlation books can be huge (note that if an investor buys EUR 10 mn of a 3-7% bespoke tranche, i.e., just 4% of the full portfolio, the structuring desk has the correlation risk of the remaining EUR 240 mn on the books), mark-to-market losses especially in the unhedged super senior area rose to a substantial amount. This, in turn, triggers hedging activities (i.e., buying protection in the unhedged positions), which pushes super senior spreads out further.

However, there was another, more fundamental issue that hit the super senior part of the capital structure. Since the subprime losses were initially a problem of the financial community, spreads in the financial universe experienced a tremendous blowout. This, in turn, had a serious impact on the pricing especially of super senior tranches. As we have discussed in chapter 2, the upper part of the tranche capital structure has a high sensitivity towards the constituents in the underlying portfolio that trade at tighter spread levels. As a consequence, super senior spreads experienced widening pressure due to the overall spread widening as well as the spread widening in the tighter names. And the latter was enormous, as financial spreads were hit hard during the crisis.

However, LSS transactions have been based not only on corporate credit portfolios, but also on CDO and ABS portfolios. And from this universe came also one of the first failed LSS deals. In late October, S&P downgraded the so-called Foraois Funding transaction to CCC and kept the deal on watch negative. This rating action came only about nine months after the deal was set up, as the transaction was closed in February 2007 and had an initial rating of AAA. But S&P managed not to downgrade the transaction from AAA directly to CCC, as the rating agency already lowered its rating in August 2007 to BBB- and placed the ratings on watch negative.

4.3 Constant Proportion Debt Obligations

Constant Proportion Debt Obligations are among the latest innovations in the corporate credit arena. They hit the screens in late 2006 and triggered an unprecedented euphoria and skepticism at the same time. We have hardly seen any other credit derivative product that attracted similar attention, dividing investors drastically into supporters and opponents. The impact of these instruments on the market was huge. The iTraxx spread in Series 6 (the on-the-run series at that time) tightened from 31 bp to 23 bp, the cyclical low that was reached on November 5, 2006, within only six weeks. Although this might not appear too impressive given the spread volatility in the summer of 2007, in late 2006 a spread tightening of 8 bp was indeed impressive, as it simply doubled the YTD spread performance of the iTraxx in just a few weeks. Moreover, we should also not forget that this 23 bp level was already very close to the all-time low in iTraxx on-the-run index spreads of 20 bp, which was reached on June 5, 2007.

So what was the miracle behind these enigmatic instruments? CPDOs allow a leveraged exposure to liquidly tradable credit indices such as the iTraxx and the CDX. The central idea of this product is very similar to the LSS tranches. They come in a note format, and the arranger of the transaction sells protection in the targeted CDS indices on a notional amount that is a multiple of the underlying notional of the CPDO note. For example, a CPDO note referring to the iTraxx and the CDX with a volume of EUR 10 mn and a leverage of 10 involves index investments of EUR 50 mn in the iTraxx and EUR 50 mn in the

CDX. Moreover, the CPDO leverage mechanism involves a gap risk that has to be mitigated via structural features. Furthermore, the market values of several CPDO transactions also dropped rapidly during the crisis, despite their initial AAA ratings. CPDOs differ from LSS tranches in that they typically involve a dynamic leverage factor which is a function of the performance of the deal and consequently varies over time. In order to prevent extreme leverage values, the CPDO documentation specifies a maximum leverage factor. However, this leverage is model-based and is typically not actively managed.[19,20]

The capital structure of a CPDO transaction involves a reserve account. This account is used to accumulate excess spread income that exceeds the regular coupon payments. A brief example demonstrates this feature. We assume that the transaction was launched at an average market spread of 20 bp. We also assume that the deal involves a coupon payment of 200 bp and a current leverage of 15. The index investment will generate a spread income of 300 bp with respect to the note's notional (300 bp = 15 * 20 bp). Since 200 bp have to be paid out to the noteholder, the reserve account can accumulate 100 bp excess spread. This reserve account can then be used to mitigate mark-to-market losses or to deleverage the note once the amount accumulated on the reserve account is sufficient to satisfy all future coupon payments. This risk mitigation technique is taken from the cash-flow CDO universe, in which such reserve accounts are frequently used to provide an additional level of security for senior investors. In this context, the reserve account is filled by excess spread that belongs to subordinated investors but which is only paid out at maturity if no losses for the senior investors have occurred. However, CPDOs do not involve a tranched capital structure, such as a CDO (see below).

In order to keep the so-called *gap risk* – that is, the risk that the losses on the leveraged position exceed the notional of the note which is provided as collateral – a CPDO typically involves a so-called cash-out event. If the accumulated losses on the index position exceed a specified loss threshold, either due to mark-to-market losses or due to default event, then the note is unwound and the note investor bears all losses. Assuming the above-mentioned example of a EUR 10 mn investment and a cash-out level of 10%, then the note is unwound if the accumulated losses exceed EUR 9 mn. However, in a cash-out event, the loss for the investor is also EUR 9 mn, or 90%. This cash-out event is very similar to the trigger structure in an LSS transaction. But unlike in the LSS, it is not defined in terms of a specific spread but by the net asset value in the portfolio, which is given by the mark-to-market value of the index investments plus the amount in the reserve account. As a consequence, the cash-out event also depends on the historic performance of the transaction. However, besides the cash-out event, there is also a cash-in event. This is triggered if the amount accumulated on the reserve account is sufficient to satisfy all future coupon payments. We continue our example and assume that the transaction has a lifetime of 10 years. Moreover, we assume that the spread level in the underlying risky asset remains constant at 20 bp, in other words, that there are no mark-to-market gains or losses. Hence, we can accumulate 100 bp per year. Ignoring any compounding on the reserve account this means that after seven years we accumulated 700 bp excess spread. However, for the remaining three years until maturity of the deal, we only need 600 bp (3*200 bp coupon payments). We can therefore pay all of the contracted coupon payments out of the reserve account. A risky asset is therefore no longer needed and the leverage factor can be reduced to zero (which means that the risky position is closed). However, in reality such deleveraging will not occur in such an abrupt manner (leverage from 15 directly to 0) but in a smoother process. The exact dependency of the leverage factor as a variable of the value on the reserve account is one key feature of CPDOs. In second and third- generation CPDOs, this leverage formula was optimized with respect to the risk or chances of cash-out and cash-in events. Nevertheless, a common property across all CPDOs is that the leverage increases when the net asset value of the structure declines due to mark-to-market or default losses. This can be understood in the following way. In case the structure suffered under spread widening, the loss incurred on the valuation side can be offset by a higher spread income. If the leverage is increased in a spread widening, the investor benefits from the higher spread income. This means that in this respect the CPDO acts countercyclical, which, by the way, should dampen spread volatility. From a modeling perspective, this countercyclical dependency exploits the mean reversion property of credit spreads (or at least of credit spread models that are used to evaluate these deals). In order to optimize this offsetting property, the duration of the risky asset is typically much shorter than the duration of the deals. Most of the known CPDO deals had a lifetime of 10 years, while the risky asset referred to 5Y indices. However, with respect to the cash-out event (i.e., the mark-to-market trigger), CPDOs are procyclical instruments. When the trigger is reached due to spread widening, the liquidation of CPDOs pushes spreads further out.

The underlying portfolio of credits is constantly adjusted in order to keep at an investment-grade level. The implementation of the rule is very simple. Since CPDOs are linked to investment-grade CDS indices, the risky position in the CPDO simply has to be rolled into the new series of the index once it is available. Since non-investment grade names are removed from the indices the portfolio is usually not very much exposed to non-investment grade names. Because these rolls occur every six months, this sub-investment-grade risk is quite limited. However, this rolling feature has a tremendous impact on the modeling of CPDOs. Two important things come into play at this point: one that impacts the default risk assessment and one that influences the anticipated P&L of the risky investment. We discuss the default risk assessment first. Due to the index rolling, a default loss in the CPDO occurs only if a name migrates to the default state from an investment-grade state within six months. This, however, is very unlikely, not only from a rating agency perspective. Hence, when modeling the default probability, this index roll is used as an argument in order to assess default risk only for consecutive six-month periods. However, accumulating these six-month probabilities always with respect to an investment grade default probability leads to a significantly lower accumulated default probability compared to a scenario when we allow for all rating migration (i.e., from AA to BB in the first six months and then from BB to default in the second six months). Consequently, the risk for a CPDO investor that stems from default events is marginal. Let us move to the second crucial point. Typically, investment grade spread curves have a "normal" shape. This means that spread levels increase with an increasing time horizon. For the constantly rolled index investment, this results in a positive P&L contribution. At the date when the exposure is rolled into a new series, the index contract has a remaining time to maturity of 5.25 years (this is a feature of the iTraxx and CDX indices). At the next roll date half a year later, the remaining time to maturity is then only 4.75 years. But if the level of the spread curve does not change, selling protection in the 5.25Y contract and closing the position when it has only 4.25 years involves a spread tightening (since the curve is upward sloping). This is called the curve roll-down, and in fact it is an important part of the P&L of credit portfolio managers. However, the first consequence of the index roll (limited default risk is more or less acceptable), relying on the second (i.e., assuming a constant spread contribution due to the curve roll-down) is a serious mistake. We will discuss our concerns below. Another potential consequence of the rolling feature that was discussed among market participants was the impact on the roll spread. Given a tremendous acceptance of the CPDO idea among investors, huge volumes would have to be rolled forward at each roll date. Moreover, since this roll is a technical (i.e., unmanaged) feature, (the CPDOs are forced to roll even if the levels quoted in the market would be ridiculous), it could be exploited.

However, since the emergence of CPDOs, several index rolls already occurred, and up to date there have been no signs of an anomaly.

As already stated several times, a CPDO usually invests in a CDS index and not in a tranche. This means that there is no risk mitigation due to subordination, as for example with the Leveraged Super Senior. As a consequence, there is no default correlation risk and investors do not need complicated portfolio models to analyze the exposure. On the other hand, unlike in a LSS, there is an immediate default risk. If a default event occurs in the on-the-run series of a CDS index, the corresponding loss will hit the leveraged investment directly. Hence, the underlying assets of a CPDO are typically not rated AAA, compared to LSS. This property caused the following joke among market participants: "What is the average rating of the iTraxx? BBB. And what is the average rating of the iTraxx when you leverage fifteen times? AAA." To make this point clear, a potential AAA rating on a CPDO transaction is only driven by the structural features implemented in a CPDO: the constant roll into a new series and in the reserve account.

By the way, now that we have discussed the basic mechanism of CPDOs, the name of these instruments – Constant Proportion Debt Obligation – appears quite odd. In fact, it is a quite artificial, marketing-driven name, as it is neither "CP" nor "DO". The "CP" part of the name tries to put the product close to CPPIs (Constant Proportion Portfolio Insurance (CPPI)). However, a CPPI involves a defensive investment strategy, since it automatically reduces exposure to risky assets when the asset value of the structure declines. CPDOs do exactly the opposite. When the net asset value of the portfolio declines due to spread widening in the underlying CDS indices, the exposure to these indices increases, following the old trader rule "If you are in trouble – double". Hence CPDOs are not defensive instruments. Moreover, since the leverage factor changes over time, the "constant proportion" part of the term is also confusing. This caused some investment banks to market their variants with the name Variable Proportion Debt Obligation (VPDO). The "DO" part of the name attempted to place the product close to CDOs. However, CPDOs are also portfolio derivatives, since they refer to a portfolio of CDS. But unlike CDOs, they do not involve any kind of tranching. There is no mitigation of default risk via selecting a higher tranche that is protection protected by subordinated tranches. In this respect, a different name would have been more transparent, such as "Dynamic Leverage Index Note", but admittedly that does not sound very sexy.

So what is the investment rationale of a CPDO, besides perhaps a somewhat blending spread of 200 bp on an AAA-rated security? The central idea behind a CPDO is to allow a leveraged exposure in order to extract the risk premium in market prices. Just consider the following example. The average cumulated default probability for a BBB-rated exposure on a 5Y time horizon is 1.5%. Assuming a recovery rate of 40%, we can approximate that in the long run this would break even in respect to default losses if the portfolio would earn a credit spread of about 18 bp. From such a point of view, a market spread that exceeds this level offers a positive return. At first glance, CPDOs allow one to extract exactly this spread difference. However, several "buts" accompany such a strategy. First, the actual default rate on the on-the-run index positions will be lower, as downgraded names are excluded (we highlighted this above). Second, the rolling process involves a mark-to-market risk due to potential downgrades (spreads in the new series will be lower than spreads on the older ones, which contain the downgraded names; we highlighted this as well). And third, the CPDO involves a cash-out event. Even if the default losses would be zero, the investor would realize a large loss if the underlying credit spreads would widen dramatically so that the cash-out event is triggered. This is especially the case if this spread-widening occurs quite soon after closing the transaction, since the structure will not have been able to accumulate sufficient reserves to buffer the losses. This is exactly the problem that hit CPDOs, as the credit market turmoil started only seven months after initiation of the first transactions.

But how can one analyze CPDOs properly? For this purpose, a framework is needed that captures the central risk factors. Besides the stochastic nature of the average credit spread and the default risk, one needs to model the spread dynamics which are incurred by the roll from one series to the other (to capture the above-mentioned downgrade risk) and the steepness of the credit curve (to capture the curve roll-down). Moreover, for all instruments that involve a trigger risk, the underlying stochastic process needs to reflect the jump risk, for example, via a jump-diffusion process.

How large is the risk for a cash-out event? Let us refer to our previous example: a CPDO which pays a 200 bp coupon, a leverage of 15, an initial spread of 20 bp, and a risky duration of the underlying asset of about 4.5. The cash-out event should be at 10% NAV. In this setup, we would earn an excess spread of 100 bp. Hence, the cash-out event would be reached if the NAV would decline to 9% after one year. Given the above-mentioned leverage and duration, a drop of 91% translates into a spread-widening of 135 bp = 0.91 / (15 * 4.5). Not possible? Just consider the twenty-five financials in the CDX.NA index. Their average 5Y CDS spread widened as much as 170 bp during the crisis. It is therefore not very surprising that the CPDOs referencing financial basket structures were among the worst performers. Series 103 of the CPDO Financial Basket Tyger Note, issued by UBS' ELM vehicle, was downgraded by Moody's to C (initial rating Aa3) on November 23, 2007, as the cash-out trigger of 10% was reached due to a widening of the weighted average spread of the underlying portfolio to 170 bp on November 21, 2007. However, a significant portion of the deal was already repurchased and cancelled by the issuer before the cash-out event occurred. Besides the strong systematic spread widening in financial spreads during the crisis, there is another problem that affected financials CPDO. Because the financials sub-indices of the CDX and the iTraxx contain only twenty-five financial institutions, the underlying CPDO portfolio – only fifty names altogether – contains a significant amount of idiosyncratic risk. This hurts one of the central key drivers for the expected stability of CPDO transactions. Our example revealed that there is one risk that can impair this product: fast and large-spread movements, or in other words *jumps*. However, since the underlying nature of credit risk is an event risk, single-name credit spreads tend to jump on headline risk. The portfolio effect of the CDS indices mitigates this idiosyncratic jump risk. But if the portfolio is too small and has only exposure to one single industry, the diversification vanishes and the risk of reaching the cash-out event increases. In total, Moody's rated about EUR 500 mn of financial CPDOs in eight transactions issued by UBS and ABN Amro, with a leverage of between 5 and 11 and initial ratings between Aaa and Aa3 (five with Aaa, one with Aa2 and two with Aa3). By the end of November, only two transactions were affirmed at Aaa, while two have been downgraded to A2, three to Baa3 and one to C (the one with the cash-out trigger). The total amount of CPDO volume analyzed by Moody's amounted roughly to EUR 2.5 bn.[21,22]

But there hasn't been only bad news about CPDOs. In November 2007, Moody's upgraded a CPDO issued by Aphex Pacific Capital which referenced to the iTraxx Europe and the CDX.IG (in 5Y maturities each) to Aaa from Aa1. The rating action followed a cash-in event in the transaction. Due to the strong tightening in iTraxx and the CDX spreads, following the 50 bp rate cut at the FOMC meeting in September 2007, the NAV of the transaction, which was closed in August 2007, increased so much that the deal could be restructured by changing the scheduled maturity to November 2011 and fixing the notes' spread to 2.05%. As the deal no longer involves default risk, Moody's upgraded it to Aaa.

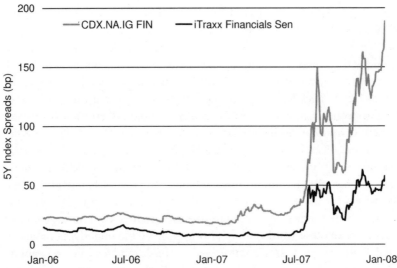

Fig. 4.3: iTraxx and CDX Financials spreads
Source: MarkIT

4.4 Structured Investment Vehicles

Besides *subprime*, the major buzzword of the second half of 2007 was *structured investment vehicle*. However, despite the fact that these vehicles were almost only known to involved specialists at the beginning of 2007, they are actually quite old investment instruments. The first SIV – Alpha Finance Corporation – was already launched by Citibank in 1988.[23] Only one year later Citibank launched its second SIV, Beta Finance Corporation. While Alpha was wound down by Citibank in 1998, the SIV boom gained momentum in the second half of the 1990s, with the launch of eight SIVs that were still existing in 2007. Since the start of the first SIV, several vehicles were launched and were subsequently shut down again. While Alpha, the first SIV, was operating with a fixed leverage, subsequent structures became significantly more complex. They involved dynamic capital structures with portfolios that changed over time with respect to the assets held, the rating qualities and the time to maturity. When the subprime crisis moved into full swing in the summer of 2007, the existing SIVs had senior debt outstanding in the amount of USD 340 bn. This compares to a total volume of USD 24 bn in capital notes outstanding (which is essentially the equity of an SIV) and results in an average leverage factor of 14.

The biggest player was Citigroup with seven SIVs with an aggregated volume of senior debt of almost USD 90 bn, followed by HSBC with a total amount of USD 42 bn in two vehicles, Dresdner Kleinwort with almost USD 30 bn and Bank of Montreal with USD 26 bn in two vehicles. The biggest non-bank SIV manager was Gordian Knot with its SIV Sigma Finance, which was established in 1995 and which had a volume of senior debt of USD 53 bn, the biggest of all existing SIVs.

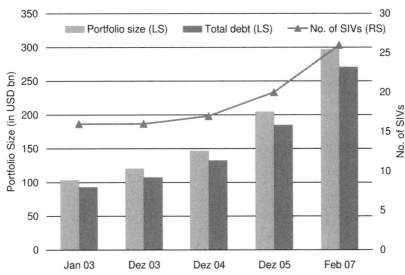

Fig. 4.4: Development of SIVs (Volume and number of vehicles)[24]
Source: Standard & Poor's

Since the beginning of 2003, the SIV universe has been growing rapidly, with the portfolio size tripling until 2007 and the number of vehicles expanding from 16 to 26 (by February 2007). Moreover, in 2007 four more SIVs with a senior debt volume of almost USD 25 bn were ramped up (see table 4.1). In addition to the SIVs, the so-called SIV-lite hit the screens in 2005. The SIV-lite transactions compiled in table 4.3 involve a total debt of almost USD 19 bn. The most recent addition to the SIV-lite universe was Sachsen Funding I, which was launched in June 2007, a few days before the turmoil started. In December 2007, S&P downgraded the capital and senior notes of the transaction to CCC-.

Tab. 4.1: Structured Investment Vehicles (SIVs); *As of August 15, 2007. **As of December 07, 2007.[24,25] (Source: Moody's, Standard & Poor's)

SIV	Manager	Initiation date	Senior debt (USD mn)*	Sub/Sen rating*		Sub/Sen rating**		NAV (Moody's) Nov/Sept 2007
				S&P	Moody's	S&P	Moody's	
Beta Finance Corp.	Citibank International PLC	8-Sept-89	20,175.95	NR/AAA	Baa1/Aaa	NR/AAAn	Caa3/Aaa (On review)	60% / 87%
Sigma Finance Corp.	Gordian Knot Ltd.	2-Feb-95	52,641.87	NR/AAA	NR/AAAn	BBB/AAAwn	NR/Baa3	54% / 61%
Orion Finance Corp.	Eiger Capital Management	31-May-96	2,298.43	BBB/AAA	NR/Aaa			
Centauri Corp.	Citibank International PLC	9-Sept-96	21,838.84	NR/AAA	Baa1/Aaa	NR/AAAn	Caa3/Aaa (On review)	60% / 85%
Dorada Corp.	Citibank International PLC	17-Sept-98	12,484.15	NR/AAA	Baa1/Aaa	NR/AAAn	Caa3/Aaa (On review)	62% / 87%
K2 Corp.	Dresdner Kleinwort	1-Feb-99	29,056.47	A/AAA	A3/Aaa	BBwn/AAAn	Caa2/Aaa (On review)	
Links Finance Corp.	Bank of Montreal	18-June-99	22,301.10	NR/AAA		NR/AAAn	NR/Aaa (On review)	78% / 94%
Five Finance Corp.	Citibank International PLC	15-Nov-99	12,843.06	BBB+/AAA	NR/Aaa	CCCwn/AAAn	NR/Aaa (On review)	63% / 74%
Abacas Investments Ltd.	N.S.M. Capital Management/Emirates Bank	8-Dec-99	1,007.95	A/AAA		A/AAA		
Parkland Finance Corp.	Bank of Montreal	7-Sept-01	3,414.43	NR/AAA		NR/AAAn		
Harrier Finance Funding Ltd.	WestLB	11-Jan-02	12,343.37	NR/AAA	Baa2/Aaa	NR/AAAwn	NR/Aaa	
White Pine Corp. Ltd. (merged with Whistlejacket Capital Ltd.)	Standard Chartered Bank	4-Feb-02	7,854.63	BBB+/AAA	NR/Aaa	B-wn/AAAn	Ca/Aaa (On review)	61% / 85%
Victoria Finance Ltd.	Ceres Capital Partners	10-July-02	13,243.95	BBB+/AAA	Baa2/Aaa	CCwn/AAAwn	Caa3/Aaa (On review)	63% / 83%
Premier Asset Collateralized Entity Ltd.	Societe Generale	10-July-02	4,312.70	BBB/AAA	Baa2/Aaa	CCC-wn/AAAwn		

Tab. 4.1: Continued

SIV	Manager	Initiation date	Senior debt (USD mn)*	Sub/Sen rating* S&P	Sub/Sen rating* Moody's	Sub/Sen rating** S&P	Sub/Sen rating** Moody's	NAV (Moody's) Nov/Sept 2007
Whistlejacket Capital Ltd. (merged with White Pine Corp. Ltd.)	Standard Chartered Bank	24-July-02	8,844.63	BBB+/AAA	Baa2/Aaa	BB-wn/AAAn	NR/Aaa (On review)	69% / 80%
Tango Finance Corp.	Rabobank International	26-Nov-02	14,039.75	BBB+/AAA	Baa1/Aaa	Bwn/AAAn	Caa3/Aaa (On review)	69% / 88%
Sedna Finance Corp.	Citibank International PLC	22-June-04	14,415.28	A/AAA	NR/Aaa	B-wn (second priority senior)/AAAn	NR/Aaa (On review)	56% / 85%
Cullinan Finance Ltd.	HSBC Bank PLC	18-Jul-05	35,142.00	BBB/AAA	Baa2/Aaa	B-wn/AAAn	Ca/Aaa	56% / 78%
Cheyne Finance PLC	Cheyne Capital Management Ltd.	3-Aug-05	9,726.18	A/AAA		D/D	C/B2	
Eaton Vance Variable Leveraged Fund	Eaton Vance	23-Sep-05	542.76	NR/AAA		NR/AAA		
Carrera Capital Finance Ltd.	HSH Nordbank	30-Jun-06	4,283.48	NR/AAA	Baa2/Aaa	NR/AAAn	Baa2/Aaa	
Kestrel Funding PLC	WestLB/Brightwater Capital	2-Aug-06	3,315.86	BBB/AAA	Baa2/Aaa	CCC-wn/AAAwn	NR/Aaa	
Zela Finance Corp.	Citibank International PLC	18-Sep-06	4,188.70	A-/AAA	NR/Aaa	B-wn/AAAn	NR/Aaa (On review)	61% / 76%
Cortland Capital Ltd.	IXIS/Ontario Teachers	1-Nov-06	1,344.19	NR/AAA		NR/AAAn		
Vetra Finance Corp.	Citibank International PLC	15-Nov-06	2,616.94	NR/AAA		NR/AAAn		
Hudson-Thames Capital Ltd.	MBIA	5-Dec-06	1,767.33	BBB/AAA	Baa3/Aaa	CCC-wn/AAA	Ca/Aaa (On review)	
Nightingale Finance Ltd.	Banque AIG	15-Mar-07	2,330.23	BBB/AAA	Baa2/Aaa	BB-wn/AAAn	B3/Aaa	81% / 95%
Axon Financial Funding Ltd.	Axon Asset Management Inc.	30-Mar-07	11,193.76	A+/AAA		D/D		
Rhinebridge PLC	IKB Credit Asset Management GmbH	13-Apr-07	2,199.63	A/AAA		D/D		
Asscher Finance Ltd.	HSBC Bank PLC	11-May-07	7,330.00	BBB/AAA	A2/Aaa	CCC-wn/AAAn	Caa2/Aaa	63% / 84%

Tab. 4.2: SIV Manager and institutional type[24]
Source: Standard & Poor's

Manager	Institutional Type	No. of vehicles	Volume
Citibank International PLC	Bank	7	88,562.92
HSBC Bank PLC	Bank	2	42,472.00
Dresdner Kleinwort	Bank	1	29,056.47
Bank of Montreal	Bank	2	25,715.53
Standard Chartered Bank	Bank	2	16,699.26
WestLB	Bank	2	15,659.23
Rabobank International	Bank	1	14,039.75
Societe Generale	Bank	1	4,312.70
HSH Nordbank	Bank	1	4,283.48
IKB Credit Asset Management GmbH	Bank	1	2,199.63
Gordian Knot Ltd.	Non-Bank	1	52,641.87
Ceres Capital Partners	Non-Bank	1	13,243.95
Axon Asset Management Inc.	Non-Bank	1	11,193.76
Cheyne Capital Management Ltd.	Non-Bank	1	9,726.18
Banque AIG	Non-Bank	1	2,330.23
Eiger Capital Management	Non-Bank	1	2,298.43
MBIA	Non-Bank	1	1,767.33
IXIS/Ontario Teachers	Non-Bank	1	1,344.19
N.S.M. Capital Management/Emirates Bank	Non-Bank	1	1,007.95
Eaton Vance	Non-Bank	1	542.76

But how is a SIV structured? In principle, a SIV is supposed to be a bankruptcy-remote special-purpose vehicle that implements leveraged investments in high-quality assets. The liabilities of these investment vehicles usually consist of (subordinated) capital, (senior) asset-backed commercial paper (ABCP) and medium-term notes. Traditional SIVs are open-end vehicles (the newer SIV-lites, a.k.a. SIV CDOs, have a fixed lifetime, see below). The subordinated capital is provided in the form of tranched or untranched capital notes. Untranched notes or more senior parts of tranched capital notes may even be rated. The structure is typically set up in a way that the senior debt and the commercial paper programs of the SIV are rated AAA and A-1+, respectively. Since ABCP typically mature between 90 and 270 days, these funds have to be constantly rolled over. Under normal conditions, maturing debt is repaid by issuing new debt. In order to prevent liquidity issues in case of a market disruption, the SIV may also involve liquidity facilities in order to repay maturing debt timely.

In order to assign AAA ratings, the rating agencies typically require certain restrictions. Assets which are eligible for a highly-rated SIV need to meet certain criteria, such as minimum ratings (investment grade), minimum level of liquidity and maturity limitations. However, depending on the documentation, SIVs were allowed to hold small portions of sub-investment grade ratings, if certain holdings have been downgraded. Restrictions applied not only to the single assets, but also to portfolio characteristics, as well as to individual asset limitations: the weighted average rating factor (WARF) and the weighted average life (WAL) may be limited and asset class diversification requirements may be specified. The latter can be implemented in the form of a maximum holding limit for specific asset classes, such as RMBS, CMBS, together with some regional restrictions. The weighted average life of the assets is usually limited to the earlier of seven years or the maturity of the latest capital note.

SIVs have very limited interest rate risk (usually referred to as *market risk*; however, we prefer to name it *interest rate risk*, since spread risk – the reason why the structures got into trouble – is also a kind of market risk), as assets as well as liabilities have quite short interest rate duration, since they were swapped or directly traded as floating rate securities. The risk involved in the balance sheet of a SIV was with respect to the credit or spread risk of assets and the ability to refinance via short-term debt. The basic purpose of SIVs is to fund long-term assets with short-term debt and to create an additional layer of leverage via this term mismatch. Typically, SIVs use a mixture of debt instruments with various maturities, such as commercial paper, medium-term notes and equity in the form of shares or so-called capital notes (the latter was the most common form of capital). Since a too-aggressive mismatch between the WALs of assets and liabilities can create a risk for the stability of the structure, SIVs are also restricted to a minimum WAL of six months on the liability side. Furthermore, SIVs need to have access to backstop liquidity facilities. However, in the SIV universe these backstop facilities do not cover 100% of outstanding senior debt, but only 5-10% of the amount of outstanding senior debt. As liquidity facilities are costly, this is a cost advantage for SIVs over other structures that need to have full liquidity support, such as arbitrage conduits. The reason for the reduced requirements for liquidity facilities was the reliance of investors, collateral managers and rating agencies on the inherent liquidity of the assets held in the portfolio.

The business model of a SIV is very similar to that of a very generic bank. Investing in long-term assets and funding via short-term debt – under normal circumstances – involves lower funding costs. The advantage of using a SIV instead of a real bank balance sheet is a regulatory one. While banks are closely monitored by regulators that restrict banks from employing leverage that is too aggressive, SIVs are totally unregulated. Besides the investors who provide the funds (and should, by the way, perform careful due diligence), the only organizations which monitored SIVs have been the ratings agencies. However, the emphasis the rating agencies put on the quality and the experience of the SIV manager highlights their former risk perception: the soundness of the functioning of a SIV depends on an appropriate implementation of the risk management procedures, rather than on the business model itself. However, this view was terribly wrong, as the SIVs collapsed due to their business model and not as a consequence of failures in its implementation.

In contrast to a normal CDO, a SIV is a dynamic structure in which the balance sheet – on the asset as well as on the liability side – may change significantly. The portfolio manager may issue new debt to purchase new assets, replace assets that no longer fulfill certain investment criteria and hedge the portfolio against unwanted risks (e.g., interest rate risks from fixed rate assets or currency risks). The central feature of a SIV is its operational state. These operational states are defined in a way to ensure appropriate risk-reduction measures in times of stress. Common SIVs may have involved some of the following operational states:

- **Normal**: In the normal operational state, the SIV can pursue its normal activities, such as selling debt and buying assets according to the predefined investment and risk-management guidelines.
- **Restricted Investment**: In this operational state, the SIV is prohibited from issuing debt – CPs and medium-term notes (MTN) – other than for repaying maturing debt. This risk of the structure cannot be increased; assets can only be switched into less riskier ones and payments to the subordinated capital notes are prohibited.
- **Restricted Funding**: This operational state is similar to the "Restricted Investment" state, except that issuing new debt (CP and MTN) is prohibited and assets can only be exchanged for cash. Moreover, payments are restricted to only CP, MTN or other senior debt.
- **Enforcement**: In this operational state, the vehicle is prohibited from issuing CP and MTN or making payments other than to CP, MTN or other senior debt. All committed liquidity lines are drawn and assets have to be liquidated in order to redeem maturing debt.

In case breaching of the test that triggers "Restricted Investment" or "Restricted Funding" has been resolved, the SIV can re-enter a higher state, that is, it can go back to the normal state. However, once the structure enters the "Enforcement" state, the SIV will be unwound, as "Enforcement" is irreversible. Triggers for an enforcement may be a failure to pay interest or principal on senior notes, or a default event in the collateral pool, etc.

Tab. 4.3: SIV-lite[26] (* As of December 2007. ** The transaction was restructured subsequently. Restructured debt was rated AA/AAA.)
Source: Standard & Poor's

SIV-lite	Initiation Date	Collateral Manager	Total Debt (USD mn)	Capital Note (Orig. Rating)	Capital Note (Current Ratings*)	Senior (Orig. Rating)	Senior (Current Rating*)	Rating Action Date
Golden Key	18-Nov-05	Avendis Financial Services	5,498.00	BBB	D	A-1+/AAA	D	27-Nov-07
Cairn High Grade Funding I	31-Jan-06	Cairn Financial Products	1,587.00	BBB-	D	A-1+/AAA	D**	31-Aug-07
Duke Funding High Grade II	17-Mar-06	Duke Funding Management LLC/Ellington Global Asset Management LLC	327.00	BBB	CCwn	AAA	D	19-Dec-07
Mainsail II	24-Jun-06	Solent Capital	4,519.00	BBB-	D	A-1+/AAA	D	27-Nov-07
Sachsen Funding I	15-Jun-07	SachsenLB	7,000.00	BBB-	CCC-wn	A-1+/AAA	A-3wn/-CCC-wn	3-Dec-07

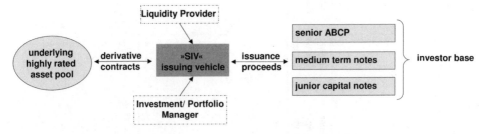

Fig. 4.5: Structural features of a SIV

One of the latest product ideas in the structured finance universe that hit the screens before the crisis has been so-called SIV-lites (see table 4.3 for examples). These closed-end structures can be seen as a combination of a SF-CDO (Structured Finance CDO) and a SIV; that's why they were also called SIV-CDOs. To characterize SIV-lites, we first highlight the central difference between SIVs and CDOs and then show how the originators of SIV-lites wanted to benefit from the new structure. Please note that, in this context, we refer to SF-CDOs, which differ from corporate credit CDOs. A main difference between a SIV and a SF-CDO is that SIVs have easy access to cheap funding through the ABCP market. Furthermore, SIVs need to have an operating-type company structure in order to make sure that the ongoing risk management operations work properly. This is crucial for a SIV as it is an open-end vehicle. Moreover, SIVs tended to change their portfolio structures significantly; they increased and decreased leverage and continuously optimized the funding structure by moving from US CPs to European CPs or from ABCP funding to medium-term notes, etc. In contrast to these characteristics, CDOs are typically set up in a special-purpose vehicle, which does not involve large overhead costs, and the capital structure of a CDO transaction is usually not actively managed over the lifetime. But perhaps the most striking feature of SIVs was that their CP programs did not have to be fully backed by liquidity facilities. In order to achieve a high rating for a SF-CDO that uses CPs as a funding source, rating agencies request sufficient liquidity facilities in place. Since such facilities are quite expensive, this feature was a huge advantage of SIVs over traditional SF-CDOs, especially when margins are low. However, the disadvantage of SIVs was that they involved quite high "equity" cushions in the form of thick capital note tranches. Hence, dealers tried to combine the best of both worlds: the cheap set-up and the high gearing of CDOs with a cheap funding of SIVs. The SIV-lite was born. As a consequence, a central difference between a SIV and a SIV-lite is the significantly higher leverage in

Tab. 4.4: Capital structures of selected SIV-lites (in EUR mn)[26]

Debt	Golden Key	Cairn	Mainsail II	Sachsen Funding I
Senior	5,000.00	1,424.00	4,000.00	6,550.00
Tier1 Mezzanine	222.00	90.00	271.00	250.00
Tier2 Mezzanine	138.00	36.00	136.00	100.00
Capital Note	138.00	36.00	112.00	100.00
Total Debt	5,498.00	1,586.00	4,519.00	7,000.00
Leverage (Capital Note)	39.84	44.06	40.35	70.00
Leverage (All sub debt)	11.04	9.79	8.71	15.56

the latter. While SIVs involve an equity leverage between 10 and 15, the leverage in SIV-lite could be as high as 70 (see table 4.4). And since this huge leverage did not appear to be sufficient to the involved managers, they geared up the risk additionally by refinancing long-term assets with short-term debt. Moreover, managers of SIV-lites were more skewed to higher-yielding assets, and the underlying portfolios have been significantly less diversified across asset classes. While traditional SIVs invested in a broad range of securities, SIV-lite were clearly focused on RMBS (96%), while the remaining assets were CDOs (2.1%) and CMBS (1.9%). As can be seen in table 4.5, traditional SIVs had only a RMBS exposure of below 30%. This strong focus on RMBS also explains the rapid deterioration of SIV-lites, when the credit crisis moved into full swing and liquidity in structured finance markets dried up. Furthermore, Golden Key, for example, was focused on US home equity loans.

One of the central players in the SIV-lite arena was Barclays Capital, which arranged all SIV-lite structures shown in table 4.3 except for Duke Funding.[27] The first deal it arranged and underwrote was Golden Key (with a volume of USD 5.5 bn) for the Geneva-based investment firm Avendis in November 2005. Just two months later followed Cairn High Grade Funding I, a USD 1.6 bn deal for London-based Cairn Capital, and in June 2006, Barclays helped to ramp up Mailsail II (USD 4.5 bn) for Solent Capital. However, the biggest transaction, the USD 7 bn large Sachsen Funding I for SachsenLB, was launched just a few days before the subprime turmoil started in mid-June 2007. Except for Sachsen Funding I, which receives support from its parent all other SIV-lites are already in default. Ironically, Sachsen Funding I contains by far the highest leverage. The ratio between total debt and capital note volume stands at 70 for SachsenLBs troubled SIV-lite, while for the three other deals that were arranged, the leverage amounted to "only" 60% of Sachsen Funding I's gearing. However, these leverage factors compare to an average leverage in the traditional SIV universe of 14 (USD 340 bn senior debt versus USD 24 bn of capital notes).

The first deal that defaulted was the Cairn High Grade Funding I, the one with the second-highest leverage. On August 31, 2007, S&P lowered its ratings for all original debt securities to D. However, since it was the first and the smallest SIV-lite that defaulted, the transaction was restructured with the support of Barclays, the arranging bank. In order to bail out the troubled fund, the liquidity facility was increased to 100% from 25% and was therefore sufficient to redeem all outstanding ABCPs as they matured. Furthermore, the restructured tier 1 and tier 2 notes bear no interest but will enjoy excess cash flows from the collateral pool. In essence, the SIV-lite was transformed into an ordinary cash flow CDO, without the involvement of short-term debt. The intention of Barclays to bail out the defaulted Cairns transaction might have been an attempt to rescue its SIV-lite idea. However, with the default of Golden Key and Mainsail II in late November 2007, it became evident that this product was definitively dead. Hence, these structures did not receive external support, and according to S&P the net asset value – the difference between assets and senior debt in the portfolio – is below zero.

Let us return to the traditional SIVs. In table 4.5, we cite some portfolio characteristics as of October 2007 aggregated over all SIVs listed in table 4.1. At this point in time, structured finance assets made up 70% of all SIV assets, with RMBS being the largest structured finance segment with 28.5%, followed by ABS with 17%. Financial bonds comprised 29.8% and non-financials were negligible with 0.17%. However, this breakup by sectors differs slightly from the one in February 2007. Structured finance assets made up only 57% (compared to 70%), while holdings of financial credits were significantly larger with 39.6% (compared to 29.8%). However, in February, SIV portfolios were invested in non-financials with 1.8% and in sovereigns with 1.5%. These changes reflect the stress in the market, as SIV managers sold off all assets that remained fairly liquid (financials and non-financials, bonds and sovereigns) but had to keep the illiquid ones (structured finance assets). Hence, percentage holdings in the first three sectors declined, while percentage holdings in the latter increased.

The rating distribution of the SIV holdings is also quite interesting, as it changed only marginally from February 2007 to October 2007. More than 2/3 of all SIV holdings are rated AAA (67.9% in October and 67.6% in February). The portion of junk bonds and non-rated assets increased to only 0.3%, and the percentage of BBB-rated assets rose from 0.2% to 0.3%. The only more pronounced change was that the portion of AA-rated assets declined by about

Tab. 4.5: SIV portfolio characteristics (by sector and ratings) as of October 2007
Source: Standard & Poor's

Sector		Rating	
ABS aircraft	0.51%	AAA	67.88%
ABS auto	1.36%	AA+	1.92%
ABS credit card	5.58%	AA	4.59%
ABS other	3.97%	AA-	13.65%
ABS student loan	5.54%	A+	6.25%
CDO corporate bonds	3.40%	A	4.64%
CDO CRE	0.72%	A-	0.46%
CDO market value corporate	0.05%	BBB+	0.20%
CDO of ABS	2.99%	BBB	0.11%
CDO of CDO	0.29%	BB+	0.03%
CDO of emerging market	0.05%	BB	0.00%
CDO of Trups	1.10%	BB-	0.04%
CDO other	2.00%	B	0.08%
CLO	6.26%	CCC	0.00%
CMBS	7.68%	NR	0.14%
Corporate debt	0.17%		
Financial institutions debt	28.04%		
Insurance debt	1.78%		
Non-US RMBS prime	12.34%		
Non-US RMBS subprime	1.65%		
US RMBS Alt-A	6.74%		
US RMBS closed-end second lien	0.64%		
US RMBS other	0.21%		
US RMBS prime	0.96%		
US RMBS subprime	5.97%		

4%, while the amount of single-A rated assets increased by 4.7%. Focusing only on the credit-quality distribution of the SIV portfolios does little to reveal any sign of stress. However, some hints of the trouble emerge when one digs a little deeper into the portfolio. About 6% of the assets are invested in US subprime RMBS, the US Alt-A RMBS buckets amount to 6.7%, and 0.6% is invested in US RMBS comprising second lien loans. Moreover, 3.3% is invested in CDO on ABS and CDO^2, and 1.7% is allocated in non-US subprime. Hence, about 18% of the SIV funds are invested in assets that are under suspicion. Furthermore, spreads for financials were also hit hard during the crisis, and SIVs are exposed to this asset class with 28% on average.

The central problem that SIVs ran into is highlighted by charts 4.6 and 4.7. Between December 2003 and February 2007, the average leverage increased from 12.5 to 13.5, while in the same period the average spread earned on the SIVs'

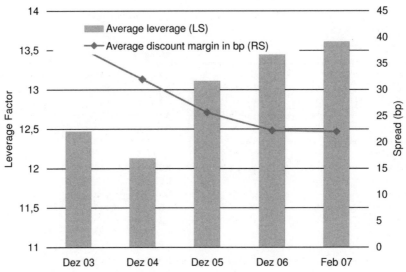

Fig. 4.6: Increasing average leverage in SIVs, accompanied by decreasing spread income on assets
Source: Standard & Poor's

assets declined from 40 bp to almost 20 bp (chart 4.6). But the collateral managers not only geared up investments using higher debt levels to cope with the tremendous compression in credit spreads, they also increased the mismatch between the weighted average life on the assets and on the liabilities. As can be seen from chart 4.7, the duration of the assets increased between December 2004 and February 2007, while the duration of the liabilities declined, at least since 2006, approaching the critical level of six months, which ratings agencies demand. This means that, in addition to higher leverage, collateral managers purchased longer-dated assets with shorter-dated funds in order to squeeze the last few basis points out of already extremely tight markets. The SIVs have been the victim of their own success. Due to extreme demand for high-quality assets – recall that just SIVs accumulated highly-rated assets with a volume in the area of USD 400 bn and including related vehicles, such as arbitrage conduits, the amount would be significantly higher – spreads for these asset classes have been put under extreme tightening pressure. It is quite obvious that such a trend would come to an end at some point in time. The problem for SIVs was that this end came very fast and that by design SIV managers were not able to adapt to such a change, as deleveraging was not possible simply because of the sheer size of their portfolios.

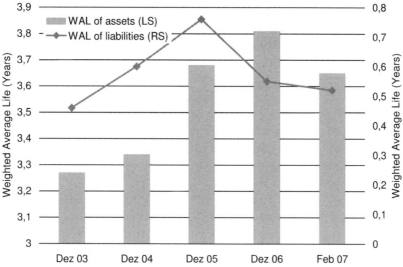

Fig. 4.7: Weighted average life on assets and liabilities of SIVs
Source: Standard & Poor's

In the first few weeks of the market turmoil in the summer of 2007, market participants in the SIV universe remained quite confident that the crisis would not hit these structures. On 20 July 2007, Moody's issued a special report containing an alarming summary about the extreme concentration especially of SIV-lites in RMBS assets with lower credit quality, including charts that showed the already pronounced deterioration in net asset values for SIVs and SIV-lites under the curious title "SIVs: An Oasis of Calm in the Sub-prime Maelstrom".[28] Moreover, on 15 August 2007, S&P published a note with the title "Structured Investment Vehicle Ratings Are Weathering the Current Market Disruptions", in which it said,

> These investment vehicles have weathered the difficult credit conditions of 1990-1991, the Long-Term Capital Management collapse, and the Sept. 11, 2001, terrorist attacks. SIVs responded to each event by diversifying into multiple funding markets, such as Europe and the US, and by having access to the best available liquidity sources, including banks and easily traded assets. SIVs also maintained access to the CP and MTN markets through each crisis during those 19 years.[29]

However, at this time – according to data provided by S&P – the aggregated net asset value (NAV) of all SIVs had fallen to 80% from 102% at the end of June 2007. The NAV is the difference between the value of the assets and the outstanding debt in relation to the outstanding amount of capital notes. It measures the extent to which the assets of the collateral pool of the SIV can be used to pay back capital noteholders after the senior noteholders have been repaid. A NAV above 100% means that the value of the collateral pool is sufficient to repay all outstanding claims of the capital note investors, while a NAV of 80%, for example, indicates that in case the portfolio will be completely unwound at current market prices, these investors will receive only 80% of their original investment.

However, by the end of October, the average NAV had fallen below 75%. In table 4.1, we cited the net asset values for selected SIVs (calculated by Moody's) for September and November 2007. During these two months, the net asset values dropped even further, for some vehicles even below 60%. Just a few weeks after the still quite positive comments about the prospects of structured investment vehicles, the worst case occurred. On October 19, 2007, seven weeks after the successful restructuring of the SIV-lite Cairn High Grade Funding I, S&P downgraded Cheyne Finance (with a senior debt volume of USD 9.7 bn) and IKB's Rhinebridge PLC (with a senior debt volume of USD 2.2 bn) to the default level. Rhinebridge defaulted after 189 days of existence. Moreover, on 27 November 2007, Axon Financial Funding (USD 11.2 bn of senior debt) was also downgraded to the default level. Axon managed to survive 242 days after its initial rating had been assigned in March 2007.

How sensitive the whole structured investment business was in respect to market risk can be shown by the following very simple, back-of-the-envelope calculation. Given an average leverage of 13.5, we assume that this figure from February 2007 did not change through the crisis; and referring to an average NAV of 73%, we can estimate that the value of the SIV holdings declined to 98% from an assumed initial par value.

This calculation proceeds as follows. The equity value of a SIV at t_0 is given by $Eq_0 = A_0 - L_0$ with A_0 the value of the assets and L_0 the liabilities. The leverage is calculated as $Lev_0 = A_0/Eq_0$. For t_1 the corresponding equation is $Eq_1 = A_1 - L_1$. However, we assume that from t_0 to t_1 the capital structure remains fixed, which means that $L_0 = L_1 = L$ (the volume of debt does not change). As a consequence, we can calculate the debt volume as $L = A_0 - A_0/Lev_0$. Moreover, assuming no *overcollateralization* (i.e., the net asset value of at t_0 is 100%), we can derive the value of the equity at t_1 as $Eq_1 = NAV_1 * Eq_0$.

Knowing the equity value, we can back out the value of the value of the assets at t_1: $A_1 = Eq_1 + L$. Now we can calculate the percentage value of the asset at t_1 compared to the ones for t_0: $A_1/A_0 = 1 - (1 - NAV_1)/Lev_0$. For the latter result, one has simply put all findings together. However, this analysis assumes that the deterioration of the NAV stems 100% from a decline in asset values, as the amount of the liabilities remains unchanged, which means that we do not take any changes in the cost of the liabilities into account.

Furthermore, considering a weighted average life of 3.6 in the portfolio, a 2% decline in asset valuation translates into an average spread widening of about 55 bp. This is indeed the magnitude of spread changes that markets witnessed in 2007. However, this outcome should not be underestimated. The trouble in the SIV universe, which affected more than USD 340 bn debt and triggered the collapse of SIV business, was caused by an average spread widening of about 55 bp in the underlying portfolios. This is the impact of leverage.

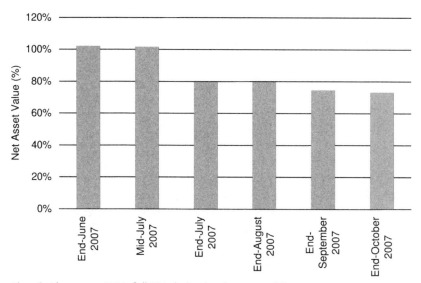

Fig. 4.8: The average NAV of all SIVs declined in the course of the crisis
Source: Standard & Poor's

During the crisis, SIV managers and sponsoring institutions suggested several actions in order to bail out the troubled vehicles. First, collateral managers tried to respond to rising requests for repayment of maturing short-term debt by using the available backstop facilities or by selling liquid assets. Such measures belong to the normal activities of SIV management. However, it became rapidly clear that repayment requests accelerated so fast that normal management procedures would not help the structures to cope with the requests. The problem was that by construction – heavy leveraging with short-term debt and only partial coverage of maturing debt via backstop facilities – SIVs do not involve mechanisms to "buy time" if the internal liquidity is not sufficient to satisfy all repayment requests. Hence, collateral managers attempted to buy time from their CP investors by convincing (perhaps even forcing) them to roll their investments over. To support these attempts, the biggest SIV player – Citigroup – together with some other banks suggested the establishment of another vehicle, the so-called Master – Liquidity Enhancement Conduit (M-LEC), a.k.a. Super-SIV,[30] that should bring back liquidity into the market. The rationale behind these attempts was simple. 'The market disruptions in the structured finance universe following the subprime crisis are just a temporary phenomenon. The spread volatility and declining market values are fundamentally unfounded, and the stress will ease once liquidity will return to the market. The SIV idea will survive, when we are able to wait a few months.'

In this respect, it was quite interesting at which point in time the M-LEC idea hit the screens. It was just a few weeks after the Fed cut interest rates by 50 bp in September and triggered reflation fantasies that pushed stock markets and credit spreads towards pre-crisis levels. The only area that refused to "normalize" was the structured finance market. It appears that the banks behind the M-LEC wanted to jump-start this still-troubled market by announcing an ill-conceived quick-and-dirty fix of the problem. However, the idea failed to trigger the return of liquidity into the troubled structured finance market. Too many investors had already realized that the SIV idea was fundamentally broken.

While some SIV managers tried to deny this simple truth, more and more SIVs switched to a wind-down mode. But even for collateral managers who accepted the bitter reality, there have been serious problems in order to implement an orderly wind-down. Just offloading all of the assets at any price was not in the interest of the capital note investors, as their recovery rate would have most probably have been reduced to zero in such a fire-sale. Hence, SIV managers developed other ideas to prevent fire-sales and to unwind these structures.[31,32]

- **Repo agreement**: In this transaction the SIV gains liquidity by entering into a repurchase agreement. The SIV manager agrees to sell assets to a repo counterparty and receives a cash inflow. After a predefined period of time, the SIV will repurchase the assets from the repo counterparty. From an economic point of view, this repo agreement is collateralized cash lending from the repo counterparty to the SIV. Usually, the collateral involved a haircut, which means that on every dollar amount of face value of assets only 95% or so cash is lent to the SIV. However, such a repo transaction is again just buying time, as it has to be repaid. Moreover, depending on the seniority of the claim of the repo counterparty (pari passu or subordinated to senior noteholders) such a transaction will impact the recovery rate of senior bond investors in case of an enforcement event.

- **Vertical slice transaction**: In this transaction, the holder of the capital note buys a percentage of assets from the collateral pool relative to his position in the capital note. Assuming that an investor holds 10% of the capital note, he would buy 10% of all assets at the current market value, and his exposure to the capital note would be redeemed at the NAV of the portfolio. Since the vertical slice transaction occurs at market prices and at the NAV of the SIV, the situation for the remaining investors – in senior as well as in subordinated debt – does not change. However, the cash inflow from this transaction enables the portfolio manager to repay 10% of the senior debtholders. This essentially means that, if all capital note volume would be returned in such a vertical slice transaction, the SIV would be completely unwound. But why should a capital noteholder get involved in such a transaction, since on a mark-to-market basis he realizes exactly the calculated loss? The advantage is that after the vertical slice transaction, the investor can choose to sell the assets later. If the market value of the assets would recover to par, then the capital note investor would not incur any losses. However, the bitter pill is that now the investor has to fund the assets, and if his funding is higher than the return on the book value of the assets, then he realizes a loss due to this spread differential. Nevertheless, this solution enables the capital note investor to control the unwinding process. However, in reality it is not always possible to transfer exactly 10% of all assets, as the number of assets in a SIV portfolio can be large. In this case, the collateral manager chooses a representative sample of the assets that will be transferred. However, this creates the risk that a slice contains a greater portion of less stressed assets, posing a disadvantage for the remaining investors. So vertical slice transactions might also involve a first mover advantage.
- **Restructuring and active support from sponsoring banks**: This is the ultimate solution for an orderly winding-down of a distressed SIV. This can be, for example, implemented by the bank by acquiring the

outstanding capital notes (if they do not own them already) and subsequently implementing a vertical slice transaction. The SIV's assets will then be temporarily or permanently consolidated onto the bank's balance sheet. On December 13, 2007, Citibank gave up its idea of the M-LEC and announced that it will consolidate the assets and liabilities of the SIVs it sponsored onto its balance sheet. From the original USD 88.6 bn volume in its seven SIVs, the portfolio managers have been actively reducing the size of the portfolio by USD 21 bn through the sale of assets to the market and subsequent redemption of maturing debt and by USD 16 bn through vertical slice transactions. The remaining portfolio was taken over by Citigroup. With this step, Citibank followed the example of several other banks, such as HSBC, which supported its two SIVs Cullinan and Asscher with an aggregated volume of senior debt of USD 42.5 bn, that choose to bail out their structures themselves and to abandon participation in the M-LEC. Although restructuring distressed SIVs comes at a cost for the capital noteholder, the examples of the defaulted SIVs Cheyne, Rhinebridge and Axon show that under this "solution" their losses are even higher, as the collateral managers for these vehicles declared that the pool of assets will not be sufficient to cover all claims from senior noteholders. This reduces the prospects for the sub-noteholder essentially to zero.

What is the impact on banks from the breakdown of the SIV universe? There are obviously three different ways that banks might be afftected.[33]

- First, banks might be invested in capital notes that suffer significant losses. The existing SIVs have a total volume of USD 24 bn capital notes outstanding. Due to the lack of transparency about the holders of the capital notes (most probably not only banks), it is difficult to assess the impact from this risk on individual banks. However, Moody's said in one of its teleconferences that that some Asian banks disclosed SIV capital note exposure that is large compared to the banks' earnings.
- Second, banks might be involved in the winding down of SIVs since they provided liquidity lines. However, due to the limited amount of liquidity facilities that are accessible by SIVs, this risk appears to be manageable by liquidity providers.
- Third, the sponsoring banks are first in line when it comes to a bailout of a troubled SIV. Banks that sponsored SIVs are Bank of Montreal, Citigroup, Dresdner Bank, HSBC, HSH Nordbank, Rabobank, Societe

Generale, Standard Chartered, and WestLB AG. However, given that KfW already had to take over responsibility for the risks involved in Rhineland Funding and Rhinebridge, IKB's ability to support its vehicles is obviously limited. Rating agencies reacted to the deteriorated outlook for financials. Citigroup, for example was downgraded from Aa1 to Aa2 on November 5, 2007, and then to Aa3 on December 13, 2007.

Finally, we want to outline the similarities and differences between arbitrage (ABCP) conduits and SIVs. At first glance, arbitrage conduits and SIVs look very similar. Indeed, both structures exploit the yield difference between longer-dated assets and short-term liabilities. While there are some similarities, the design of ABCPs and SIVs differs significantly:

- Both structures invest mainly in AAA or AA structured finance paper. However, the investment strategies differ slightly:

  - SIVs: about 60% of the asset pool is related to structured finance (mainly RMBS (23%), CLO/CBO (11%) and CMBS (8%)) and about 98% is rated AAA or AA. The remaining 40% of the portfolio involves the financial sector (8% AAA, 24% AA, 8% A). Note that these numbers differ from table 4.5, as they reflect portfolio compositions before the crisis.

  - Arbitrage ABCP: almost 100% of the portfolio is related to highly rated ABS bonds (about 98% are AAA / AA rated). The ABS composition is on average as follows: CDO/CLO (38%), RMBS (33%), CMBS (12%).

- ABCP exclusively uses senior secured short-term debt ("commercial paper") for funding, while a SIV can also make use of "medium-term notes" ("MTN") and "capital notes" ("CN") to fulfill its funding needs.

  - A major difference is the amount of available liquidity support. As CPs are short-term debt, ABCP programs require strong liquidity support. Therefore, these structures have 100% liquidity support from banks (in most cases unconditionally). As discussed above, external liquidity support for SIV is limited.

  - Credit risk is handled differently too: an arbitrage ABCP relies on overcollateralization and a letter of credit ("LOC"). A SIV on the other hand is protected by its structure (senior, mezzanine and junior debt). Subordination provides a leverage of around 10-15.

- A SIV pool is more dynamic than an ABCP pool. The portfolio performance of SIVs as well as asset liability matching is highly influenced by the portfolio manager, the performance of the vehicle is monitored closely and continuously by rating agencies.

- SIVs mark-to-market their portfolios frequently on a daily or weekly basis.

- As mentioned above, SIVs feature different modes of operation depending on the structures, asset liability matching, and the performance of the underlying pool.

4.5 Collateralized Debt Obligations

CDOs have been one of the major drivers for credit markets before and during the crisis. The so-called technical bid from CDO issuance activity kept compressed credit spreads to extremely tight levels ahead of the financial market turmoil. CDOs are investment products that refer to a portfolio of credit assets. However, in a CDO transaction one does not refer to the complete portfolio, but only to a specific loss tranche. The tranches cover distinct loss ranges in the portfolio. The most junior tranche, for example, is called *equity piece*, and it absorbs the first losses in the portfolio. A 0-3% tranche, for example, would cover all losses which make up 3% of the total portfolio volume. If accumulated losses in the portfolio would exceed this 3% level, the notional of the next tranche would start to erode. This means that all higher-level tranches do not suffer any losses until all of the notional of the subordinated tranches is completely eroded.

CDOs have been issued on various different assets as underlyings and in several different formats. A CDO can, for example, refer to corporate credit risk, either in the form of bonds (a.k.a. Collateralized Bond Obligation, CBO) or in the form of an unfunded CDS, which is then called a synthetic CDO. Another type of CDO refers to loans (this structure is known as a Collateralized Loan Obligation, CLO). The loans can either be normal corporate or syndicated loans, or leveraged loans that are used in an LBO transaction. The CLO business was one of the central pillars of the explosion of LBO activity. A large portion of syndicated loans was underwritten by investment banks in order to generate volume for CLOs that have been sold to clients. Besides funded CLOs which refer to real loans, there have also been synthetic CLOs that refer to the underlying loan exposure via specifically designed Loan-CDS contracts, the so-called LCDS. More exotic

CDO structures have been referring to other asset classes as underlyings, such as hedge fund exposure (Collateralized Fund Obligations, CFO) or commodity and currency swaps (Collateralized Commodity Swap Obligation, CCO and Collateralized FX Obligations CFXO). But compared to corporate credit CDOs and CLOs, the latter play only a niche role.

Another major distinction among different CDO types is whether they are funded (i.e., cash) CDOs or unfunded (i.e., synthetic) CDOs. In a synthetic CDO, the underlying portfolio is built up using CDS contracts. The exchange of capital at initiation of such a synthetic transaction is thus not needed, neither on the asset side of the CDO nor on the debt side. In a cash CDO the portfolio of assets usually consists of real cash instruments, such as bonds or loans. There are also examples of mixtures between cash and synthetic CDO, such as a cash CDO where the portfolio was partly or completely built using CDS contracts. In such a structure, the funds that come from the CDO investors are invested in high-quality instruments, such as government bonds or other highly rated paper. The latter serves as a collateral for the counterpart of the unfunded CDS contracts. Other examples for cash-synthetic hybrids are structures where only a part of the tranches is issued as cash instruments. The rest of the capital structure is sold via unfunded instruments. A classical example is a CDO where the super-senior tranche is not sold as a cash instrument but just protected via a swap contract with a highly rated counterparty. The rationale for such a structure is that the super-senior swap covers the largest part of the CDO volume, but it involves only a very limited spread. Before the crisis, it was difficult to find investors who were willing to invest their funds in such low-yielding assets. Only selling protection in an unfunded way, without the explicit transfer of funds, appeared to be an attractive solution to this dilemma. However, during the months of extremely tight spreads just before the subprime problems became aware to everybody, even this solution was no longer attractive. Since the underlying spreads in the portfolio are so tight, the spread that could be paid on the super-senior swap very often amounted to a low single-digit number. However, instead of keeping hands off such products, investors were leveraging this risk simply in order to gain more basis points premium. The resulting products are called leveraged super-senior (see our analysis of LSS in section 4.2).

In particular, the synthetic corporate credit CDOs developed into sophisti-cated investment products. The emergence of the so-called single-tranche CDOs changed the business drastically. In traditional CDOs the issuer of the structure compiles a portfolio of credits and approaches the clients in order to sell all the resulting tranches. If all tranches were sold, the CDO deal was closed. In this approach, the sum of all tranche volumes equals the volume of the underlying portfolio. The purpose of such a transaction was that the issuer wanted to reduce exposure to the assets he had compiled in the portfolio. However, from an investor point of view this is not an optimal process, as he has no influence on the portfolio, on the tranching (i.e., the definition of the attachment and detachment points of the issued tranches) or on the issued volumes. Moreover, since several different investors had been involved in the CDO transactions, it is hardly possible to satisfy all specific wishes. The single-tranche CDO (STCDO) was the solution to this problem and opened the CDO market to a wide range of investors. In a single-tranche CDO, the arranger structures and sells only one specific tranche to an investor. The remaining tranches of the CDO portfolio are not sold. Such a single-tranche CDO can therefore not be structured by purchasing the underlying portfolio and selling all tranches. In contrast, each tranche is hedged individually in the books of the arranger. This makes the usage of very sophisticated CDO models inevitable. One of the largest marketplaces for the single-tranche CDO is the market for standardized tranches on CDS indices. Here, the dealers trade tranches on the iTraxx and the CDX in a standardized format, which involves predefined attachment and detachment points for the tranches and a price quotation and trading mechanism that aims at isolating the specific risk in tranches, the default correlation. This is also the reason why the trading desks that cover these tranches are called "correlation desks". However, besides tranches on the European and North American investment-grade indices, iTraxx Main and CDX.NA.IG, there is a growing market for standardized index tranches that cover the high-yield and Loan-CDS indices in the United States. These tranches refer to the CDX.NA.HY and the LCDX tranches, and it will be only a matter of time until similar products are available for the respective iTraxx indices. Moreover, since both index families now belong to MarkIT, we expect the emergence of tranches on global CDS indices.

Moreover, the single-tranche CDO technology not only allows investors to select a desired tranche on a specific volume; the investment banks enable investors even to choose the single-name exposure in the underlying portfolio. This is called *bespoke CDO*. Some investment banks even allow investors individually to compile CDO portfolios on web pages, analyze the risks involved and structure a transaction to their specific needs, which can then be submitted to the correlation trading desks. However, not only the investment banks recognized the revenue potential stemming from these structured credit transaction; also the rating agencies have been a central part of the business and distributed their CDO rating models to investors. With S&P's CDO Evaluator,

Moody's CDOROM and Fitch's VECTOR, investors could investigate which rating an agency would assign to a specific transaction. Hence, CDO structuring was simply optimizing the portfolio and the tranche in order to achieve a good rating and to earn a high spread. When investor and arranger decided upon a transaction, they just submitted it to a rating agency, which then officially assigned a rating. At that time, all of the analysis and parameterization has been already done by the counterparties. One consequence of this development is that a large portion of corporate credit CDO transactions involve portfolios that refer to 50% US and 50% European companies, since the portfolio models of the rating agencies penalize regional concentration. Moreover, the universe of potential names that can be used in synthetic CDOs is quite limited. All North American, European and Asian investment grade companies that can be traded with sufficient liquidity in the CDS market sum up to approximately three to four hundred names. Consequently, most of the basic CDO transactions are rather similar. CDOs can be structured involving static portfolios – that is, both counterparties decide on a portfolio which is kept unchanged until maturity – or dynamic ones. The latter opened the CDO business to the asset management community, which provided so-called *managed CDOs*. The CDO manager ad-

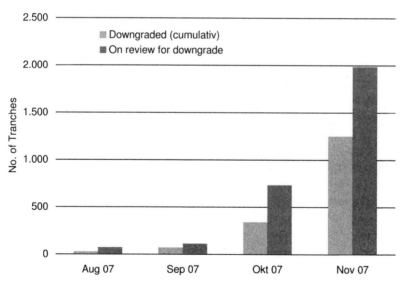

Fig. 4.9: Moody's downgrades and review for downgrades of US structured finance CDOs until November 2007[34-37]
Source: Moody's

justs the portfolio underlying a CDO transaction according to specified rules, in order to avoid default events or a deterioration of the credit quality due to downgrades.

Finally, there was another development in the CDO market which played an important role in the subprime crisis: CDOs that refer to other structured finance tranches in the underlying portfolio. To this asset class belong the so-called CDO^2, or CDOs that refer to other CDO tranches as underlyings, as well as the so-called structured-finance CDOs, or CDOs that involve RMBS and similar structured-finance instruments as underlyings. The latter are especially interesting, because they form a huge market and they suffered a horrible rating performance during 2007. By the end of November 2007, Moody's downgraded approximately 1250 structured-finance CDO tranches from 416 CDO transactions, with a total volume of USD 62.6 bn. This represented almost 30% of all rated tranches, 42% of all rated deals and 12% of the total volume. Furthermore, almost 2000 tranches (43%) from 513 transactions (52%) and USD 175 bn (32%) were put on review for potential downgrade.

In chart 4.9, we show the number of downgrades of US structured-finance CDOs and outstanding reviews for potential downgrade by the month of the rating action. It highlights that the overwhelming majority of downgrades came

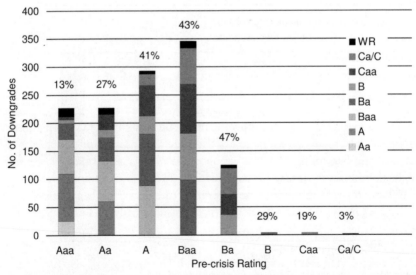

Fig. 4.10: Rating performance of US structured finance CDOs (all existing vintages) at Moody's[34-37]
Source: Moody's

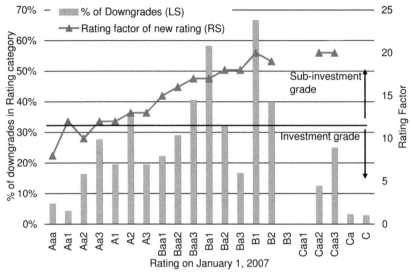

Fig. 4.11: Rating performance of US structured finance CDOs (excluding 2007 vintages) at Moody's with average new ratings. Rating factors: Aaa – 1, Aa1 – 2, ... Caa3 – 19, Ca – 20 and C – 21[34-37]
Source: Moody's

in the last two months of the analysis, and since by the end of November 2007 there were still about 2000 tranches on review for potential downgrade, there is obviously much more to come.

But it was not only the huge number of downgrades that shocked markets, it was also the number of notches that the rating agencies cut their ratings. It is devastating for an investor when formerly AAA-rated tranches are cut into junk territory. In chart 4.10, we show the rating performance of US structured-finance CDO tranches as a function of the pre-crisis rating (for tranches that existed at the beginning of 2007 we used the rating of that date, while for tranches of the 2007 vintage we used the initial rating). In addition, we broke down each pre-crisis rating into the new rating categories. This analysis reveals that 227 formerly Aaa-rated tranches (13% of all initially Aaa-rated SF-CDO tranches) experienced a downgrade event, 25 of which were downgraded to Aa, 84 to A and 62 to Baa. Furthermore, 56 of the 227 rating actions led the exposure directly to junk status or to a rating withdrawal. The data reveals also that about 138 tranches were downgraded to Ca/C, more than 60% of which had had an investment-grade rating before.

In chart 4.11, we provide a different view on the rating performance of all SF-CDOs that were outstanding at the beginning of 2007 (i.e., excluding the 2007 vintage). This analysis shows that about 7% of Aaa-rated tranches of older vintages experienced a downgrade event, and that these were downgraded on average to a Baa1 rating (which corresponds to a rating factor of 8). Moreover, except for very high-rated tranches (up to Aa2), all other rating actions led on average to a junk rating. All downgraded tranches that were rated Baa3 and below – and as can be seen from this analysis, a significant percentage of tranches in this level experienced downgrades – were cut on average to Caa and below. When including the 2007 vintages, the situation gets even uglier.

As shown in chart 4.12, structured finance CDOs and high yield CDOs have been the major drivers of the tremendous growth in CDO issuance activity before the crisis. Since the beginning of the crisis, this market collapsed almost entirely due to the reluctance of investors to purchase any kind of structured credit product, although they are not linked to subprime.

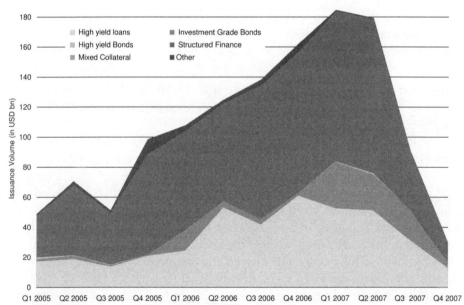

Fig. 4.12: CDO issuance volume by asset class
Source: Moody's

4.6 Structured-Squared Madness

In the summer of 2007, the structured credit market went from wonderland to nightmare. But why is it that the subprime infection filtered through to the money market within a few weeks? The strategies we analyzed in this chapter are the central pieces in this puzzle. With the booming US housing market, the volume of mortgage loans was expanding rapidly – in prime as well as in the subprime area. However, in order to keep the fire burning, liquidity was needed and banks were seeking ways to refinance the growing exposure. The cheapest source of funding is the money market. But money market investors will most likely not be very keen on distributing their funds into this asset class. Hence, banks developed a layered process involving several different structured credit vehicles, forming a chain that starts with mortgage loans and ends with the money market.

In the first layer of this process (see figure 4.13), banks pooled mortgage loans and structured RMBS. The latter are refinanced with different RMBS tranches on the senior, the mezzanine and the equity level. However, the vehicles we discussed in the previous sections were designed to be optimal buyers of most of the primary RMBS tranches. The equity or first-loss pieces were bought by banks, hedge funds, or so-called permanent capital vehicles. These investment vehicles typically invest in equity pieces (mostly CDO equity pieces). They also involve leverage, but the leverage is not implemented in the vehicle itself, but directly by the underlying instruments. PCVs are also set up as SPVs and are typically listed on a stock exchange. They use the equity they receive from investors to purchase the assets, while the return on their investment is allocated to the shareholders via dividends. The target return amounts, in general, to around 10%. The portfolio is managed by an external manager and is marked-to-market. The share price of the company depends on the net asset value (NAV) of the portfolio and on the expected dividend payments.

The mezzanine tranches of the primary structured-finance assets have been typically purchased by structured-finance CDOs. As highlighted above, these structures pooled mezzanine tranches of primary structured assets classes, such as prime and subprime RMBS or ABS on car loans, student loans or credit card exposure and funded these assets by issuing tranches. As a part of the capital structure of structured-finance CDOs was also issued as senior and super-senior debt, these vehicles offer cheap funding for the mezzanine pieces of the primary RMBS and ABS. However, their equity and mezzanine tranches was also purchased by banks, hedge funds and PCVs.

Finally the senior part of the capital structure of the primary RMBS was acquired by SIVs, SIV-lites and arbitrage conduits. This could be done either directly or via leveraged super-senior tranches. Moreover, such high-quality investors also purchased senior pieces of structured-finance CDOs and therefore helped to refinance also the mezzanine level of the primary assets. In the end, the risks of the mortgage loans arrived in the money markets, since SIV and related vehicles funded their investments by issuing asset-backed commercial paper.

Other products involved in this layered process which do not appear on chart 4.13 are the so-called Credit Derivative Product Companies (CDPCs).[38] A CDPC is a rated company that buys credit risk via all types of credit derivative instruments, primarily super-senior tranches, and sells this risk to investors via preferred shares (equity) or subordinated notes (debt). Hence, the vehicle uses super-senior risk to create equity risk. The investment strategy is a buy-and-hold approach. Investors are primarily exposed to rating migration risk, to mark-to-market risk, and, finally, to the capability of the external manager. The rating agencies assign, in general, an AAA-rating on the business model of the CDPC, which is a bankruptcy remote vehicle (SPV). The business models of specific CDPCs are different from each other in terms of investments and thresholds given to the manager. The preferred-asset classes CDPCs are invested in predominantly single-name CDSs, bespoke synthetic tranches, ABSs and all kinds of CDOs. CDPC's main investments have been allocated to corporate credits, but they extended their universe to ABS and CDO products before the crisis. The implemented leverage is given through the vehicle and can be in the range of 15-60x. On average, the return target was typically around 15% return on equity, paid in the form of dividends to the shareholders.

Admittedly, we simplified this analysis in order to keep it straightforward, but it demonstrates the principles of the interrelation between the different investment vehicles that emerged in the recent years and highlights the infection channel from the subprime crisis to the ABCP market. From the current perspective it might appear odd that people believed that this mechanism could be sustainable. But since the different layers involved equity cushions in the vehicles, market participants thought that this construction would be stable enough to withstand a crisis. And in fact, this transformation process bears only slight differences to the traditional one, where banks play the role of the intermediaries. In the traditional process banks also use short-term debt to refinance their loan exposure. However, this crisis showed that the traditional intermediation process provides much more security and stability for the financial system than

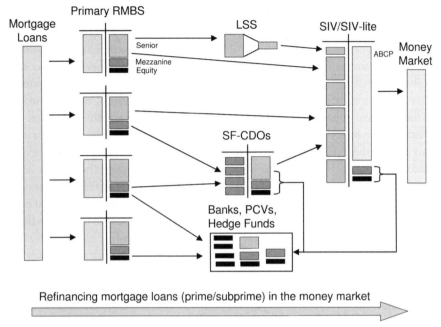

Primary RMBS

Mortgage Loans

LSS

SIV/SIV-lite

Money Market

Senior
Mezzanine
Equity

ABCP

SF-CDOs

Banks, PCVs, Hedge Funds

Refinancing mortgage loans (prime/subprime) in the money market

Fig. 4.13: The structured-squared madness, or how to refinance subprime loans in the money market

a cascade of unregulated, lean and highly leveraged special-purpose vehicles (and this cascade involves many stages where managers and arrangers extract the risk premium via fees). Banks, in contrast to SIVs and the like, are flexible in their business model; they have sufficient capital and manpower to fight against the troubles of a flawed strategy. Perhaps they lose money, but they will not just disappear, like SIVs did. Moreover, this crisis proved that the risk limitations that stem from an efficient regulation of the banking system are inevitable for the proper functioning of a complex financial system. Exaggerations such as SIV-lite, which use a leverage factor of 70 (Sachsen Funding I) and contain assets in a significant amount compared to the balance sheet of the sponsoring banks, have to be avoided in the future.

However, the traditional intermediation process in which banks used their balance sheets for the transformation of risks and provided their capital as a cushion for their debt investors has been considered as outdated for years. A large number of banking strategy research and business consultants suggested that banks have to be transformed from an "originate to hold" approach (which is essentially an "originate and manage" approach) to a "originate to sell" business model. In these concepts there was a sustainable role for only two types of banks: the ones with a retail network that can originate assets, and those that do the transformation, structuring and placement in the financial market. The refinancing of the assets was supposed to be done by non-banking investors. The problem of intransparency and complexity of these "retail" risks that make it difficult for outside investors to understand and manage the risks was intended to be solved by applying structuring technology. However, this "if you buy structured products, then you don't need to worry" approach essentially boils down to the view that the structured products manage their risks automatically, which is not the case. Ironically, the system did not collapse because the "traditional" system was still intact, and banks bailed out a significant portion of their distressed vehicles simply by taking their exposure back onto their balance sheets, that is, returning to the traditional approach of banks doing the intermediation. However, the return of the traditional approach can already be seen in the market. One consequence of the turmoil in the structured finance markets is the huge demand for a very old-fashioned product: the covered bond. In Germany for example, mortgage lending was traditionally refinanced via *Hypothekenpfandbriefe*. This instrument provides cheap funding for the issuer and very high security for the investor. In the covered bond universe, refinancing does not involve bankruptcy-remote vehicles from which the sponsor can simply walk away in times of stress, since the investor has a dual claim against the bank and against the covered pool. Hence, in contrast to an RMBS, a covered bond loses only in a double default scenario: when the bank is in default and when the covered pool suffers.

Hence, one consequence of the subprime crisis might be that the good old mortgage-lending business, which became the focus of investment bankers and hedge fund managers, will return to its roots. A traditionally run, high-volume, low-margin business – which will not be too attractive for Wall Street.

5
The Anatomy of a Credit Crisis

5.1 Introduction

> *A credit crunch occurs when, for a given price of credit, lenders sub-*
> *stantially reduce the volume of credit provided to a group of borrowers*
> *whose risk is essentially unchanged. That is, a credit crunch is caused*
> *by a reduction in lenders' willingness to make risky investments or by*
> *a 'flight to quality' by lenders. In terms of a standard supply and de-*
> *mand diagram, a credit crunch is a substantial decline in the volume*
> *of credit caused mainly by a leftward shift of the credit supply curve,*
> *when the shift is not due principally to an increase in the riskiness of*
> *borrowers. This definition is similar in spirit to that of Bernanke and*
> *Lown (1991), who define a crunch as "a significant leftward shift in*
> *the supply for bank loans, holding constant both the safe real interest*
> *rate and the quality of potential borrowers."*[39]

In the yellow press, the buzzword *financial crisis* is used for almost everything that triggers a more pronounced drop in the asset value of a specific market segment. The traditional definition is stricter. In any case, financial crises are a typical phenomenon in financial markets rather than a six-sigma event. Price-setting in financial markets is not always a smooth adjustment process, but it does indicate a jump to a new equilibrium. This is even more the case if there is huge leverage in the market, such as via the excessive use of derivatives.

The complexity of investments in general seems to be closely coupled with the appearance of a financial crisis, as the vulnerability of the financial system is closely linked to transparency and efficient risk allocation. Many crises (LTCM, the 1987 stock market crash, and, in the end, the subprime turmoil) were linked to the excessive use of derivatives. Although nobody denies that derivatives support the functioning of financial markets in normal times, they certainly add to volatility when exogenous shocks hit the market.

A major topic in this respect is the role of regulators. If the regulatory environment is weak, the financial system is obviously more vulnerable than it is in a well regulated financial market. The remaining question is: what does

Credit Crises. J. Felsenheimer and P. Gisdakis
Copyright © 2008 WILEY-VCH Verlag GmbH & Co. KGaA, Weinheim
ISBN: 978-3-527-50375-9

the term *weak regulatory environment* really mean? The lesson we learned from the subprime turmoil was that even in a well regulated system, namely, the German banking system, financial distress in the banking sector can occur. A good example is IKB and SachsenLB. This problem was at least partly linked to the fact that these banks had set up rather complex off-balance sheet vehicles (or *conduits*) which carry not only huge liquidity risks but also a large portion of pure credit risk (i.e. spread risk and default risk). The answer as to what weak means in the context of describing a regulator is very simple: it is the relative strength of the innovative power in the market versus the strength of the regulator to cope with these instruments and vehicles.

Financial crises are complex situations, including pretty tricky transmission mechanisms which are not visible in a normal market environment. The complexity of the financial system and the transmission mechanisms behind it become more apparent in crisis scenarios. This comes often as a surprise to the majority of the financial community, as in "normal" times only a small fraction of the community is aware of tail-event risk. In case these events occur, panic selling from so-called Goldilocks investors is a logical consequence. And panic selling aggravates the decline in asset values further.

These effects which accompany a crisis causes the phenomenon that the initial damage directly related to a crisis is just a small part of the total costs of the crisis. Total costs includes costs triggered by so-called second or third order effects, which cover the indirect costs of the crisis triggered by contagion via the infection mechanism of a financial crisis. In any case, there is always an irrational momentum incorporated in these effects, while one could argue that also the development before the crisis (asset price inflation and the burst of a bubble) are irrational moves. But this is important to understand and shows that focusing on fundamentals is not enough to analyze a financial crisis appropriately.

5.2 Crisis classification

Financial crises are a common phenomenon in history that hit the market from time to time. There are some similarities and there are always some specifics. In practice, we classify a financial crisis primarily by referring to the area from which it originates. Using this approach, four major financial crises can be identified:

The Anatomy of a
Credit Crisis

- **Currency Crisis:** A speculative attack on the exchange rate of a currency which results in a sharp devaluation of the currency; or it forces monetary authorities to intervene in currency markets to defend the currency (e.g., by sharply hiking interest rates).
- **Foreign Debt Crisis:** a situation where a country is not able to service its foreign debt.
- **Banking Crisis:** Actual or potential bank runs. Banks start to suspend the internal convertibility of their liabilities or the government has to bail out the banks.
- **Systemic Financial Crisis:** Severe disruptions of the financial system, including a malfunctioning of financial markets, with a large adverse effect on the real economy. It may involve a currency crisis and also a banking crisis, although this is not necessarily true the other way around.

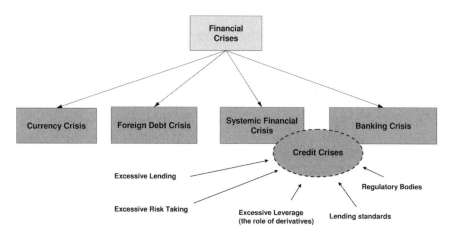

Fig. 5.1: Crisis classification

In many cases, a crisis is characterized by more than one type, meaning we often see a combination of at least two crises. These involve strong declines in asset values, accompanied by defaults, in the non-financials but also in the financials universe. The effectiveness of government support or even bailout measures combined with the robustness of the economy are the most important determinants of the economy's vulnerability, and they therefore have a significant impact on the severity of the crisis. In addition, a crucial factor is obviously the amplitude of asset price inflation that preceded the crisis.

Depending on the type of crisis, there are different warning signals, such as significant current account imbalances (foreign debt crisis), inefficient currency pegs (currency crisis), excessive lending behavior (banking crisis), and a combination of excessive risk taking and asset price inflation (systemic financial crisis). A financial crisis is costly, as there are fiscal costs to restructure the financial system. There is also a tremendous loss from asset devaluation, and there can be a misallocation of resources, which, in the end, depresses growth. A banking crisis is considered to be very costly compared with, for example, a currency crisis.

We classify a credit crisis as something between a banking crisis and a systemic financial crisis. A credit crisis affects the banking system or arises in the banking system; the huge importance of credit risk for the functioning of the financial system as a whole bears also a systemic component. The trigger event is often an exogenous shock, while the pre-credit crisis situation is characterized by excessive lending, excessive leverage, excessive risk taking, and lax lending standards. Such crises emerge in periods of very high expectations on economic development, which in turn boosts loan demand and leverage in the system. When an exogenous shock hits the market, it triggers an immediate repricing of the whole spectrum of credit-risky assets, increasing the funding costs of borrowers while causing an immense drop in the asset value of credit portfolios.

A so-called credit crunch scenario is the ugliest outcome of a credit crisis. It is characterized by a sharp reduction of lending activities by the banking sector. A credit crunch has a severe impact on the real economy, as the basic transmission mechanism of liquidity (from central banks over the banking sector to non-financials corporations) is distorted by the fact that banks do not provide enough liquidity for the non-financials segment. This results in a liquidity squeeze, finally resulting in rising default rates. A credit crunch is a full-fledged credit crisis, which includes all major ingredients for a banking and a systemic crisis, spilling over onto several parts of the financial market and onto the real economy. A credit crunch is probably the most costly type of financial crisis, also depending on the efficiency of regulatory bodies, the shape of the economy as a whole, and the health of the banking sector itself.

5.3 A brief history of credit crises

5.3.1 The sage of spillover effects and who is leading whom?

After a financial crisis materializes, one of the major questions is whether there are spillover effects from financial markets onto the real economy. That idea implies that there is a specific threshold a financial crisis has to reach before the crisis spills over onto the real economy; in other words, the financial market has an impact on the economy. But this picture is misleading. There are always interdependencies between financial markets and the real economy. Spillover effects always exist and are not linked to a certain level of severity of the crisis. Although the interdependencies between financial markets and the real economy appear in many economic indicators, they are not visible if they are only behind the comma. Markets start to recognize such effects only when they are before the comma.

There is no established classification of spillover effects, but in general we are talking about second and third-round effects. These effects are very important given their immense loss potential. Direct effects from a financial market crisis are effects (i.e., losses) which stem directly from the initial shock. For example, all losses linked to subprime-related products (the market itself, RMBS, subprime-linked RMBS, etc.) are direct effects of the subprime turmoil. In general, investors tend to calculate losses based on the direct effects. Unfortunately, direct effects are only a small portion of the total losses that stem from spillover effects onto other segments of financial markets or even from a negative impact on economic activity.

- *Second-round effects*: These includes effects that are direct contagion effects; negative spillovers from one segment onto another in financial markets. If the global ABS market is virtually closed on the back of the subprime crisis and there are mark-to-market losses on ABS books, outflows from non-subprime-linked CDO funds, or a decline in primary market activity in the securitization universe, then we can categorize these effects as second-round effects.
- *Third-round effects*: These describe more severe long-lasting implications of the crisis; second-round effects of second-round effects (or second-squared effects). We can summarize all economic effects of a financial crisis into third-round effects, but also some specific events which are not directly linked to the initial problem at first glance. If a bank encounters funding problems due to closure of the ABS market, which is

again linked to the fact that a specific market segment (subprime) is in trouble, then we could call it a third-round effect.

The effect itself does not say anything about this categorization: a sharp drop in equity markets can be classified as a second-round effect in a credit crisis, whereas we would call them direct effects, for example, in an equity-linked crisis.

In the end, the crucial question is, Who is leading whom? Is the real economy leading financial markets or vice versa? There are many good arguments for both directions. In general, we assume that financial instruments are linked to the fundamental development. Regarding credit markets, this means that an improving fundamental environment is causing the higher earnings generation power of companies, triggering improving credit metrics and, in the end, leading to a lower risk of default. All in all, this should support credit markets, as reflected in tighter spreads. The credit market is obviously following the economic trend. Hence, analyzing credit markets requires a close monitoring of economic indicators, and a spread forecasting model should include macroeconomic parameters to account for the fundamental environment. However, we also find good arguments for the thesis that financial markets are leading the economic development, and again the subprime crisis is a good example for this thesis. When we use financial instruments (CDOs) as a funding tool, such as to generate more risk in the underlying market (subprime loans) because they allow us to allocate risk onto more shoulders, the overall leverage in the market is increasing. If, for example, the housing market is in a correction mode, this correction could be aggravated by the excessive use of derivatives via "leveraged selling pressure" from this side, which finally has an impact on the underlying market itself. We doubt whether the price correction in the US housing market in the aftermath of the subprime crisis would be the same without the use of innovative structured credit instruments to finance the boom.

To sum up, we do not like the idea that something is leading something else. The real economy is closely linked to financial markets and vice versa. Spillover effects between both are imminent and persistent, while both go hand in hand rather than one is leading the other. This brings us to a very important conclusion: analyzing economic developments to forecast the performance of financial markets is as good as or as bad as using financial markets as an indicator for economic trends ("the market knows best"). Only a full-fledged macroeconomic model which allows us to incorporate financial markets can be seen as the appropriate way of forecasting financial market developments and economic trends.

5.3.2 Financial crises – some examples

As shown before, there are many different types of financial crises. We briefly discuss the credit aspect within the context of the savings & loan crisis in the United States at the end of the 1980s, the Long Term Capital Management (LTCM) Crisis, the 2001/2002 Credit Crunch, and the Correlation Crisis in 2005.

This is a very interesting sample of crises, as it includes completely different scenarios, which, however, led to wider spread levels. The initial trigger of these spread-widening phases, however, was completely different. Hence, the causality of a crisis is not a one-dimensional problem. For example, the IMF generates a vulnerability indicator for financial crises on a regular basis, which is based on some stress indicators. However, the following examples show that there is not only a wide range of potential trigger events but also a variety of transmission mechanisms through which the initial source of a crisis is spilling over onto financial markets and, in the end, onto the real economy.

In chart 5.2, we point out the spread of long-term US industrial spreads from the beginning of the 1960s. Credit spreads showed huge swings over this period, because there were several shock events and crisis scenarios over this period. Looking at these long-term data, it seems as if credits are a mean-reverting asset class. It is obviously hard to disagree on this topic when we refer to the specific chart. Nevertheless, mean-reversion is obviously a function of time. What we can learn, however, is that there is a floor for spread tightening (the natural floor for a credit default swap is naturally zero), while also the spread widening seems to be capped. Spread indices which refer to a whole universe (portfolio) of credit-risky instruments will not exceed a specific spread level even in a credit turmoil. There is some value left, as rising default rates as well as declining recovery values are limited, assuming the survival of the financial system. Before the net asset value of a specific part of the credit universe drops to zero, the respective stock universe would have to drop to zero long before (given the higher seniority of debt instruments). The assumption of equity markets dropping close to zero is definitely not very realistic. Hence, there are at least some boundaries for credit spreads, which are also reflected in historical patterns. From this perspective, one could argue that spreads are mean-reverting, which is simply related to the nature of the credit market. Calculating the average on a data series which is capped on both sides while moving over time following a stochastic process will trade close to the mean from time to time. It is, however, far from being

A brief history of
credit crises

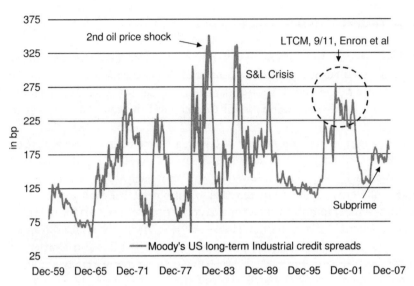

Fig. 5.2: Long-term credit spreads: not as stable as one might think

a profitable trading strategy! In addition, this assumption is not true for single credits as it ignores the risk of default.

The savings & loan crisis: A typical housing slump

The Savings & Loan Crisis is a perfect example of how potential threats for the economy can occur due to a mismanagement of mortgage risks. Savings and loan institutions have a long history as community-based institutions for savings and mortgages in the United States, dating back to around 1800. For a long period of time it provided stability to the market, until one of the worst crises ever hit the housing market, sending the US economy in a deep and ugly recession at the beginning of the 1990s. However, the story began a few decades earlier. In the 1970s, hyperinflation in the United States triggered a significant outflow from these deposits, which paid only a small interest. Many investors shifted money at this time into higher-yielding assets, for example into money market funds, which provided attractive returns. S&L institutions simply played the yield curve: they invested at the long end of the curve at high yields and funded at the short end of the curve at low yields.

Being invested at the long end of the curve at fixed rates while relying on short-term funding is a strategy that is obviously highly vulnerable to rising yields. S&L institutions experienced significant marked-to-market losses on

The Anatomy of a
Credit Crisis

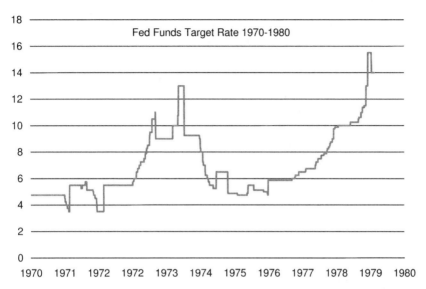

Fig. 5.3: FED Funds target rate in the 1970s

their long-term mortgage loans that were written at fixed-interest rates when rates rose (see chart 5.3); in other words, their investments traded significantly below their face value. For example, a 20Y mortgage bond with a coupon of 5% trades at a market value of around 50% in price terms when yields are at 10%. That said, an investment in the exemplary 20Y mortgage bond is losing 50% when yields rise from 5% to 10%. Consequently, the value of these loans, which were the institution's assets, was worth less than the deposits used to make them, and the savings and loans' net worth was being eroded. In chart 5.3 we show the dramatic surge of the Fed Funds Target Rate (FFTR) between 1970 and 1980, which even accelerated in the late 1970s. While the FFTR stood at 6% at the beginning of 1976, it climbed above 15% in 1979. The worst case happened from the perspective of S&Ls.

As a response to the challenging environment in the late 1970s, caps on mortgage rates were lifted, and the amount covered by insurance (finally provided by the government) was increased from 70% to 100%. This is a traditional moral hazard problem as the rising coverage by insurance also permitted managers to assume more risk. At the beginning of the 1980s, almost 87% of 3,800 S&Ls were not profitable. Hence, in 1982, the St Germain Depository Institutions Act was designed to make S&Ls more competitive and more solvent. They were now allowed to pay higher market rates for deposits, to borrow money from the

Federal Reserve, to make commercial loans, and to issue credit cards. In the end, the S&Ls developed from their initial purpose to being able to provide savings and mortgages. This should help to diversify business and reduce the dependency on the mortgage market. However, the changed regulatory environment did not make banks out of S&Ls. Consequently, the next fatal error happened: To take advantage of the real estate boom in the United States, S&Ls increased lending and entered more risky business segments. In addition, S&Ls knew that the government will take care of them, whereas insolvent banks would have been shut down quickly by bank regulators.

The vicious cycle continued when so-called deposit brokers, who are paid a commission by the customer to find the best certificate of deposit (CD) rates and place their customers' money in those CDs, entered the arena. Short-term CDs can be shifted very quickly, and hence only a small change in rates by one institution can attract a large number of deposits. It forces institutions to provide attractive terms, in the end resulting in more risky investments.

All these specific developments in the markets made the system even more vulnerable to rising interest rates, and unfortunately exactly this happened when the Fed started to fight inflation at the end of the 1970s. Rising rates triggered increasing funding costs, which even exceeded the yield of the long-term mortgage loans the S&Ls were invested in, simply increasing the asset-liability mismatch. The only way out is to focus on more risky, higher-yielding transactions (similar to the subprime meltdown).

As a reaction, the US government started to allow S&Ls to sell their mortgage loans and use the cash generated to seek better returns in 1981. What we would call "repackaging" today was already practiced many years before: the losses on the mortgage books were amortized over the life of the loan and any losses could also be offset against taxes paid over the preceding ten years. Consequently, S&Ls sold their loans primarily to Wall Street firms which paid distressed debt prices (significantly below the face value of the loans) and then transformed the loans by bundling them more or less as government-backed bonds (using guarantees from Freddie Mac and Fannie Mae). At this stage of the S&L crisis, the similarity to the subprime situation is becoming obvious.

S&Ls were among the investors who bought these bonds (holding USD 150 bn by 1986), paying substantial fees for the transactions. This put additional pressure on S&Ls in combination with rising bankruptcies of S&L costumers. As a consequence, around a fourth of S&Ls collapsed during the first third of the 1980s. The US government agency Federal Savings and Loan Insurance Corporation then had to repay all the depositors whose money was lost.

Finally, the S&L crisis lasted the whole decade, triggering a recapitalization of the US banking system and having had a significant impact on the US economy. The collapse of a system existing for almost two centuries was caused by a combination of regulatory changes that triggered excessive lending and risk taking, a changed structure of the financial market itself (deposit brokers, the rising power of Wall Street), and an adverse interest rate environment. These are the usual ingredients of a severe financial crisis, which took place interestingly in one of the most developed countries regarding regulatory environment and the financial system itself. This underpins the thesis that there are built-in mechanisms in financial markets that lead (from time to time) to a severe crisis. Such a crisis is based on many developments that – on their own – would not have been strong enough to rock a highly developed financial system. What is interesting to note are the similarities here to the current subprime crisis. Although the (financial) weapons have changed, the course of the battle was quite the same: overlending and excessive risk taking supported by a risk-taker-friendly regulatory framework, with rising rates as a trigger event. Mortgage crises are similar in many aspects. There are some general characteristics which can be found in the subprime and the S&L crisis, but also in the real estate bubble in Japan in the early 1990s.

LTCM: The arbitrage saga

The failure of the LTCM hedge fund (probably the most famous hedge fund ever) is still one of the most cited stories during discussions about the need for regulation in the hedge fund industry. Long-Term Capital Management (LTCM) was a hedge fund founded in 1994 by John Meriwether (the former vice-chairman and head of bond trading at Salomon Brothers). Besides Wall Street veteran Meriwether, who enjoyed the status of being a legend in fixed- income trading, Myron Scholes and Robert C. Merton, who shared the 1997 Nobel Prize in Economics, were on the fund's board of directors. Scholes and Merton acted as the academic conscience of the fund, underpinning the sophisticated approach the fund was implementing to generate profits through arbitrage trading, a strategy promising high returns accompanied by limited risk. While LTCM was initially enormously successful, with annualized returns of over 40% during its first years, it lost USD 4.6 bn in less than four months in 1998.

The basic idea behind the company was to take advantage of fixed-income arbitrage positions, which were based on complex mathematical models. The focus was on convergence trades in the most liquid segments in the FI market, US, Japanese, and European government bonds. Simply spoken, convergence trades mean that various positions will end up at the same price in the long run, while short-term price deviations are an often-seen phenomenon. Consequently, exploiting these short-term misevaluations in the market will, in the end, lead to an almost risk-free profit in the future. In other words, these trades have been non-directional, which means that the market direction does not have an impact on the P&L of the position. As the price deviations in general were rather small, huge volumes were traded to generate a sufficient return in absolute figures. The success of the company triggered enormous inflows and posed a problem for LTCM: there were simply not enough investment opportunities in its traditional universe of potential trade positions to invest the entire fund's money. Hence, LTCM started to implement trading strategies outside its expertise, which were also non-market directional, but they were not convergence trades as such. For example, LTCM was a major player in S&P 500 options to bet on the long-term volatility of US stock markets.

The fact that all these positions offered nearly risk-free profits was unfortunately accompanied by the fact that the expected return was also rather small (compared to directional trading strategies). This brings a factor into play that is also an important factor in the correlation crisis (to be discussed later): leverage! LTCM was forced to take highly leveraged positions to make a significant profit. At the beginning of 1998, the firm's equity amounted to USD 4.72 bn, while it borrowed more than USD 120 bn. This leverage of around 25 (which is also not unusual for the hedge fund community today) guarantees a highly attractive return on equity, while it makes the fund highly vulnerable to a liquidity crisis, in other words, large fund withdrawals. The off-balance-sheet derivative positions amounted to USD 1.25 tn, primarily related to interest rate derivatives. But there were only USD 4.7 billion in equity to cover potential losses in case of an emergency!

The fund was especially designed to benefit from arbitrage opportunities. As a matter of fact, such opportunities primarily arise during a short-term crisis in the market, because rational price discovery is replaced by panic selling! An investor who sticks to a rational, program-driven strategy should generate windfall profits in such a scenario. Times seemed to be favorable for such strategies at the end of the 1990s. The 1997 East Asian financial crisis was followed by the Russian financial crisis in August and September of 1998. At this time, the Russian government defaulted on its government bonds. LTCM had already shown some negative months before the Russian crisis hit the market. In May and June 1998, the fund lost 6.42% and 10.14% respectively, reducing LTCM's capital by USD 461 mn. In contrast to what we said before, the

Russian default was a worst-case scenario for LTCM. Although it offered huge opportunities in theory for funds that had not yet been invested, it also triggered tremendous losses on the existing convergence positions of LTCM. Panic selling among investors triggered a sell-off in Japanese and European bonds, while US Treasuries benefited from their safe-haven status. LTCM bet on the convergence of these bonds, while they diverged dramatically on the Russian default. The fund had lost USD 1.85 bn in capital by the end of August. The next step of the domino effect was a confidence shock, which led to a significant liquidity crisis. In the first three weeks of September 1998, LTCM's equity dropped from USD 2.3 bn to USD 600 mn, while the portfolio size remained unchanged. Consequently, leverage increased further.

LTCM's trading strategies generally showed no or almost very little correlation. In normal times or even in crises that are limited to a specific segment, LTCM benefited from this high degree of diversification. Nevertheless, the general flight to liquidity in 1998 caused a jump in global risk premiums, hitting the whole financial system. All (in normal times less-correlated) positions moved in the same direction. Finally, it is all about correlation! Rising correlation reduces the benefits from diversification, in the end hitting the fund's equity directly. This is a similarity with CDO investments (i.e., mezzanine pieces in CDOs), which also suffer from a high (default) correlation between the underlying assets. Consequently, a major lesson of the LTCM crisis was that the underlying Covariance matrix used in Value-at-Risk (VaR) analysis is not static but changes over time.

The risk of a domino effect (LTCM has to liquidate its assets, triggering a further drop in prices and forcing other companies to liquidate also) brought the Fed into play after LTCM rejected an offer from Goldman Sachs, AIG, and Berkshire Hathaway to buy out the partners and to inject cash to the fund, although LTCM's operations should be run within Goldman Sachs' trading unit. The Federal Reserve Bank of New York organized a bailout of USD 3.625 bn by the major creditors to avoid a wider collapse in the financial markets. All major players in the market participated, including Bankers Trust, Barclays, Chase, Deutsche Bank, UBS, Salomon Brothers, Smith Barney, J.P.Morgan, Goldman Sachs, Merrill Lynch, Credit Suisse, First Boston, and Morgan Stanley. Also Société Générale, Crédit Agricole, and Paribas participated, while Lehman Brothers and Bear Stearns declined to help out LTCM. An interesting side note is that during the first subprime wave in the summer of 2007, Bear Stearns was in the middle of speculations that the bank is in deep trouble (also because of the two Bear Stearns hedge funds that marked the starting point of the crisis).

However, Wall Street still remembered Bear Stearns' reaction during the LTCM crisis, triggering speculation that support from other US investment banks would remain limited if Bear Stearns were the next bailout candidate.

Compared to the subprime meltdown, the losses from the failure of LTCM were almost negligible, which was also related to the fact that no severe spillover effects occurred and markets returned to business-as-usual relatively quickly. Total losses amounted to USD 4.6 bn, allocated to interest rate swaps (USD 1.6 bn), equity volatility (USD 1.3 bn), emerging markets debt including Russian (USD 430 mn), directional trades in developed countries (USD 371 mn), yield curve arbitrage (USD 215 mn), S&P 500 stocks (USD 203 mn), and USD 100 mn in junk-bond arbitrage. This is only a fractional amount compared to the losses that occurred during the first wave of the subprime crisis, but also compared to the other crises we briefly discuss in this section.

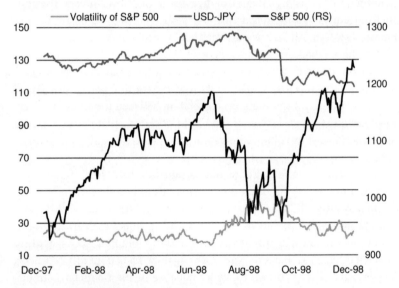

Fig. 5.4: The LTCM Shock

The banks that participated in the bailout even made a small gain on the positions when the panic abated. In the long run, the basic investment principle of LTCM proved right. However, "in the long run, we are all dead!" (J.M. Keynes). Even if there are arbitrage opportunities in the sense that two positions that trade at different prices right now will definitely converge at a point in the future, there is a risk that the anomaly will become even bigger. However, typically a high leverage is used for positions that have a skewed risk-return profile, or a high likelihood of a small profit but a very low risk of a large loss. This equals the risk-and-return profile of credit investments but also the risk that selling far-out-of-the-money puts on equities. In case a tail event occurs, all risk parameters to manage the overall portfolio are probably worthless, as correlation patterns change dramatically during a crisis. That said, arbitrage trades are not under fire because the crisis has an impact on the long-term risk-and-return profile of the position. However, a crisis might cause a short-term distortion of a capital market leading to immense mark-to-marked losses. If the capital adequacy is not strong enough to offset the mark-to-market losses, forced unwinding triggers significant losses in arbitrage portfolios. The same was true for many asset classes during the summer of 2007, when high-quality structures came under pressure, causing significant mark-to-market losses. Many of these structures did not bear default risk but a huge liquidity risk, and therefore many investors were forced to sell. This is especially true for some money market funds which have had a huge portion of ABS on their books. While LTCM cannot be compared with the subprime meltdown from a fundamental point of view (the latter is much more severe regarding spillover effects onto the real economy), some mechanisms are rather similar. The use of leverage makes not only trading positions but also investment books more vulnerable against exogenous shocks, triggering panic selling and irrational behavior. The excessive use of derivatives to build up leverage happens always in times when markets are discounting a scenario close to the "best of all worlds". Exogenous shocks, however, do not care about what markets discount.

An external shock to the system: 9/11

Exogenous shocks are events that do not have their origin in the financial system itself. Political events and natural catastrophes are the major sources of external shocks. The worst exogenous shock during the last decade was 9/11. Exogenous shocks pose a risk for financial markets and for the real economy as a whole via psychological effects as well as via fundamental ones.

Psychological effects are rather short lived, but they might be a trigger for a kind of domino effect in financial markets. The first reaction on September 11, 2001, when the first airplane crashed into the World Trade Center, was shock. As it became obvious that it was not an accident when the second airplane hit the second WTC tower, markets came under severe stress. The collateral damage of such an event is primarily the personal agony of the human beings directly involved, while the direct economic effect is rather negligible. From a pure economic perspective, accidents or natural catastrophes could be even supportive of growth in case the loss in productive capital and the growth deficit linked to it is smaller than the additional growth triggered by restoring the destroyed infrastructure. The psychological effect, however, is in many cases immense. This is especially true for political crises. The potential risk of political changes also bears the risk of significant changes in the relative pricing of securities. This uncertainty triggered by a shock event is responsible for pronounced changes in global risk premiums. However, if the fears do not materialize, the repricing back to pre-crisis levels happens as fast as the shock sent prices for risky assets downward. This was exactly what happened in the aftermath of 9/11. Stock and credit markets recovered within a few weeks, and negative effects on some segments (travel industry) were offset by some positive effects on other industries (security business). There is, in general, no lasting impact on the economy from these psychological effects.

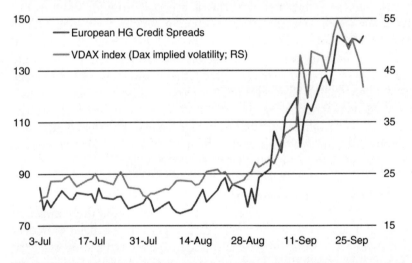

Fig. 5.5: The 9/11 Shock

The opposite is true for the second type of effects: fundamental ones. Exogenous shocks often trigger rising oil prices (at least, this was true for the previous three decades, a time which was dominated by the Middle East conflict), which obviously have an impact on economic growth. In this case, the exogenous shock is leading to a changed fundamental environment, as it influences the relative pricing for many asset classes. Higher oil prices, for example, have an impact not only on input prices for many industries but also on FX markets, on interest rates (via potential inflationary effects), and on geographical risk premiums. Natural catastrophes which lead to a shortage of specific commodities is a further example of the fundamental impact exogenous shocks can have.

There is a huge difference between these two most common exogenous shocks. Although the human agony of earthquakes and floods is often tremendous, the impact on the financial system is very limited. This is often driven by the fact that most of these events occur in undeveloped countries, which do not have a huge importance for the global economy. Nevertheless, the flood in New Orleans in the aftermath of Hurricane Katrina in 2005 also did not cause a meltdown of financial markets. Financial markets, as a matter of fact, do ignore any personal issues.

Exogenous shocks are, in general, not as bad as other financial crises. Spillover effects are less severe, as there is no systemic failure which leads to self-fulfilling processes that finally hit the economy. Exogenous shocks, however, can trigger the emergence of a systemic problem. Global imbalances, for example, can persist for a long period, while an exogenous shock can cause an abrupt repricing in the FX market, which, in the end, causes a sharp adjustment of financial markets to incorporate a fundamental problem which was imminent.

Accounting scandals: Enron and others

Known as Enronitis, the crisis in the US non-financial segment in 2001/2002 was a typical micro-fundamental crisis triggered by accounting scandals. The US energy company Enron, which filed for Chapter 11 in late 2001, took center stage in this crisis and has become the most popular symbol of corporate fraud and corruption. Enron was one of the world's leading companies supplying electricity, natural gas, pulp and paper, and communications and had been named "America's Most Innovative Company" for six consecutive years by Fortune. Enron lost this title in 2001, when it became clear that that its reported financial condition was sustained mostly by institutionalized, systematic, and creatively planned accounting fraud. The scandal also caused a discussion about accounting firms, as Arthur Anderson, Enron's accounting firm, was obviously not able to avoid fraud either.

As Enron had been considered a blue chip stock, this was an unprecedented and disastrous event in the financial world. Enron's plunge occurred after it was revealed that much of its profits and revenue were the result of deals with special-purpose entities (limited partnerships which it controlled). The result was that much of Enron's debt and the losses it suffered were not reported in its financial statements. To point out the quick fall of the formerly most innovative company in the United States, we quote our colleagues from UniCredit's (formerly HypoVereinsbank) credit research department below to provide a "real-time impression" of the crisis. The Enron debacle came as a surprise not only for investors, but also for the financial community as a whole!

- **October 30, 2001: Moody's lowers the company's senior unsecured long-term debt ratings from Baa1 to Baa2 and keeps the ratings on Watchlist negative.** The rating action reflects the deterioration in Enron's financial flexibility; the company announces significant write-downs as well as equity charges in previously undisclosed partnership investments. This results in a substantial loss in investor confidence that cuts Enron's share price in half and creates difficulties in rolling over commercial paper. In response to these events, Enron shores up its near-term liquidity position by drawing down all of its committed revolving credit facilities and buying back its outstanding commercial paper. In addition, Enron is in the process of arranging additional bank financing to support its core wholesale trading operations. In light of these uncertainties, we recommend to remain cautious. Enron's Eurobonds have widened sharply over the last few weeks and already discount Enron, eventually becoming sub-investment grade in the future.

- **November 6, 2001: Fitch downgrades Enron's senior unsecured debt to BBB- from BBB+ and keeps the ratings on Rating Watch negative.** Fitch states that it would consider further downgrades if Enron would be unable to make progress in reducing debt. According to Fitch, the rating action reflects the difficulties Enron faces in managing its liquidity position in the face of eroding investor confidence. This follows the recognition of a substantial diminution in value of its global merchant investments, which were partly financed with an aggressive use of off-balance sheet vehicles. Fitch also underlines the additional uncertainty that results from the investigation of certain Enron-sponsored partnerships by the US Securities and Exchange Commission (SEC). We do not regard the current widespread levels of Enron's bond issues as an investment opportunity as long as high uncertainty persists.

- **November 9, 2001: Stay away from Enron's Eurobonds as long as no concrete takeover announcement has been made.** Enron restates its balance sheet for the past four years due to the USD 1.2 bn charge against its equity to cover losses at some of its partnerships. Enron had already announced the charge, which has resulted in investor concerns about the soundness of the company's balance sheet. Dynegy, a US energy and communications company, announces that it may acquire Enron. Dynegy possibly would pay about USD 8 bn in stock for the company, whose shares have fallen 89% this year due to a loss of investor confidence. So far, no agreement could be reached, as Dynegy might be afraid of acquiring a troubled company that could lose its investment grade ratings, putting additional pressure on Dynegy's own ratings. In the energy-trading business, an investment-grade rating is important for receiving credit lines with trading partners. For Enron it is still important that a solution is found soon, as some trading partners have withdrawn their business from Enron, which again undermines the latter's ratings. While the company is cleaning up its act, its management is still subject to an SEC investigation. As long as the situation is uncertain, we recommend staying away from Enron's Eurobonds despite elevated spread levels.

- **November 12, 2001: Dynegy agrees to acquire Enron for USD 8.85 bn in stock and assume another USD 14 bn in Enron's debt, still preserving Enron's investment grade rating.** The Enron downgrade was prompted by the credit implications of the company's restatement of financial statements going back to 1997 due in part to a legal and accounting review of certain related-party transactions by a special committee of Enron's board of directors. The investment-grade rating is based on the prospect of improved credit quality with the acquisition by the financially stronger Dynegy and the near-term liquidity enhancement through the injection of USD 1.5 bn of equity capital by ChevronTexaco that came with the signing of the merger agreement. The credit quality of the post-merger Dynegy can be maintained if the company can accomplish the sales of Enron's non-core assets in an effective and orderly manner and produce the expected improvement in financial measures. S&P warns that Enron could still become a non-investment grade company if liquidity and the value of the company's trading business are not maintained during the merger process. However, regulatory uncertainties remain. In any case, buying Enron would still leave some risks for Dynegy regarding Enron's dubious partnerships and the ongoing SEC investigation.
- **November 22, 2001: Despite Dynegy's bid for troubled Enron, investors remain concerned about the latter's financial liquidity.** Yesterday, Enron shares dropped by a third and bonds dropped even below levels seen before Dynegy's bid. On Monday, Enron announced that it would have

to pay back debt of USD 9.15 bn by 2003 and a USD 690 mn note due next week. This has created concerns that Enron could run out of cash before the merger is completed (expected by October 2002). A potential drop into high-yield territory would trigger the repayment of another USD 3.9 bn in debt issued by affiliated companies. Dynegy's bid could still fail if lawsuits against Enron related to its affiliates total more than USD 2 bn.

- **December 3, 2001: S&P has lowered its long-term corporate credit rating on Enron Corp. to CC from B-.** The CreditWatch implications were changed to "negative" from "developing". The rating action reflects S&P's expectation that following the dissolution of Enron's announced merger with Dynegy Inc., burdensome debt restructuring requirements, negligible liquidity, and limited access to capital will likely cause Enron to seek bankruptcy protection (which it has already done). The change in CreditWatch implications to "negative" reflects Standard & Poor's belief that such a filing in the very near term is probable.

- **Enron's filing for Chapter 11 causes downgrade by agencies. Enron sues Dynegy for USD 10 bn. Chances of success seem limited.** Enron recently sued Dynegy for USD 10 bn, accusing Dynegy of withdrawing a takeover offer to remove a competitor; it seems, however, that chances of success are very limited. By not disclosing the liabilities, Enron had breached its obligation to disclose all material obligation, which gave Dynegy the right to withdraw its offer, according to a Dynegy spokesman. Some experts predict that the bankruptcy filing and related lawsuits will take years to resolve. In a response, Dynegy also demands that Enron either hand over control of a disputed pipeline or return the USD 1.5 bn that Dynegy invested in it. Although the outcome of lawsuits is difficult to predict, we do not think that Enron will receive a significant amount in damages. Like Moody's, we also expect recovery values to be low and recommend investors to avoid Enron bonds at current levels.

The Enron scandal shook investors' confidence in Corporate America, which for a long time was the hoard of stability, proper regulation, and exemplary accounting standards. It was the worst micro-fundamental confidence crisis that credit markets have ever experienced. It triggered concerns of investors regarding balance sheet figures in general, while it was also accompanied by further scandals, WorldCom and Parmalat being the most famous.

Besides Enron, WorldCom was the other famous company dominating headlines for a while due to accounting scandals. WorldCom had been the second-

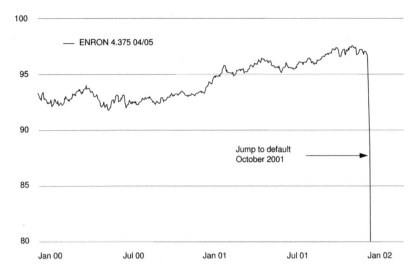

Fig. 5.6: The end of the Enron Debacle

largest long distance phone company behind AT&T in the United States. World-Com's growth strategy was primarily driven by acquisitions during the 1990s and reached its peak with the acquisition of MCI in 1998, resulting in the USD 37 bn merger to form MCI WorldCom. This was the largest merger in US history at this time. In October 1999, the next step in the "mergermania" of the company was announced, when Sprint Corporation and MCI WorldCom stated a USD 129 bn merger agreement between the two companies. The deal again would have been the largest corporate merger in history up to that time. However, the deal did not go through because of concerns by the US Department of Justice and the EU that it would create a monopoly. WorldCom's growth strategy suffered a serious blow when it was forced to abandon its proposed merger with Sprint in late 2000. This was the beginning of the end for MCI WorldCom. From 1999 to May 2002, the company used fraudulent accounting methods to mask its declining financial condition by painting a bright picture of financial growth and profitability to support its stock price. The company obviously undertook several strategies to enhance its financial statement. MCI WorldCom underreported interconnection expenses with other telecommunication companies by capitalizing these costs on the balance sheet rather than properly expensing them. Moreover, it inflated revenues by booking accounting entries from "corporate unallocated revenue accounts". The company's audit department uncovered around USD 3.8 bn of the fraud in June 2002 during a routine examination of capital expenditures. KPMG (which replaced Arthur Andersen, the external auditors during the fraud) withdrew its audit opinion for 2001, and the SEC launched an investigation into these matters. In the end, MCI WorldCom had inflated total assets of around USD 11 bn. On July 21, 2002, MCI WorldCom filed for Chapter 11, the largest filing in US history.

The most famous corporate scandal in Euroland was Parmalat, when a EUR 8 bn hole was discovered in Parmalat's accounting records at the end of 2003. It was a spectacular case also because it was the first credit event that hit the newly introduced index swap universe Trac-x, which was the predecessor of the iTraxx universe. In 2003, Parmalat was the leading global company in the production of ultra-high-temperature (UHT) milk. Today, the company is still specialized in UHT milk and milk derivatives with more than 36,000 employees. In 1997, Parmalat entered the globalization carousel by financing several international acquisitions with debt. Unfortunately, in 2001, many of the new divisions produced losses, while the company financing shifted to the use of derivatives, apparently at least in part with the intention of hiding the extent of its losses and debt. In February 2003, the company unexpectedly announced a new EUR 500 mn bond issue. This came as a surprise both to the markets and to the CEO, who began to suspect that the company's total debt was more than double the amount on the balance sheet. The crisis became public in November 2003, when questions were raised regarding mysterious transactions with a Cayman-based fund linked to Parmalat. This triggered a huge sell-off in Parmalat stocks. The company was not able to repay its debt and fulfill coupon payments, and the company's bank, Bank of America, released a document showing that EUR 3.95 bn on a bank account was a forged. Moreover, Parmalat sold credit-linked notes referencing its own credit worthiness in order to generate some windfall profits. The company defaulted at the end of 2003; the recovery rate was in the low double-digit area in the end.

The problem with accounting scandals is that investors are completely losing confidence in the micro-fundamental situation of companies. This is especially true for bondholders, who invest in the senior part of the capital structure; hence, tail events are the major risk factors (defining fraud as a tail event is unusual but appropriate). Moreover, the risk that these micro-fundamental developments spill over onto the economy is rather high. Micro-fundamental crises can therefore easily trigger a credit-crunch scenario.

2001/2002: A full-fledged credit crunch

A combination of rising risk premiums in general in the aftermath of 9/11 (and ahead of the second Iraq invasion in 2003), so-called Enronian economics, the burst of the tech bubble (starting in Q1 2000), and a general weakening of economic growth patterns triggered a full-fledged credit crunch in 2001/2002. At the time it was the most severe crisis for credit markets since the beginning of the 1980s. This is true if we only look at spread levels as indicators for the severity of a crisis; however, the overall impact on the real economy, the combination with very weak equity markets, and the tremendous loss in confidence made the 2001/2002 crisis one of the worst in the younger history of financial markets.

A *credit crunch* is defined as a situation when growth in debt is slowing significantly, for example, due to surging risk aversion that is triggering a strongly declining provision of debt financing (e.g., via tighter lending standards of banks, which, in the end negatively affects the real economy. A credit crunch is the worst outcome of a credit crisis, as it means that all transmission mechanisms of a credit crisis are getting into full swing, ending up in a scenario where a drop in debt growth is a burden for economic growth. In the textbook definition, traditional characteristics of a credit crunch are the following:

- Lax lending standards resulting in a misallocation of capital; lending institutions do not charge low-quality borrowers an appropriate risk premium. This can have many reasons, for example, a moral hazard situation. This was the case in the subprime crisis, when CDOs were used as funding vehicles for subprime mortgages. In any case, it is a rather typical behavior of banks that act pro-cyclically. Banks tend to overlend in boom periods, while they tend to be too restrictive in times of crisis. Hence, banks add to the cyclicality of the credit market; in other words, they tend to aggravate cyclical swings.
- A credit crunch is accompanied by a financial crisis as the result of asset price inflation and the burst of a bubble in financial markets. This is definitely worse than a liquidity crisis, which is rather a temporary distortion of an otherwise well functioning market. A liquidity crisis does not directly bear the risk of insolvencies, defaults, bankruptcies, and the like. At least, this is true if a liquidity crisis is temporarily limited. However, a credit crunch is generally accompanied by a liquidity squeeze. A credit crunch always triggers some defaults, as the reduced growth of the money supply caused by a credit crunch can bankrupt marginal borrowers and threaten the solvency of marginal lenders.

- This also means that there is a fundamental problem. A credit crunch is not a "technically triggered" crisis but a severe economic problem, either on the macro- or on the micro-fundamental side. We cannot explain a credit crunch by the misbehavior of single institutions or market players, and we cannot blame a single industry (with hedge funds being the most popular victim of being made accountable for a crisis).
- A full fledged credit crunch includes many developments that are well known in financial theory: lemming-like behavior, moral hazard, financial panic. Self-fulfilling prophecies are also an often-seen phenomenon in credit crunch scenarios. A credit crunch leads to a significant price collapse in many segments of the financial market, and it takes a long time to recover. The costs of a credit crunch are enormous, especially including second and third-order effects. A credit crunch is clearly categorized as a banking crisis.

Does this scheme fit with the 2001/2002 credit crunch scenario? Lax lending standards have been a problem at the beginning of the new millennium, primarily related to the new economy boom. At this time, some technology, internet, or new-economy companies had a market capitalization that was far above what traditional valuation approaches would call fair value. High double-digit price-earnings ratios have been the standard for new-economy stocks, because the bet was that future earnings potential is tremendous, easily exceeding that previously known from the old economy. However, the problem in the new economy was the valuation of equity rather than of debt. There was no severe credit crisis in the new economy. Leverage in the credit market at this time had been driven by companies from the old economy, for example in the telecom sector. The auction of UMTS licenses, for example, lead to ridiculous prices for licenses that ultimately proved to be worth much less than previously anticipated. A good example of this development is Deutsche Telekom (DT), still the largest German telecom company. In chart 5.7, we show the share price and 5Y CDS spreads of DT during the period between 1999 and 2003. DT was in the middle of the credit crunch in the old economy as the company significantly increased leverage to bid for UMTS licenses in Germany, which was reflected in a strong new issue pipeline in the years 1999-2001. The previously fully state-owned company tapped the IPO market three times, and the share price peaked at above EUR 100 in February 2000. The burst of the bubble in the new economy also hit high-leveraged old economy players, and the share price dropped below EUR 20 at the end of 2001 (see chart 5.7). At the same time, DT's credit spreads

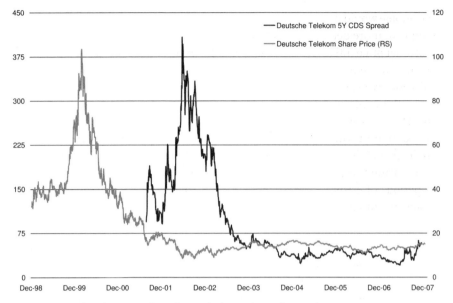

450										120
				——Deutsche Telekom 5Y CDS Spread						
				——Deutsche Telekom Share Price (RS)						
375										100
300										80
225										60
150										40
75										20
0										0
Dec-98	Dec-99	Dec-00	Dec-01	Dec-02	Dec-03	Dec-04	Dec-05	Dec-06	Dec-07	

Fig. 5.7: Deutsche Telecom stocks and spreads during the credit crunch

widened dramatically, also significantly increasing its funding costs. 5Y CDS on the name jumped to almost 450 bp!

Lending obviously became expensive for many companies. The more general increase of the premium for credit-risky assets on the back of rising political tensions in the aftermath of 9/11 triggered an increasing systematic spread widening, while Enronian economics added uncertainty to the market, also causing investors to demand a higher risk premium for taking credit risk in general. As the banking industry got hit hard by the ongoing weakness in stock markets, the failure of some icons of the new economy, and the economic slowdown, it strongly tightened its lending standards. Pro-cyclical lending and investment behavior of banks clearly worsened the situation in 2001-2002.

The bursting of the bubble has had severe consequences for the real economy. First of all, there is no doubt that we have seen a bubble in the new economy, with some non-profitable new economy companies having had a higher market cap than some very profitable old-economy companies, which, however, have been obsolete on the buying lists of investors, as they did not promise a double-digit earnings growth for the next decades (as the new-economy firms did). Unfortunately, the existence of a bubble can be adopted only ex-post; otherwise,

A brief history of
credit crises

the bubble would never come true! We will describe the emergence of a financial bubble in more detail in the following section, while no one would really doubt that asset price inflation was a major reason for the severity of the new-economy crash. It was obviously accompanied by the most critical liquidity squeeze since a decade. We show this effect in the chart 5.8 for US corporate bond markets. Since the beginning of the 1990s, US corporate bonds have experienced a constant increase in net purchases of foreigners. This trend still persists. The only period in which we have seen a decline in net purchases was during the credit crunch in 2001-2002. However, purchases remained in positive terrain even during this period. That said, there is always demand for credit risk, even in periods of crisis. However, demand in a crisis period is not strong enough to absorb supply. That is the real definition of a *liquidity squeeze*.

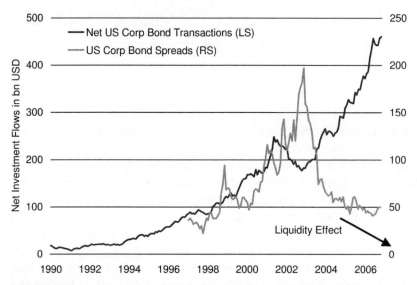

Fig. 5.8: The liquidity effect on credit spreads

Nevertheless, asset price inflation does not mean that this is only a technical, or valuation, problem. The fundamental problems from 2000-2002 have risen steadily, as reflected in accounting scandals, record-levered companies, declining growth patterns, and so on. However, the economic cycle itself was not the trigger for the 2000-2001 credit crunch; it was rather a combination of excessive leverage, excessive lending, and excessive risk taking. Although we

The Anatomy of a
Credit Crisis

argued that a credit crunch is characterized by a huge fundamental problem, the technical side in the market has a significant impact on the severity of such a crisis. The 2001-2002 pattern shows an ugly alliance of a combination of both deteriorating fundamentals and weak technicals.

Self-fulfilling processes, moral hazards, and financial panic have also been observed during the burst of the tech bubble. Self-fulfilling processes were also a topic in 2002. Although credit spreads already started to price in rising default probabilities in 2000, realized default probabilities increased insignificantly before 2001 and 2002. This is a phenomenon often seen in credit markets. Investors anticipate rising default rates and demand a higher risk premium for holding credit risk. This is causing wider spread levels, which overcompensate for the current default risk (but not for future default risk). This forces companies to fund themselves at higher levels, which can lead to a liquidity squeeze, especially for lower-rated companies. This eventually translates into higher default rates, and the initial spread-widening was justified. Moral hazard was observable in the credit crunch especially from a micro-fundamental perspective. Many institutions have been accused of not having seen the fraud. This is especially true for Enron, as many market players had an intrinsic notion that Enron was performing well! Finally, financial panic triggered the last wave of selling in the stock market, when investors reduced exposure to all companies without differentiating between good and bad ones.

In conclusion, the 2001-2002 credit crunch was the most severe credit crisis in the new millennium-although the subprime turmoil has a good chance to dethrone the burst of the tech bubble in this respect.

Correlation Crisis in 2005: Do not play with fire!

The first widely recognized crisis in the credit derivatives universe occurred in May 2005. The so-called correlation crisis got its name from the fact that specific strategies in the standardized tranched iTraxx universe, *correlation trades* (please refer to section 2.5), caused significant distortions in the underlying credit market, pushing spreads significantly wider. This was a rather technically driven spread widening; from a fundamental perspective, the spread widening (iTraxx spreads doubled in a few weeks' time) was not justified at all. The correlation crisis happened in the United States (CDX indices) and in Europe (iTraxx) at the same time, with an almost similar outcome. In this section, we explain the chronology of the crisis by referring to the iTraxx indices for two reasons: (i) these indices are the most liquid instruments in the global credit market, and (ii) we already introduced these instruments in section 2.5.

A brief history of
credit crises

The background to the crisis was the positioning of market participants in the credit derivatives market. The predominant market view at the beginning of 2005 was that of a moderate spread widening in the course of the year, which would hit the market as a whole without a dramatic increase in idiosyncratic risks. This means that implied default correlation should remain relatively high, which favors the equity piece. Against this background, a delta-hedged tranche trade was the appropriate investment strategy for many correlation traders. This trade includes a long position in the iTraxx 0-3% tranche and an appropriate short position in the iTraxx 3-6% tranche (junior mezzanine tranche). In contrast to the equity piece, the mezzanine tranche is vulnerable to rising default correlation, that is, the price of the tranche declines (or the tranche spread rises) if default correlation increases. Delta hedged means that the P&L of the combined positions is not affected by a widening of the underlying index spread, triggered by an equivalent spread widening of the index constituents. That said, the spread sensitivity of the invested amount in the equity piece is similar to the spread sensitivity of the invested amount in the mezzanine piece, and consequently, the short and the long positions offset each other in respect to spread changes. In practice, the spread delta of the equity piece at this time was around 20, while the sensitivity for the mezzanine piece amounted to around 5. Consequently, the hedge ratio between the equity and the mezzanine piece is 4. A EUR 10 mn long position in the 0-3% tranche can be immunized against spread changes in the underlying universe by a EUR 40 mn short position in the 3-6% tranche. The good news was that this trade generates positive carry (the spread for the long position exceeds the spread the investor was forced to pay for the hedge) at the beginning of 2005. In other words, the spread an investor receives for holding a long position in the equity piece is more than four times the spread he has to pay to buy protection on the mezzanine tranche. This is, however, only true if we assume a simultaneous widening of all the names in the underlying index, that is, if there are not a few names that trigger a widening in the index while others remain unchanged. In other words, the spread dispersion (the spread difference between the single-name index constituents) remained unchanged.

Unfortunately, we saw a completely different scenario in May 2005. Against the backdrop of resurfacing LBO fears regarding UK retailers, as well as negative spillover effects from the tumbling carmakers GM and Ford in the United States, the spread dispersion increased dramatically.

In contrast to the shareholders' perspective, leveraged buyouts are a potential burden for bondholders. Consequently, spreads widen on LBO fears. In May

2005, a couple of UK retail companies experienced significant spread widening as rumors resurfaced that these companies will become LBO targets. The rest of the credit universe remained relatively unimpressed, as this is an idiosyncratic (or sector-specific) risk factor which obviously leaves the rest of the credit market unaffected. In other words, the correlation between these names and the others declined strongly, which translates into losses in long equity tranche positions. Declining implied default correlation is especially hitting the first loss piece as the survival probability declines ("someone will default in any case"). Chart 5.9 depicts the spread dispersion at the beginning of March and in May at the peak of the crisis. While the spread of all constituents widened from 28.3 to 50.9 bp (a shift of the dispersion curve to the right), especially the spread dispersion changed dramatically. This is reflected in a changed curvature of the slope of the dispersion curve and shows a rising heterogeneity of the iTraxx constituents, making idiosyncratic risk a more dominant factor. That is exactly what makes (index) delta hedges inefficient! In other words, it indicates that hedges on an index level are not the appropriate tool to keep a correlation trade spread neutral. The spread blowout of potential LBO candidates, in fact, caused the single-name deltas to change dramatically.

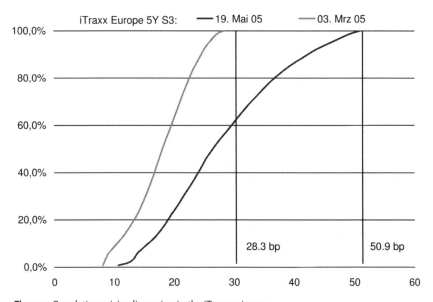

Fig. 5.9: Correlation crisis: dispersion in the iTraxx universe

An even more interesting footnote in the correlation crisis was the impact from Ford and GM on the European tranched market. At this time, Ford and GM traded at distressed levels (5Y CDS jumped above 1,000 bp for some reference entities) as the operational performance was disappointing, while some other problems weighted on the companies (pension liabilities, etc.). In addition, private investor Kirk Kerkorian bought an equity stake in GM, underpinning rumors that a restructuring of the company will favor shareholders at the cost of bondholders. Moreover, restructuring was defined as a credit event in some US CDS contracts. The occurrence of a credit event (irrespective of its restructuring or default) will eat directly into the equity tranche. These fears resulted in a significant jump in the upfront payment for the equity piece in the US CDX HY universe to more than 90%! This means that the first insurance fee paid by a protection buyer on the equity piece paid more than USD 9 mn. Moreover, this panic selling of equity risk spilled over onto the European market, with the 0-3% tranche in iTraxx jumping to above 50%, although GM and Ford were not included in the underlying index!

These effects also caused a significant increase in spread volatility. Another reason for the high spread volatility is rather simple: the spread widening of the index only means that the expected loss increased, hence that higher tranches move in-the-money! A spread level in the iTraxx Europe of 60 bp goes hand-in-hand with an expected loss of roughly 3% in a five-year period, which is the attachment point of the BBB (3-6%) tranche. As the gamma (the delta of the delta) of a tranche investment reaches its high exactly when the expected loss passes through the "at-the-money point" (attachment point) of the tranche, delta-adjustment trades have been necessary in order to keep correlation positions delta-neutral.

The most interesting point is if we compare the moves during the correlation crisis with the effect of the subprime crisis on the tranched universe. While the spread widening of the underlying index universe was rather similar during both crises, the impact on the tranches was exactly complementary. While the first wave of the correlation crisis in 2007 was driven by fears that single-name defaults will directly eat into the equity piece (declining correlation), the subprime crisis was characterized by rising systematic risk (increasing correlation). Hence the equity piece came significantly under pressure in the former, while the senior part of the capital structure was the major loser in the latter.

5.4 What can we learn from existing crises models?

5.4.1 Bubble theory & credit markets

Speculative bubble and *irrational exuberance* are some of the buzzwords in financial markets, especially during times of crisis. A *bubble* is defined as a deviation of market prices from what fundamentalists would call "fair value". However, as a "fair" valuation is a pretty unstable and not very well known technique, investors tend to argue that the fair value is underestimating the future price and therefore, it makes sense to buy the asset from a risk and return perspective.[40]

A good example of a speculative bubble was the technology bubble especially in US and European stock markets, which peaked in 2000. At this point in time, some new economy companies' stocks traded at a triple-digit price-earnings ratio, compared to a low-double-digit ratio which we would call fair simply using the long-term average of P/E ratios. Moreover, some of these companies did not generate any profit at this time and earnings were close to zero. Therefore, analysts started to modify "old-school ratios" that they have used for decades to generate relative value analysis for single stocks. They introduced these new measures (like future profitability figures, etc.) to account for the tremendous future earnings growth, although ratios calculated for current figures looked very ugly. A current example is the Chinese stock market, as there are also many companies which trade at high double-digit P/E ratios, which is far above what investors expect to be a fair value in established markets.

The argument for the high valuation in the Chinese market is, however, similar to what analysts stated during the new economy bubble: it is not appropriate to use traditional measures to deduce a fair valuation, as there are special situations. During the technology bubble, the implementation of completely new business models underpins hopes of endless growth. But the Chinese market is growing at rates which are far above those in the Old World. At least for the tech bubble, we can say that these expectations were overdone. However, at a specific point in time, investors, analysts, and even the companies believe in those bright forecasts. From this perspective, a bubble is not irrational; it is only based on wrong expectations. That said, it would be too easy to conclude that irrational behavior of some investors is triggering asset price inflation that finally leads to a speculative bubble, which – sooner or later – will burst. The emergence of a bubble can also be introduced in models which are based on rational expectations. Finally, the uncertainty about what the intrinsic value of an asset is sufficient to create a speculative bubble.

Unfortunately, the problem is that we can identify bubbles only ex post. Actually, the majority of investors do not think that a bubble is emerging, and therefore they continue to fill the bubble with their speculation. If the majority of investors would have known that asset price inflation occurred, they would have reduced their holding in the specific asset/market, and in the end there would not have been a bubble and also not a burst of it. This also underpins those theories which deny the validation of fundamental models in a bubble, as the price mechanism is not driven by typical demand and supply patterns. That is the reason why some academics characterize the emergence of a bubble as irrational. Traditional demand and supply patterns that are well-known from a micro-economic theory also in "normal" market times do not accurately explain price moves. Consequently, why should we trust them in crises times?

There are many different explanations for the emergence of a speculative bubble in academic theory. The most popular one is that bubbles are just reflecting the *greed and fear phenomenon*, which means that extremely bullish investors trigger an irrational exuberance, which ends up in a bubble. These investors obviously overstate potential returns, while they underestimate the accompanied risk. Based on the fact that speculative bubbles also occur in well-developed markets, including high transparency, information efficiency, and sufficient liquidity, this argument is especially true for very complex, less-developed segments in financial markets. The price-finding process in the structured credit market ahead of the subprime shock is a very good example for this argument. Some investors bought many complex instruments although they were not able to appropriately monitor and value those products. They relied on the market price only, and when liquidity in structured credits dropped to zero during the summer of 2007, those investors could not even derive valuation prices. They were forced to rely on performance updates provided by investment banks that sold them those products. CPDOs are a very good example in this respect. We think that less sophistication in risk analysis is a factor which fuels the emergence of a speculative bubble, but it is by far not sufficient to explain the whole phenomenon.

There is another approach, which is known as a *greater fool explanation*. The idea behind this explanation is that even if market participants are able to price an instrument/market correctly, overshooting in financial markets is simply triggered by the fact that a "fool" sees the chance to sell the asset at a higher price to a "greater fool". That means that price discovery in financial markets does not rely on appropriate valuation but only on the fact that there are very heterogeneous investors, and more sophisticated ones are trying to benefit from less-sophisticated ones. In the end, the bubble grows until the "greatest fool" in the market buys the asset and thus, no investor is left to fuel the upward spiral, or asset price inflation. The next logical step is a significant decline in asset prices as demand drops to zero. Despite the fact that the assumption of heterogeneous investors makes sense, a necessary prerequisite for such a vicious cycle is a highly liquid market with huge turnover. This is definitely not true for the credit markets, and especially not for the structured credit market. Many structured credit instruments are designed for buy-and-hold investors, and hence secondary markets are highly illiquid. This assumption simply does not fit with the institutional design of the credit market as a whole.

Last but not least, a major argument for the existence of bubbles is a rather psychological one: *lemming-like behavior of investors*. A very good example is the asset manager industry, in particular if we assume benchmark-oriented behavior: The individual success depends on the performance of all other competitors, as the fund performance is a relative one rather than an absolute one. The decision-making process of one fund manager therefore is not only two-dimensional: outperforming or underperforming the rest of the asset managers, but this also includes a psychological component. In case the asset manager agrees with the overall view in the market, he will set up his portfolio in line with his competitors. Assuming that the fund will benefit from the market directions in the future, everyone performed well and there is no reason to rethink the strategy. But even if there are adverse market conditions and the fund manager is losing money, the loss is in line with that of all his competitors, which is a good excuse for all investors. That said, even if the fund performs poorly in absolute terms, buying the "herding" (buying the benchmark) is the appropriate strategy from the portfolio manager's perspective. This is true because if the fund manager is taking the opposite view on the market as the rest of the world, he runs the risk of underperforming when everyone else is performing, while he has the chance of outperforming when everyone else is generating a negative return. However, even if we imply that the probability to under- and outperform is similar (which means the portfolio manager is on average as good as the huge majority of the market that is predicting exactly the opposite), we would be forced to skip the assumption that the asset manager is risk averse. Lemming-like behavior or herding is a major factor in FX markets, especially in currency crises, that is, speculative attacks (please refer to the financial panic section below). Nevertheless, we doubt that this is the right template for credit crises. Herding is an often-seen phenomenon from a short-term trading perspective, which can also be observed in credit markets. An important data release, for example, often causes a financial "J-curve" effect, which means that the initial reaction to the data release is more than offset subsequently. This only means that some opinion leaders are driving the market while no one is betting against them. However, we do not think that herding is playing a major role in asset price inflation, although it gains importance significantly when the bubble bursts. "Everyone is trying to get out through the same door" is even more severe in markets which are rather illiquid. This was also a phenomenon we experienced in 2007.

All in all, we would call the above-mentioned approaches additional driving factors behind the mechanism of credit crises that have a significant impact on the severity of a credit crisis. They are not mandatory in the sense that if these factors occur, they consequently lead to a credit crisis. The good news is that these approaches can help us understand the outcome of crises, and this is also true for credit markets. The basic problem is that asset price inflation is an often-seen phenomenon, but it is not always followed by a crisis. Nevertheless, asset price inflation is the dominating issue. Thus, what drives asset price inflation? The most important parameter is obviously excess liquidity provided by central banks!

A mainstream argument is that the cause of bubbles is excessive monetary liquidity in the financial system. Central banks flood the market with liquidity to support economic growth, also triggering rising demand for risky assets, causing both good assets and bad assets to appreciate excessively beyond their fundamentally fair valuation. In the long run, this level is not sustainable, while the trigger of the burst of the bubble is again policy shifts of central banks. The bubble will burst when central banks enter a more restrictive monetary policy, removing excess liquidity and consequently causing investors to get rid of risky assets given the rise in borrowing costs on the back of higher interest rates.

This is the theory, but what about the practice? The resurfacing discussion about rate cuts in the United States and in Euroland in mid-2005 was accompanied by expectations that inflation will remain subdued. Following this discussion, the impact of inflation on credit spreads returned to the spotlight. An additional topic regarding inflation worth mentioning is that if excess liquidity flows into assets rather than into consumer goods, this argues for low consumer price inflation but rising asset price inflation. In late 2000, the Fed and the European Central Bank (ECB) started down a monetary easing path, which was boosted by external shocks (9/11 and the Enron scandal), when central banks flooded the market with additional liquidity to avoid a credit crunch. Financial markets in general benefited from this excess liquidity, as reflected in the positive performance of almost all asset classes in 2004, 2005, and 2006, which argued for overall liquidity inflows but not for allocation shifts. It is not only excess liquidity held by investors and companies that underpins strong performing assets in general, but also the pro-cyclical nature of banking. In a low default rate environment, lending activities accelerate, which might contribute to an overheating of the economy accompanied by rising inflation. From a purely macroeconomic viewpoint, private households have two alternatives to allocate liquidity: consuming or saving. The former leads to rising consumer price inflation, whereas the latter leads to asset price inflation.

Ahead of the subprime turmoil, we have already seen some inflationary effects, however, not in traditional terms. While core CPI growth figures remain in relatively moderate terrain, asset prices rose significantly. This is not only true for the United States but also for Euroland. In chart 5.10 below, we point out that the missing link between inflation of consumer goods and spreads was replaced by the increasingly strong link between spreads and other asset classes. While consumption remained strong during recent years (especially in the United States), particularly riskier asset classes benefited from declining risk aversion and the improving global liquidity situation. Asset price inflation,

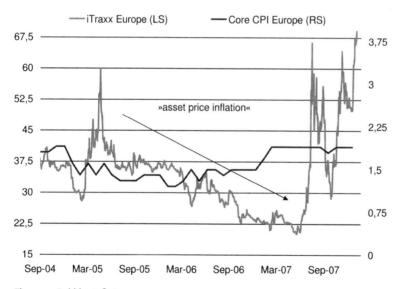

Fig. 5.10: Bubbles inflation

in general, is not a phenomenon which is limited to one specific market but rather has a global impact. However, there are some specific developments in certain segments of the market, as specific segments are more vulnerable against overshooting than others. Therefore, a strong decline in asset prices which are not directly linked to credit markets will lead to negative spillover effects on all risky asset classes due to the reduction of liquidity.

This is a very important finding, as it explains the mechanism behind a global crisis. Spillover effects are liquidity-driven and liquidity is a global phenomenon. Against the background of the ongoing integration of financial markets, spillover effects are inescapable, even in case there is no fundamental link between specific market segments. How can we explain decoupling between asset classes during financial crises? During the subprime turmoil in 2007, equity markets held up pretty well, although credit markets got hit hard.

- First, measuring spillover effects is a tough task as we obviously do not know what would have happened in case there would not have been a crisis in a specific segment. This argument is particularly important to explain the decoupling between equity and debt markets in 2007. Credit spreads widened significantly over the year, while global equity markets traded close to all-time-highs. However, we do not know where they would have traded in absence of any turbulence on the credit front. This would be important in order to quantify the negative impact from credits on equities in 2007.
- Second, asset price inflation is not an absolute problem but a relative one! This means that there are relative inflationary tendencies in a specific asset class compared to other asset classes. But it also means that asset price inflation has to be regarded as relative to consumer price inflation, that is, to the growth of money supply. This relative inflation approach supports the idea of "relative bubbles". During the subprime turmoil, asset price inflation especially in credits was the major problem, while other asset classes have shown this trend towards inflation to a much lesser extent. Hence, a burst of a bubble can trigger diverging effects in different market segments – not with respect to the direction, but with respect to the amplitude.

To sum up, the bubble argument is often used, as it is hard to confute the thesis that after a prolonged period of rising asset prices we face a bubble, since no one knows the true value of the underlying asset exactly. Always when asset prices reach historical highs, bubble aficionados resurface and argue that a potential burst of the bubble is right around the corner. When 10Y Bund yields dropped to 3.0% in Euroland (below 4% in the United States), many economists discussed if subdued yield levels in the United States and Euroland reflect irrational exuberance. Based on an econometric approach (based on short-term interest rates, inflation expectations and the business cycle), the fair value for government bond yields should be much higher. However, many concluded that there are several structural factors which underpin the current valuation; for example, demand from Asian central banks, the recycling of petrodollars and growing demand due to changed accounting standards. When credit spreads traded near historical lows in Q1 2007, spreads tightened significantly for a four-year lasting period. However, just looking at the absolute spread tightening is not a sufficient argument for a bubble. One could have used the same argument one year before, as credit spreads already traded close to the cyclical lows.

In the end, a simple two-dimensional chart analysis is not sufficient for an appropriate statement regarding bubble theories. In a first step, we have to analyze what a bubble is. The textbook definition is rather simple, stating that an asset-price bubble occurs when "Security prices move wildly above their true value". Unfortunately, this definition is not very helpful, as a few questions remain unanswered:

- What is the "true value" of credit spreads? Using historical data from rating agencies, we can derive a fair compensation for building up credit risk, which depends on the expected loss. The expected loss is simply the default probability multiplied by the loss given default $(1 - \text{Recovery rate})$. Hence, one can argue that the credit spread is determined by the required compensation for the risk of default. There is no obvious reason why we should believe in history repeating itself. Taking current default and recovery rates into account, spreads do not trade below the level sufficient to compensate for the expected loss! But what about the premium for the unexpected loss?

- What does "wildly" mean? There is no theory which provides certain levels of overvaluation. Even if we assume that we know the "fair value" of credit spreads, the absence of any theoretical construct to model overvaluation, we do not know to what extent it can deviate from the fair value. In our view, an absolute valuation does not make sense, because demand-supply patterns (and, in the end, asset prices rise only because demand exceeds supply) in financial markets are not focused on a single market but are rather driven by relative valuation. Consequently, we have to analyze relative prices from a cross-asset class perspective rather than based on absolute valuation levels.

While credit markets often look too dear from a fundamental point of view, strong market technicals explain ongoing demand for spread products. What is definite is: Technicals will not be able to withstand fundamentals forever! In the end, the business cycle will dominate structural developments in the market. From 2003 to 2007, the strong growth of derivatives markets (the technical bid) and the entry of new market participants (long-only investors looking for carry) argued for a tightening bias in credit spreads, although markets already started to look overbought at the end of 2005 from a pure fundamental perspective. If we believe that fundamentals will keep the upper hand in the medium to long term, there is something we can learn from bubble theories: the bigger the deviation of technical-driven markets from fundamental valuations, the stronger the necessary reaction to bring markets in line with fundamentals. In any case, adjustments are not necessarily reflected in the burst of a bubble; it can also be a very smooth process. Last but not least, asset price inflation has an impact on specific asset classes even if it does not apply to these segments at a specific point in time. Excess liquidity (provided by central banks) can trigger forced-to-invest behavior. Independent of the market a bubble bursts in, it removes liquidity from the global financial system. Finally, this will hurt all asset classes, with the exception of safe havens which benefit from flight-to-quality, as central banks are expected to cut rates in such a scenario.

5.4.2 The overshooting phenomenon

Closely linked to the bubble theory, Rudiger Dornbusch's famous overshooting paper[41] set a milestone for explaining "irrational" exchange rate swings and shed some light on the mechanism behind currency crises. This paper is one of the most influential papers written in the field of international economics, while it marks the birth of modern international macroeconomics. Can we apply some of the ideas to credit markets? The major input from the Dornbusch model is not only to better understand exchange rate moves; it also provides a framework for policymakers.[42] This allows us to review the policy actions we have seen during the subprime turmoil in 2007.

The background of the model is the transition from fixed to flexible exchange rates, while changes in exchange rates did not simply follow inflation differentials as previous theories suggest. On the contrary, they proved more volatile than most experts expected they would be. Dornbusch explained this behavior of exchange rates with sticky prices and an instable monetary policy, showing that overshooting of exchange rates is not necessarily linked to irrational behavior of investors ("herding"). Volatility in FX markets is a necessary adjustment path towards a new equilibrium in the market as a response to exogenous shocks, as the price adjustment in the domestic markets is too slow.

The basic idea behind the overshooting model is based on two major assumptions. First, the "uncovered interest parity" holds. Assuming that domestic and foreign bonds are perfect substitutes, while international capital is fully mobile (and capital markets are fully integrated), two bonds (a domestic and a foreign one) can only pay different interest rates if investors expect compensating movement in exchange rates. Moreover, the home country is small in world capital markets, which means that the foreign interest rate can be taken as exogenous. The model assumes "perfect foresight", which argues against traditional bubble theory. The second major equation in the model is the domestic demand for money. Higher interest rates trigger rising opportunity costs of holding money, and hence lower demand for money. In the contrary, an increase in output raises demand for money, while demand for money is proportional to the price level.

In order to explain what overshooting means in this context, we have to introduce additional assumptions. First of all, domestic prices do not immediately follow any impulses from the monetary side, while they adjust only slowly over time, which is a very realistic assumption. Moreover, output is assumed to be exogenous, while in the long run, a permanent rise in money supply causes a proportional rise in prices and in exchange rates. The exogenous shock to the system is now defined as an unexpected permanent increase in money supply, while prices are sticky in the short term. And as also output is fixed, interest rates (on domestic bonds) have to fall to equilibrate the system. As interest-rate parity holds, interest rates can only fall if the domestic currency is expected to appreciate. As the assumption of the model is that in the long run rising money supply must be accompanied by a proportional depreciation in the exchange rate, the overshooting model suggests that initial depreciation of the exchange rate must be larger than the long-run depreciation! That said, the exchange rate must overshoot the long-term equilibrium level. The idea of sticky prices is in the current macroeconomic discussion fully accepted, as it is a necessary assumption to explain many real-world data.

That is exactly what we need to explain the link to the credit market. The basic assumption of the majority of buy-and-hold investors is that credit spreads are mean-reverting. Ignoring default risk, spreads are moving around their fair value through the cycle. Overshooting is only a short-term phenomenon and it can be seen as a buying opportunity rather than the establishment of a lasting trend. This is true, but one should not forget that this is only true if we ignore default risk. This might be a calamitous assumption. Transferring this logic to the first subprime shock in 2007, it is exactly what happened as an initial reaction regarding structured credit investments. For example, investment banks booked structured credit instruments in marked-to-model buckets (Level 3 accounting) to avoid marked-to-market losses. The idea behind such transactions is that losses are only temporary, while in the long run spreads (and hence, prices) will move back to the fair value (i.e., the long-term equilibrium level). Consequently, the overshooting model should not be misunderstood as a justification to hold distressed securities; the overshooting approach explains exchange-rate movements completely ignoring default risk. This is less of a problem as the credit risk in the Dornbusch model is only linked to governments, while this might be a huge problem in credit markets.

However, the mechanism behind the model is also interesting for credits from a different perspective. What the model describes as an unexpected increase in money supply in real-world terms means that central banks do react to exogenous shocks independent of what we would call the long-term fundamental trend. In the long term, we can assume that central banks provide the economy with liquidity so that the output can be maximized using all input factors efficiently and under some conditions, in general an inflation targets. In the short term, nevertheless, central banks can be forced to flood the market with additional liquidity independent of the fundamental output trend. Exactly this happened in September 2001 as a reaction to the terror attacks, but also in 2007, when global central banks provided record liquidity injections to support the money market, which was virtually closed as a reaction to the subprime turmoil. This also means that these impulses from the money supply can trigger overshooting and further distortions in the market. If we follow the overshooting model, it definitely means that markets are far from being in an equilibrium stage at the end of 2007. Hence, a credit crisis itself can cause a reaction of central banks, which finally will lead to significant adjustment processes in other markets, like the FX market. A credit crisis therefore can be the trigger point of overshooting in other markets. This is exactly what we have observed during the subprime turmoil in 2007.

This is a crucial point, especially from the perspective of monetary policy makers. Providing additional liquidity would mean that there will be further distortions. Healing a credit crunch at the cost of overshooting in other markets. Consequently, liquidity injections can be understood as a final hope rather than the "silver bullet" in combating crises. In the context of the overshooting approach, liquidity injections could help to limit some direct effects from credit crises, but they will definitely trigger spillover effects onto other markets. In the end, the efficiency of liquidity injections by central banks depends on the benefit on the credit side compared to the costs in other markets. In any case, it proved not to be the appropriate instrument as a reaction to the subprime crisis in 2007.

5.4.3 Financial panic in credit markets

In contrast to the overshooting approach, financial panic models follow the basic idea of bubble theory, assuming that overshooting simply reflects an over-reaction of investors to sell in panic during a currency crisis. In this context, investors fully ignore fundamentals. From a credit perspective, however, we are especially interested in a specific feature of such models, as, for example, suggested by Obstfeld (1996).[43] This feature is the self-fulfilling character of such models, which can be easily transferred from currency to credit markets.

Financial panic models are based on the idea of a principal-agent: There is a government which is willing to maintain the current exchange rate using its currency reserves. Investors or speculators are building expectations regarding the ability of the government to maintain the current exchange-rate level. As an answer to a speculative attack on the currency, the government will buy its own currency using its currency reserves. There are three possible outcomes in this situation. First, currency reserves are big enough to combat the speculative attack successfully, and the government is able to keep the current exchange rate. In this case, there will be no attack as speculators are rational and able to anticipate the outcome. Second, the reserves of central banks are not large enough to successfully avert the speculative attack, even if only one speculator is starting the attack. Thus, the attack will occur and it will be successful. The government has to adjust the exchange rate. Third, the attack will only be successful if speculators join forces and start to attack the currency simultaneously. In this case, there are two possible equilibriums, a "good one" and a "bad one". The good one means the government is able to combat the currency peg, while the bad one means that the speculators are able to force the government to adjust the exchange rate. In this simple approach, the amount of currency reserves is obviously the crucial parameter to determine the outcome, as a low reserve leads to a speculative attack while a high reserve prevents attacks. However, the case of medium reserves, in which a concerted action of speculators is needed,

What can we learn from existing crises models?

is the most interesting case. In this case, there are two equilibriums (based on the concept of the Nash equilibrium): independent from the fundamental environment, both outcomes are possible. If both speculators believe in the success of the attack, and consequently both attack the currency, the government has to abandon the currency peg. The speculative attack would be self-fulfilling. If at least one speculator does not believe in the success, the attack (if there is one) will not be successful. Again, this outcome is also self-fulfilling. Both outcomes are equivalent in the sense of our basic equilibrium assumption (Nash). It also means that the success of an attack depends not only on the currency reserves of the government, but also on the assumption what the other speculator is doing. This is the interesting idea behind this concept: A speculative attack can happen independent from the fundamental situation. In this framework, any policy actions which refer to fundamentals are not the appropriate tool to avoid a crisis.

Self-fulfilling processes are a major characteristic of credit crises and we can learn a lot from the idea presented above. The self-fulfilling process of a credit crisis is that short-term overshooting might end up in a long-lasting credit crunch – assuming that spreads jump initially above the level that we would consider "fundamentally justified"; for instance, reflected in the current expected loss assumption. That said, the implied default rate is by far higher than the current one (e.g., the current forecast of the future default rate from rating agencies or from market participants in general). However, the longer the spread remains at an "overshooting level", the higher the risk that lower-quality companies will encounter funding problems, as liquidity becomes more expensive for them. This can ultimately cause rising default rates. In the end, realized default rates justify the implied default rate at the beginning of the crisis; a majority of market participants referr to it as *short-term overshooting*. Self-fulfilling processes are a major threat in a credit crisis, as was also the case during the subprime meltdown. If investors think that higher default rates are justified, they can trigger rising default rates just by selling credit-risky assets and causing wider spreads. This is independent from what we would call the fundamentally justified level!

The other interesting point is that the assumption of concerted action is not necessary in credit markets to trigger a severe action. If we translate the role of the government (defending a currency peg) into credit markets, we can define a company facing some aggressive investors who can send the company into default. Buying protection on an issuer via credit default swaps leads to wider credit spreads of the company, which can be seen as an impulse for the self-fulfilling process described above. We can even skip the assumption of aggressive investors who are benefiting from the fact that a company defaults. If some players are forced to hedge their exposure against a company by buying protection on the name, the same mechanism might be put to work. At the end of 2007, for example, banks were forced to reduce risk-weighted assets going into 2008. Hence, there was huge demand for protection on many names, which triggered a strong flattening trend in credit curves, as these protection buyers preferred the short end of the credit curve (one or two years). Buying protection led to wider spreads in shorter maturities, reducing the spread difference between shorter and longer-dated CDS contracts. This flattening trend also means that funding costs for many companies rose across all maturities. Such a technically driven concerted action of many players, consequently, can also cause an impulse for a crisis scenario, as is the case for currency markets in financial panic models.

5.4.4 Moral hazard in credit markets

Moral hazard is an often-mentioned buzzword in a credit crisis, as always when the banking sector is involved. There are many potential moral hazard situations in financial markets, on a macro as well as on a micro level. The credit-specific characteristic of moral hazard problems is linked to the nature of credit markets. The problem is that asymmetric information, a prerequisite for moral hazard problems in over-the-counter (OTC) markets, is much greater, as is the case for exchange-traded securities. Credits, but especially structured credits, are OTC-traded, accompanied by limited liquidity and low transparency. Credit markets are characterized by asymmetric information, much more than, for example, equity, FX or government bond markets.

The most popular moral hazard situation can clearly be found in the banking sector on a national but also on an international level. As national banks know that the national central bank is (almost) forced to avoid a default in the banking industry (given the immense spillover effect onto the real economy and the foreign perception of high vulnerability of the domestic financial system), the risk & return optimization for banks is skewed to take on more risk, as would be the case if they are fully responsible for also taking on the losses. Banks can increase return by keeping risk unchanged, because they know that in a worst-case scenario, the central bank will bail them out. Financial bail-outs of lending institutions by governments, central banks or other institutions encourages risky lending, as those that take the risks know that they will not have to carry the full burden of potential losses. Banks increase risk by surging loan exposure, while the most risky loans are paying the highest return. The same is true for national central banks/governments in their relationship with global financial institutions, like the IMF, which is basically the lender of last resort.

Moral hazard can also occur on the other side: with borrowers. The borrower knows his own credit quality better than the lender. Monitoring is one instrument against this kind of moral hazard, while the credit card business is a very good example for another way to limit expected losses for the credit card company: just by limiting the amount borrowers can spend when using their cards, independent of their credit quality. In theory, this is called *statistical discrimination*. However, the motivation of the originator to reduce expected losses is obviously linked to where the risky exposure finally ends up: on its own balance sheet, or is the lender able to transfer the risk to another counterparty? Assuming the latter, the originator of the risk is less motivated to properly monitor and evaluate the risk-and-return profile of the investor. That is exactly what happened during the US housing market boom, especially in 2005 and 2006.

This moral hazard problematic is well known and broadly discussed in academic literature; hence we ignore this topic in the following argumentation. We primarily focus on credit-specific moral hazard problems. Asymmetric information can cause a market failure as it triggers adverse selection, a concept introduced by George Akerlof in the early 1970s. The short version of the model is very simple. Buyers know less than sellers of a commodity. As buyers know that the seller better knows the true quality of the commodity, the buyer is only willing to pay the price for the lowest quality available. Potential sellers will stay away from the market in case the quality of their commodities is above the lowest quality the buyer is willing to pay a fair price for. In the end, this leads to a complete shutdown of the market. A similar trend could be observed in the structured credit market during the second half of 2007.

As mentioned above, asymmetric information is a basic problem in credit markets, in general. *Asymmetric information* just means that information is not allocated evenly through investors, originators, and other parties involved in trading credit-risky instruments. If investors know that there might be others who have better information, they would require an additional risk premium for buying credits. This is true when looking at plain-vanilla corporate bonds (the company always knows its current risk-and-return profile better than the investor; the syndicating bank always knows the quality of loans better than investors), but especially for the structured credit universe. Assuming a balance sheet CDO/CLO transaction which securitizes assets a bank is holding on its balance sheet, monitoring of the credit quality is done by the bank. Consequently, it should know its credit risks better than an external counterpart. The problem of selling credit-risky instruments under asymmetric information can be resolved in various ways, but the established one is rather simple. The seller mandates an external party to assess an objective valuation of the credit risk. These agents are known as rating agencies. Unfortunately, there is also a kind of moral hazard problem including rating agencies and their assessment of credit risk.

There are many examples which underpin that markets are front-running, already anticipating a rating action before the rating agencies actually announce any rating actions. This underpins market fetishists who believe in the market's function as an information intermediary: The market knows best! From a purely theoretical standpoint, there are three parties involved: the rating agency, the rated firm, and investors. The former is a kind of intermediary, transferring information about the company to the investor. Moreover, the information from the company is converted into a rating view, which is used by investors as a pricing input. In many cases, this is even the most important pricing input, for instance, if there is a downgrade to sub-investment grade and investors are forced to sell due to investment limitations. Consequently, there is a direct link between the rating agencies' view and the price of outstanding debt of the company. Investors trust the rating agency and think that the process of converting information is efficient and leads to a correct assessment of the company. As the rating agency has inside information, the investor relies on the agency and could not (ex ante) evaluate the company on his own. Ex post, perhaps, there could be different views, as is even the case at different rating agencies, which is also reflected in the existence of split ratings. As the rating agency has an information monopoly, the investor is dependent on the agency's ability to compile a complete and accurate report. Looking only at the agency-investor relationship and assuming the agency has the competence to process information efficiently, there is no reason for any informational asymmetries, and markets tend to be efficient. However, there remain two problems: Does the agency possess the necessary information, and does the relationship between the rated company and the rating agency have an impact on rating actions?

First, analyzing balance sheet items, especially credit protection ratios, could lead to different outcomes, since there is a broad range of different opinions and not one absolute truth. If the rating terminology is publicly available and known by all participants, then there is no informational problem. If the rating agency is completely transparent, investors could follow rating actions and even anticipate future actions if they evaluate relevant balance sheet items correctly. Nevertheless, the problem remains that there could be different views (also reflected in split ratings by different rating agencies) and/or incomplete information on how the rating process works. This, in our opinion, is not a major problem and could be solved easily by simply increasing transparency. Different views are preferable from an investor's standpoint and help to improve market efficiency. We focus rather on a structural problem. The major threat for investors is linked to the institutional agreement among the company, the agency and the investor. Companies and investors have pretty different needs regarding the work of the agencies in general. Such problems reflect a typical case of game theory and could be compared to widely known, standard moral hazard examples. Assume a car dealer has the order from a customer to sell a car, getting 10% of the price as commission. Hence, the car dealer has the intention to sell the car for a high price to increase his commission, while the car owner also benefits from a higher price. Assuming further that the car owner and the car dealer have better knowledge of the condition of the car (the major price determinant) than the buyer, both have the intention to make the car sound better than it is. In any case, the loser is (most likely) the buyer. The good news is that there is a very simple solution to this problem: the car dealer has to provide a guarantee regarding the condition of the car. Translating this idea to our case, with the car dealer being the rating agency, the car owner being the company, and the buyer being the investor, the information inefficiency among the three parties could be solved via a guarantee. The rating agency must guarantee that it made a best effort to use a transparent rating methodology and will provide continuous updates on the condition of the company. This will help prevent negative surprises and will tend to clarify the reasons for different views of the rating agency and the investor. The guarantee of a rating agency is simply its reputation within the marketplace, and consequently, rating agencies have the intention to assign ratings in line with the fundamental risk assessment, which is theoretically the major factor also for the pricing of instruments in debt markets. Nevertheless, it is obvious that there are differences between markets and rating agencies with respect to information flow, which is reflected in a faster reaction of markets compared to ratings. This is rather an over shooting-like character of financial markets (as discussed above), while credit ratings are still good indicators of a company's creditworthiness in the long term.

During the first wave of the subprime crisis, moral hazard was often cited as being responsible for many problems deriving from the US housing front. The most obvious moral hazard problems in the subprime case are the following:

- The borrower tends to understate his own risk of a default by concealing relevant parameters, as the mortgage bank takes the losses in case of foreclosure. This tendency is supported by lax lending standards.
- The mortgage banks do not have an incentive to monitor the idiosyncratic risk of the single homeowner properly, as it passes on these risks to investment banks in a pooled format. This is also reflected in lax lending standards.
- Investment banks do not have an incentive to properly monitor the credit risk of the pool of home equity loans, as they pass on these risks to investors, primarily via securitization (RMBS, CDOs, etc.).
- Rating agencies benefit from the strongly growing, structured credit universe, as a rating assessment is needed by a huge majority of the investor base. The innovative power of structured credit players put rating agencies in a defensive position. They have to react to all new features included in the variety of instruments brought to the market in a very short period of time (the introduction of new instruments accelerated with the ongoing tightening of credit spreads from 2003 to 2007). A majority of the above-mentioned new features in the structured finance arena have been implemented during this period. Rating agencies have already established waiting lists in 2006 and 2007, as demand for structured credit ratings increased dramatically during this time. This does not mean that rating agencies had an incentive to asses their ratings carelessly, but at least that the pressure on rating agencies to find new models to evaluate specific structures and features increased markedly. A good example was the introduction of CPDOs in 2006 (please refer to Part I of the book for a more detailed description of CPDOs), when rating agencies clearly underestimated the risk of a more pronounced, systemic spread widening in a crisis scenario, assigning a AAA-rating to structures which generated dramatic losses during the first subprime shock in 2007 (some of them have even defaulted).
- From an ex post perspective, the business case of a monoline insurer seems to be a "no-brainer". They insured a huge amount of instruments relative to their capital base (i.e., equity). In good times, they earn a decent amount of money by providing a guarantee which will not be used. In bad times, they are the first to get into trouble! This is what we experienced in 2007.

- Many investors did not properly monitor the risk, as they invested in best qualities directly or via vehicles. Moreover, there is obviously symmetric information between the seller and the buyer of those risky structures. A "correct" valuation of such investments is often impossible for the investor without further information from the originating banks or the arranger of these structured credit products.
- In the end, one can even blame the government – that is, governmental authorities – for a lax regulatory environment, as also those institutions obviously benefited from the strongly growing US housing market.

If no one feels responsible to monitor investments and risks properly, too much risk might be generated. This is a major reason for the subprime turmoil. Moral hazard obviously plays a very prominent role in credit crises in general, but in the subprime meltdown in particular! Finally, someone has to pay the bill. Historically, this was often the taxpayer (at least to a large extent).

5.5 The credit cycle

5.5.1 The impact of derivatives on the credit cycle

The basic concept of the credit cycle is simply the idea that credit spreads should be closely linked to the business cycle. Not only spreads but also default rates, recovery values, and, in the end, expected (or realized) loss is linked to the cycle rather than being stable over time. This has already been implemented in modern econometric approaches[44] and refers to the economic rationale of credit-risky instruments. During times of economic expansion, company earnings benefit, cash-flow generation accelerates, and in the end the credit metrics of companies improves. This translates into declining default probabilities, arguing for a decreasing premium for default-risky instruments. As a consequence, spreads should tighten in an expansionary economic environment. The basic assumption is that fundamental developments determine the long-term trend in credit markets, while technical factors or structural breaks determine the short-term trend.

And what role do credit derivatives play in respect to the cyclical behavior of credit spreads? Credit derivatives do not change the credit cycle itself, but they have an impact on the frequency and the amplitude of the swing of a cycle. Derivatives improve liquidity, transparency, and allocation efficiency of markets, but they add momentum in case a tail event occurs. Markets become

The Anatomy of a
Credit Crisis

more vulnerable to exogenous shocks if the leverage increases. Traditional fundamental spread indicators lose in importance for the short to medium-term trend in credit markets, especially in a distressed environment. Market technicals primarily affect the credit cycle, especially via the credit derivatives market.

The famous *technical bid* was the buzzword for many years in credit markets, when spreads entered a four-year so-called Goldilocks period at the beginning of 2003, which was stopped by the US subprime turmoil in Q2 2007. The technical bid describes the strong demand for credits driven by the immense growth of the structured credit and credit derivatives universe. This demand kept spreads at historically tight levels, while causing a decoupling between fundamental trends in the credit market and the valuation levels for credit-risky instruments. Many banks (especially European ones) reduced risk-weighted assets in the aftermath of the credit crunch in 2001/2002. The result was a significant decline in interest income. As spreads retightened strongly at the beginning of 2003, the only alternative to boost interest income by increasing carry income on credit investments at this time was to increase leverage (as investing in lower-rated names was fairly limited given the less favorable treatment of such investments from an economic capital perspective). The innovative power in the credit derivatives universe accompanied by a rising popularity of CDOs offer an attractive solution for this investment problem of banks. Investments in mezzanine CDO pieces generated enough spread income to fulfill interest-income targets, while the capital requirement for relatively high-rated credit derivatives and structured credit transactions (AA/AAA-rated CDO investments offered a spread in line with sub-investment grade single name credits) was fairly low. The strong demand for synthetic CDOs led to an accelerating transaction volume, which peaked in the first half of 2007. Moreover, it was a major pillar of the tight spread valuation at this time. CDO arrangers (the banks that sell CDOs) are creating synthetic risk via the CDS market, which is being purchased by other banks. That said, the arranger is short-credit risk. To hedge this short position, the arranger is forced to tap the synthetic market, selling protection on single names to hedge idiosyncratic risks and on indices – like the iTraxx universe, but also on standardized tranched products – to hedge systematic risks. The tranche hedging is primarily driven by the need to hedge correlation risk. Strong demand for synthetic products translated into selling protection activities from these CDO arrangers, leading to continuous tightening pressure on credit spreads.

Despite the popular thesis that the credit cycle is dead, fundamental trends in the market will continue to drive credit spreads in the long term. The basic cyclical behavior of fundamentals is obviously beyond question, but the rising popularity we have seen over the last few years of structured credit products has an impact on the amplitude and the frequency of the swings of the cycle. The credit market experienced a dramatic structural change over the last decade. Besides the immense growth of the market, new market participants entered the derivatives arena. These market players are implementing completely new investment strategies using innovative instruments from the derivatives universe. The well-known derivatives discussion (in the 1970s regarding FX derivatives and in the 1980s/1990s concerning equity derivatives) also applies for credits: the establishment of a derivatives market improves the transparency, liquidity and allocation efficiency in normal times, while derivatives potentially add momentum to the market in case tail events occur. Against this background, the president of the ECB, Jean-Claude Trichet, stated in April 2007 that "The fear is that a large proportion of market participants may have become excessively complacent", and continued that "Dangerous herding may create risks to the financial system." Herding effects are closely linked to the use of derivatives and the trading strategies of hedge funds. The major argument that an LTCM crisis cannot happen again, as there is no single big player in the hedge fund community but rather a huge amount of smaller, independent funds, is foiled by the fact that a majority of funds are using the same models to implement the same strategies.

Consequently, in theory we assume that there should be a close link between different financial market segments, as – at least in the long run – all these

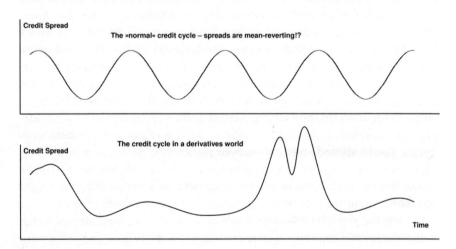

Fig. 5.11: The credit cycle

The Anatomy of a
Credit Crisis

segments should be driven by the economic environment. We highlight two basic ideas which reflect how markets are linked and why theory often fails to explain correlation patterns between specific segments.

The cyclical aspect of financial crises was also a basic assumption of the US economist Hyman Minsky's (1991-1996) theories regarding the emergence of speculative bubbles. In his ground-breaking work back in the 1970s, he disagreed with the mainstream economists at this time as he argued that booms and busts in financial markets are inevitable in a free market economy. He argued that regulation imposed by the government could smooth this "boom & bust" cycle, opposing deregulation that characterized the 1980s, especially in the US. Without explicitly mentioning it, Minsky's ideas provide also a useful explanation of the equity-debt cycle discussed below. His cyclical theory of financial crises describes the fragility of financial markets as a function of the business cycle. In the aftermath of a recession, firms finance themselves in a very safe way. As the economy grows and expected profits rise, firms take on more speculative financing, anticipating rising profits and that loans can be repaid easily. Increased financing translates into rising investment, triggering further growth of the economy, making lenders confident that they will receive a decent return on their investments. In such a boom period, lenders tend to abstain from guarantees of success, i.e. reflected in less covenants or in rising investments in low-quality companies. Even if lenders know that the firms are not able to repay their debt, they believe these firms will refinance elsewhere as their expected profits rise. While this is still a positive scenario for equity markets, the economy has definitely taken on too much credit risk. Consequently, the next stage of the cycle is characterized by rising defaults. This translates into tighter lending standards of banks. Here, the similarities to the subprime turmoil become obvious. Refinancing becomes impossible, especially for lower-rated companies, and more firms default. This is the beginning of a crisis in the real economy, while during the recession, firms start to turn to much more conservative financing, and the cycle closes again.[45]

5.5.2 Credit spreads and safe-haven yields

Our first example is the relationship between the yield curve derived from safe havens (government bonds, or *govies*) and credit spreads. Interest rates and safe-haven yields have been an important indicator for credit spreads in the past, while recent developments and correlation analysis argue for a decoupling of both figures. Only if exogenous shocks occur, flight-to-quality effects lead to

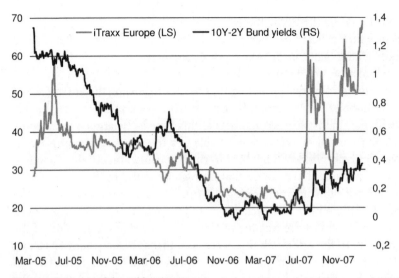

70 ‍ 1,4

────iTraxx Europe (LS) ────10Y-2Y Bund yields (RS)

Fig. 5.12: Spreads and the yield curve

the traditional pattern: lower govie yields and a flatter govie curve should be accompanied by wider spreads. There are two basic theories to explain the link between safe havens and spread products. The macroeconomic view supports a negative correlation between credit and interest rate returns. In case of an economic downturn, central banks lower rates and yields decline, generating a positive return on safe havens. At the same time, default rates should increase in an economic downturn and credit investors demand a higher risk premium. Wider credit spreads translate into a negative return of spread products. So far the theory; chart 5.12 show a different picture.

We could not observe this traditional pattern during the last few years, with spreads seeming to be completely decoupled from safe havens. Even the opposite theory, arguing that spreads should decline in case yields decline, as investors are looking for investment alternatives to generate a sufficient carry income, could not be justified by market data dating back to 2004. The simple reason for this phenomenon is that new market participants are less dependent on movements on the interest rate side. A hedge fund manager does not need to implement a traditional risk-return optimized approach, and therefore the relative return of asset classes is less important, with total return generation being the main target. Hence, theories based on allocation issues are outdated. As long as yields are in a terrain which does not argue for major macroeconomic distortions, credit spreads remain relatively unimpressed by movements in the interest rate market. However, this is not true in any case. If tail events occur, flight-to-quality effects appear and trigger a textbook-like behavior of safe havens and market spreads as we have seen in the correction which hit markets in February and March 2007. While the iTraxx Crossover widened by more than 70 bp within two weeks, 10Y Bund yields dropped by 17 bp at the same time. Obviously, correlation patterns change in crisis periods.

5.5.3 Credit Spreads and FX movements

Our next example is the currency relation between the Japanese yen and the euro. From a fundamental perspective, exchange rate moves have an impact on spread markets via two transmission channels: There is an impact on the competitiveness of globally operating companies, while FX moves directly affect the attractiveness of assets in domestic currencies. Therefore, credit spreads should be linked to FX markets. We argue that the dominating role of hedge funds in the credit market argues for another transmission channel. The major currency for European companies is still the USD. Assuming the above-mentioned fundamental links are still valid, we should observe that a declining USD should hurt European companies and trigger wider spreads. However, when we look at the correlation pattern between the euro-USD exchange rate versus the generic Crossover spread, we find that this link is rather weak. In contrast to the USD, the fundamental impact of the Japanese Yen on European companies should be rather limited, as the importance of the Japanese economy for European companies is below that of the US economy. However, historical data suggest that the opposite is true. As can be seen in chart 5.13, we plot the EUR-JPY versus the Crossover spread and derive a much better R-squared compared to the spread/USD link. Assuming statistical relevance, the argument for a declining importance of the USD versus the JPY on the European spread market can be explained by the dominating role of hedge funds in the business. Many credit hedge funds not only implement leveraged investment strategies but also leveraged funding strategies, primarily using the JPY as a cheap funding source. A weaker JPY accompanied by tighter spreads is the best of all worlds for a yen-funded credit hedge fund. However, these funds should be more linked to the JPY than to the USD. One impact is obviously that the favorable growth outlook in Euroland triggers a strong EUR and tighter spreads of European companies (which benefit the most from the improving economic environment). However, the diverging fit between EUR spreads, the USD, and the JPY, respectively, un-

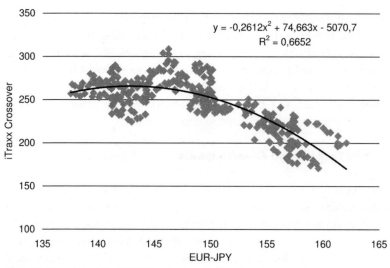

$$y = -0,2612x^2 + 74,663x - 5070,7$$
$$R^2 = 0,6652$$

iTraxx Crossover

EUR-JPY

Fig. 5.13: Spreads and the EUR-JPY exchange rate from June 22, 2004 to April 20, 2007

derpins the argument that technical factors as well as structural developments dominate fundamental trends at least in certain periods of the cycle.

5.5.4 Excursus: Decoupling of cycles

The most famous explanatory variable for credit spreads is still equity markets. The basic idea is that strong equity markets should go hand in hand with tighter credit spreads and vice versa. This idea is also the basis for capital structure arbitrageurs, who, in general, set up trading strategies using all instruments available on the balance sheet of a single company. They try to find pricing anomalies, which they aim to exploit by synthetically replicating a specific instrument which refers to the company. This trading approach is especially popular in the hedge fund industry and at proprietary trading desks in banks. From a top-down perspective, this idea can be easily transferred to an index level, being a major argument for cross-asset allocation strategies. In many real money account portfolios (insurance companies, fund managers), the share of credit-risky instruments is closely correlated to the share of equities.

Structural models date back to the seminal work of Robert Merton in 1974.[46] They derive the default probability directly from information about the company's capital structure. The central quantity that is modeled is the firm or en-

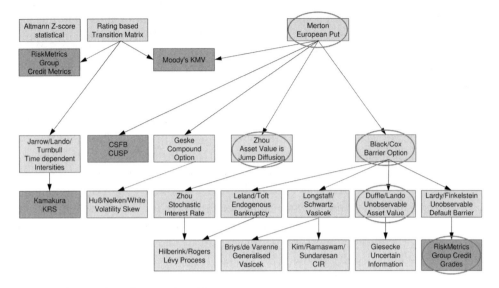

Fig. 5.14: The genealogy of structural models

terprise value. Consequently, structural models are also known as Merton-type models, or firm- or enterprise-value models. There are several models discussed in the financial literature, with the ongoing development of new approaches still being in process (please see the major model types in chart 5.14). They can be broadly classified into two groups: the classic Merton-type approach and the so-called first-passage-of-time framework, which dates back to Black and Cox.[47] The classic Merton approach assumes a firm with a very simple capital structure. The liability side comprises a single zero coupon bond with maturity T. The asset value is modeled as a geometrical Brownian motion. At maturity, the model implicitly assumes that the company's assets are liquidated and the proceeds are distributed among bondholders and stockholders following the strict priority rule. The company's debt is repaid first, and only if the asset value exceeds the face value of the debt; the remaining proceeds are distributed among the stockholders. If the asset value does not exceed the face value of the debt, the bondholders suffer a loss that amounts to face value minus asset value and the stockholders lose everything. Therefore, the payoff structure for the stockholders equals that of a European call option on the assets, with the face value of the debt as the strike price. This enables us to use standard Black-Scholes[48] methodology to price the value of the equity (the European call option) and derive the value of the defaultable debt as the risk-free value of the debt minus the value of the put option. Note that the payoff of the underlying options is only evaluated at maturity of the single debt instrument. The complete balance sheet is modeled with a finite time horizon T, which corresponds to the maturity date of the firm's liability. Therefore, we can use standard European option-pricing formulas.

In practical terms, a declining share price and rising implied equity volatility should be accompanied by wider credit spreads. In case of divergent trends, arbitrage trades are implemented to benefit from the return of volatilities, prices or spreads to the fair (model-based) pricing relationship. However, the word *arbitrage* is misleading, as these trades have a speculative character rather than generating "risk-free profits". So far the theory. In practice, these approaches have not proved stable over time, which is especially true at a company-specific level. The most famous case was the equity-debt decoupling we saw at General Motors in Q2 2005. At this time, capital structure arbitrageurs lost money by betting on General Motors, including a long position in credits, hedged by a short position in equities. Unfortunately, markets discounted restructuring rather than default, and the immense spread blowout was accompanied by a rising share price (Kerkorian's bid), which triggered losses on both sides of the position. In the default scenario, the investor receives the recovery value on the long credit position, but the short equity position will more than offset the loss assuming a share price of zero. In the restructuring scenario, in contrast, assets might be shifted to benefit the shareholder at the expense of the bondholder, and the cap' structure player realizes a double loss on the credit (losing 1- recovery) and on the equity position (due to the expected rise of the share price. The major problem of these approaches is basically two assumptions:

- In case of default, the value of equity is zero. This is unfortunately not true in any case. In the basic Merton theory, a *default* is defined as bankruptcy of a company. The company has to sell all its assets, allocating the purchase price to the creditor following strict rules regarding the seniority of the claims. As, per definition, the value (i.e., the equity) of the company is below the face value of debt (which is the definition of default in basic Merton models), there is no money left for the shareholder. The share price has to drop to zero in this case and the hedging strategy (short equity) works. However, the assumption that default is the only credit event is definitely wrong, especially when credit derivatives have been used to build up the long credit position. In a standard ISDA contract (the legal framework in the credit derivatives universe), there are other credit events than default; namely failure-to-pay and re-structuring. In particular, the latter is a potential threat for capital structure positions, as it might adversely affect the position of shareholders versus bondholders. Moreover, there are technical risk factors like succession events (which, for example, steps in if a company is splitting up business units, de-merges, etc.). There might be a loss on the credit investment, while the stock trades above zero.

- The capital structure over the investment period is determined by market moves only. In the general approach, we know the capital structure (the relation between equity and debt of a company) at the beginning of our analysis and assume that moves in the share price affect the capital structure over time. There are no other factors which drive the relative valuation of equity versus debt. In practice, this assumption is also wrong. The capital structure itself might be a target of the financial policy of the company itself. The company could, for example, implement shareholder-friendly measures, like increasing dividend payments or share buybacks. These actions have an impact on the capital structure of the company and the share price, as the only parameter for the theoretical default probability is losing explanatory power.

Besides the arguments why the implementation of structural approaches in practice does not deserve the attribute "arbitrage", there are more general and structural trends which argue against a positive correlation between equity and debt through the whole cycle. For example, the flood of liquidity central banks provided in the aftermath of 9/11 and to fight the market impact of Enronian economics played a crucial role in the asset-pricing mechanism (asset price inflation) during the last few years. This is also an important factor in the relative pricing of different instruments or market segments. We think that central banks can partly affect the amplitude of cyclical swings but not the character of the cycle itself. We will come back later to this thesis, which is also a major argument in bubble theory.

However, the basic cycle itself argues against a stable correlation between equity and debt markets, which can be simply illustrated using balance sheet parameters and their impact on the relative valuation of the capital structure. Leverage and profit growth of companies are crucial parameters for pricing equity and debt through the cycle. In chart 5.15, we highlight the investment cycle depicting the German DAX index and the iBoxx NFI spread back to 1999. The positive equity performance from 1999 until March 2000 was accompanied by a relatively stable spread environment, as rising leverage benefited shareholders while the positive sentiment offset deteriorating credit fundamentals. During 2000, the picture changed dramatically, with an increase in leverage and declining profit growth. Consequently, spreads widened and stocks entered a three-year-long bear market. Spreads reached their all-time high in Q4 2002, while stocks marked their cyclical lows in Q1 2003. Spreads are front-running in this stage of the investment cycle, as leverage starts to decline while profit growth is lagging. From 2003 to 2005, improving profitability, lower leverage, and high cash positions favored stocks and credits.

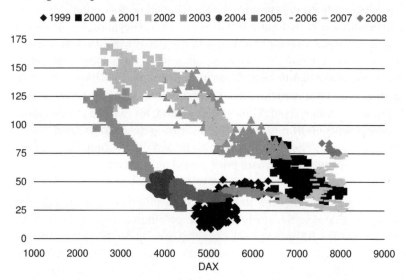

Fig. 5.15: Correlation pattern are not stable through the cycle

In the subprime crisis, the first victims of a changed correlation pattern between equity and debt were some hedge funds that implemented capital structure strategies. In early 2007, these funds implemented some long credit positions hedged by short stock market or long equity volatility positions. This proved to be a serious problem when credit spreads started to widen, while, at the beginning of the crisis, equity markets could withstand negative spillover effects from the credit market. This trend triggered tremendous losses on the books of some capital structure arbitrageurs.

From a cyclical perspective, 2006 was dominated by a renaissance of shareholder-friendly measures, while the profit growth rate already reached its peak. The credit environment was still healthy, although there were initial signals that we had already reached the peak in the cycle. Following a period with a very

The Anatomy of a
Credit Crisis

low correlation between credit spreads and implied volatility, patterns in 2007 changed dramatically, triggered by the fact that the driving factors for equities were potential threats for credits, namely rising M&A and LBO volumes. That said, credit investors cannot trust traditional patterns and rely on strong equity markets as an argument to buy credit risk, as Merton failed to foresee the relative performance of equity and credit markets at the beginning of 2007. A decoupling is either a temporary or a cyclical phenomenon. Temporary decoupling materialized, for example, in case of exogenous shocks due to a different pace of convergence to a new equilibrium in different market segments (i.e., more efficient markets are faster in discounting news). But a decoupling trend can also have a cyclical character, as equity/debt markets are not positively correlated in a specific stage of the cycle. While stock markets benefit from idiosyncratic news (especially LBO and M&A linked), companies have already started to increase leverage, implementing shareholder-friendly measures (share buybacks, record dividends). In such an environment, stocks and credits are only positively correlated if tail events occur. The subprime turmoil was a good example in this respect.

While the subprime crisis shows some similarities to previous turbulences, there are also some subprime specifics which are crucial for the relative valuation of equity and debt. In chart 5.16, we plot the spread of the iTraxx Europe

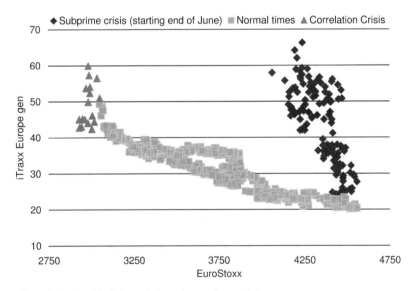

Fig. 5.16: Equity-debt linkage during crises and normal times

versus the EuroStoXX. During the correlation crisis in May 2005 (please refer to the crisis section 5.3.2 for a detailed explanation of the situation in May 2005), the usual correlation between both markets was interrupted, which is reflected in the changed correlation paradigm. This, however, can be explained by the credit-specific character of the correlation crisis, with (correlation) technicals rather than fundamentals having been the basic trigger behind the move. In the subprime crisis of 2007, the spread blowout was more pronounced, and it lasted much longer. However, the correlation pattern is distorted less, as equities did not remain unaffected. The correlation crisis only affected credits, while subprimemania had more spillover potential. A crucial question regarding the impact of exogenous shocks on the equity-debt cycle is to what extent second and third-round effects will hit the real economy, and consequently will they be a burden on the earnings of financial and non-financial companies? These effects are negative for all instruments placed on the capital structure of a company.

6
Epilogue: How can we avoid Credit Crises in the future?

We comprehensively discussed what the major drivers are behind credit crises, also showing that the trigger events of historical crises were different, while there is no general outcome of financial market crises. However, there are similar mechanisms behind crises, and we also can identify some input factors which have an impact on the vulnerability of financial markets.

All efforts to avoid crises in the future by monetary or international author-ities are focused on these vulnerability indicators, for instance, the regulatory environment, legal issues and removal of mechanisms which hinder finan-cial markets from working properly, in general. Nevertheless, crises occur in an almost regular cycle, although all market participants including the above-mentioned authorities are aware of potential warning signals. This brings us to the conclusion that financial crisis in general, and especially credit crises, are rather normal adjustment processes towards a new market equilibrium in case a tail event occurs, when structural changes distort the mechanism of finan-cial markets or when excessive tendencies trigger a deviation of market prices from what we would call fair value. There are many good reasons why what we call a *crisis* is just a necessary process which brings markets quickly to a new equilibrium.

From a purely market technical perspective, one can argue that a quick adjust-ment process is preferable to a smooth adjustment process which takes longer, as during the adjustment process markets do not work in an efficient manner. Moreover, if we analyze credit crises, we can even argue that jump processes in credit markets are pretty normal processes. Jump-to-default is a major risk parameter in all kinds of models which cover credit-risky instruments. It is a credit-inherent character that adjustment processes are not smooth, but char-acterized by jumps as well as under- and overshooting. Using the terminology of structural models, a credit-risky bond simplified equals a short put position referring to the value of the company. An idiosyncratic shock could trigger a sharp drop in the underlying value of the company, and the put is moving closer to its strike price. In such a case, the value of the put reacts sharply. The same is true for credit spreads.

Epilogue: How
can we avoid
Credit Crises in
the future?

Credit Crises. J. Felsenheimer and P. Gisdakis
Copyright © 2008 WILEY-VCH Verlag GmbH & Co. KGaA, Weinheim
ISBN: 978-3-527-50375-9

If jump processes are a pretty normal behavior of single-name credits, why should credits behave differently on a market level? Obviously, we can simply split credit risk into two parts: an idiosyncratic one (known as alpha) and a systematic one (beta). During the first wave of the subprime crisis in the summer of 2007, idiosyncratic default risk remained limited (except for US mortgage players), while also the European credit universe experienced a sharp widening in credit spreads, including mostly names which were not directly involved in subprime issues. Even for European banks, which were linked to the US housing market, the subprime problem was not an event which triggered concerns that one of the big banks could fail. However, the rising systematic risk, including malfunctioning of money markets and the like, caused a sharp adjustment process in the market. That brings us to the conclusion that not only corporate bonds but also credit markets in general tend to overshoot and show jump behavior in crisis times.

There is a rather simple explanation why the adjustment process in credit markets is characterized by huge volatility, jump processes, and overshooting. By transferring the idea behind structural models on an index level, we can argue that credit markets are highly vulnerable to exogenous systematic shocks. The subprime crisis triggered immediately a re-pricing of financial stocks, also reflecting that market participants discounted a recapitalization of the banking industry. This does have an impact on the senior part of the capital structure, reflected in a significantly rising value of the put option. And bondholders are short this put option. This is also true in case a systemic shock hits the financial system as a whole. Credit crises tend to have systemic shocks as a trigger event. This was true not only for the subprime turmoil but also for the 2001/2002 credit crunch, which many participants consider as an event which was purely linked to micro-fundamentals. However, the spread explosion in 2002 was not driven by fears that some companies besides Enron were involved in accounting scandals, but rather by fears that accounting scandals are a broad, systemic problem. These fears (in combination with some industry-specific trends especially in the telecom and the auto sectors, as well as the tremendous drop in global stock markets) led to a blowout of the whole credit market, as the systematic part of the risk premium experienced a drastic re-pricing.

We do not see the sharp spread widening in a situation which we call credit crisis as the major problem, although we do not ignore that credit crises trigger immense direct losses in the financial system on the back of the importance of credit-risky instruments for the financial sector. The major problem of credit crises is rather the fact that they have a much broader impact on the economy as, for example, a re-pricing in stock markets. Spillover effects are the most severe part of a credit crisis, as they cause by far the biggest losses within a crisis scheme; in the end, they even negatively affect basic transmission mechanisms in financial systems and in the real economy, which results in reduced or even declining growth. Not-realized growth causes enormous costs.

If spillover effects are the major problem in credit crises, while crises are a normal phenomenon in the market, the concentration of identifying vulnerability indicators does not make much sense. Spillover effects, unfortunately, are supported by globalization, capital market integration and mobility of risk capital. Nobody would seriously argue that we should limit these developments, which have a very positive impact on the financial system as a whole and, consequently, on global growth.

As usual, however, voices which call for more regulation resurface any time a crisis occurs. The first reaction to the subprime turmoil was a call for broad regulation including:

- Underwriting standards in the US mortgage market
- Accounting standards (especially regarding off-balance sheet vehicles)
- Rating agencies (following the triple-digit billion downgrades in the structured credit universe)
- And, as usual, hedge funds.

Does regulation really help? Obviously, one of the major reasons for the subprime turmoil involves lax lending standards of mortgage banks, which can be explained by the fact that banks acted as an intermediary rather than a risk taker. Banks generated subprime loan exposure only because they knew that there was somebody in the background who was taking on the risk, namely the CDO manager, that is, CDO investors. That also means that the motivation of banks to properly analyze lending activities in the subprime segments was pretty subdued from a risk perspective. Obviously, banks ignored the fact that they will be the lender of last subprime resort in any case. Forcing banks to put risk on their own balance sheets means also that these transactions have to pass through a bank's risk control systems, and hence be monitored in an appropriate way. However, the financial industry will keep its innovative power, finding ways to optimize investments and lending activities also using off-balance sheet vehicles. Any regulation limiting the innovative power of the banking industry will be contra-productive against this background.

Regulation of rating agencies is also continuously resurfacing hand in hand with the debt crisis in general. The major problem is not that rating agencies assign a triple-A rating to some structures which will be in default only a few months later. The real cause of the problem is that investors believe in AAA-ratings without knowing exactly how they were generated.

An AAA is not always an AAA, that is, there is no "master scale" for ratings among different asset classes. When we compare ratings by the Big Three (Fitch, Moody's and Standard & Poor's) and ratings for different market segments, neither the ratings of rating agencies nor the intra-ratings are consistent. In terms of default probabilities, the results can be off by a factor of ten. In contrast to common belief, the rating agencies do not internally use a master scale to gauge their models. Instead, they publish default and transition studies, which raises the question whether the ratings are consistent between different rating agencies ("inter-ratings") and among different asset-classes of the same agency ("intra-ratings"). The number of defaults is often very limited; for example, Fitch's default study of sovereign ratings identified six defaults within the last ten years. To circumvent this problem, we use rating transition matrices which refer to a much larger data base. Additionally, as we are interested in restricted investors, only high grade investments are possible. Thus, a downgrade to junk status is considered a "HY-default" (as we assume that the investor has to unwind his position). For a given transition matrix a HY-default state is introduced, and using the Markov chain-model (matrix-multiplication) the HY-default probabilities can be calculated. According to our own estimation, the inter-ratings differ dramatically in some cases. For example, the expected AAA 5Y HY default probability for corporate bonds amounts to 0.04% (Fitch), to 0.26% (Moody's) and to 0.56% (S&P). Also, the intra-ratings (between different asset classes) deviate significantly. We calculate the 5Y HY default probability for BBB-rated instruments using Fitch data: this amounts to 35% for CDOs, 21% for corporate bonds and only 2% for Western European RMBS. Rating agencies implicitly admit that their ratings depend on the type of the asset; for example, Fitch applies a bonus in its CDO model if the underlying is an ABS transaction and not a corporate bond (only exception: no bonus is applied if the ABS is a CDO).

In November 2007, a CPDO (UBS's ELM B.V. – Series 103 – Tyger Notes 2017) experienced a cash-out event after the structure dropped to 10% of the initial net asset value, being forced to sell its holdings. The structure was launched in March 2007 and referred to financials only. Within 9 months, an investor in a triple-A structure consequently lost about 90% of his investment. AAA is definitely not AAA, while AAA in structured finance does not mean that there are no significant price declines. The interesting thing with the above-mentioned CPDO is that one can lose 100% of an investment without experiencing any default in the underlying asset pool. This also means that the strategy to book all AAA-rated assets in hold-to-maturity buckets to avoid marked-to-market accounting can prove to be a disastrous strategy in a credit crisis!

Last but not least, regulatory action regarding hedge funds seems to be a favored topic every time a crisis occurs. This was also true when the subprime turmoil hit markets in 2007 until people realized that hedge funds were probably the major winners. Although the two Bear Stearns hedge funds have been identified with hindsight as the trigger event of the first major subprime wave in June 2007, the hedge funds industry had left the subprime battlefield as the winner, as the largest hit was taken by the banking industry. This was not always the case, for example, during the LTCM crisis.

Finally, regulation is not the key of wisdom for avoiding future crises, while it can help to reduce the vulnerability of the financial system and therefore the negative impact from a crisis on the real economy. But the traditional argument against regulation also holds in respect to a credit crisis, as over-regulation simply hinders capital markets from working properly, while regulation only triggers replacement strategies, which are probably not efficient from an economic perspective.

We will have to cope with crises also in the future as they are normal adjustment processes in an innovative, utility-maximizing world in which decisions under uncertainty remain the driving force behind growth. After the subprime turmoil comes to an end, the next crisis will hit markets in a couple of years. This is as certain as paying taxes and death. Denying this normal pattern means ignoring reality and missing opportunities, as there are always winners, even in a crisis. In November 2007, for example, the US hedge fund LAHDE Capital announced that it generated 1,000% return in 2007 by betting against US mortgages (via shorting the ABX market).

Bibliography

.

1 Joseph R. Mason and Joshua Rosner. How Resilient Are Mortgage Backed Securities to Collateralized Debt Obligation market Disruptions? *Hudson Institute Working Paper*, February 2007.

2 Joseph R. Mason and Joshua Rosner. Where Did the Risk Go? How Misapplied Bond Ratings Cause Mortgage Backed Securities and Collateralized Debt Obligation Market Disruptions. *Hudson Institute Working Paper*, May 2007.

3 Alan Greenspan and James Kennedy. Sources and Uses of Equity Extracted from Homes. *Finance and Economics Discussion Series Divisions of Research & Statistics and Monetary Affairs Federal Reserve Board, Washington, D.C.*, March 2007.

4 Lakhbir Hayre. *Salomon Smith Barney Guide to Mortgage-Backed and Asset-Backed Securities*. John Wiley & Sons, New York, 2001.

5 Martin Bartlam. *Structured Finance and Securitization*. Orrick, 2006.

6 Roger Merritt, John Schiavetta, John Olert, Kevin Duignan, Ahmet Kocagil, Alan Dunetz, and Ian Linnell. *Market Value Structures: Exposure Draft*. FitchRatings, December 2007.

7 Alan Greenspan and James Kennedy. Estimates of Home Mortgage Originations, Repayments, and Debt On One-to-Four-Family Residences. *Finance and Economics Discussion Series Divisions of Research & Statistics and Monetary Affairs Federal Reserve Board, Washington, D.C.*, September 2005.

8 Mark Pittman. Subprime Securities Market Began as 'Group of 5' Over Chinese (Wall Street's Faustian Bargain: Part 1 of 5). *Bloomberg*, December 2007.

9 Bob Ivry. 'Deal With Devil' Funded Carrera Crash Before Bust (Wall Street's Faustian Bargain: Part 2 of 5). *Bloomberg*, December 2007.

10 Mark Pittman. Bass Shorted 'God I hope You're Wrong' Wall Street (Wall Street's Faustian Bargain: Part 3 of 5). *Bloomberg*, December 2007.

11 Kathleen M. Howley. Rating Subprime Investment Grade Made 'Joke' of Credit Experts (Wall Street's Faustian Bargain: Part 4 of 5). *Bloomberg*, December 2007.

12 Bob Ivry. Savannah Cries About a Bicycle Left Behind in Reset of Subprime (Wall Street's Faustian Bargain: Part 5 of 5). *Bloomberg*, December 2007.

13 Yalman Onaran. Subprime Losses Reach $163 Billion With Asian Banks. *Bloomberg*, February 2008.

14 Andrew Frye. Subprime Scorecard. *Bloomberg*, January 2008.

15 Roger W. Merritt, Ian Linnell, Robert Grossman, and John Schiavetta. *Hedge Funds: An Emerging Force in the Global Credit Markets*. FitchRatings, July 2005.

16 Roger W. Merritt and Eileen Fahey. *Hedge Funds: The Credit Market's New Paradigm*. FitchRatings, June 2007.

17 Cian Chandler, Lapo Guadagnuolo, and Norbert Jobst. *CDO Spotlight: Approach To Rating Leveraged Super Senior CDO Notes*. Standard & Poor's, August 2005.

18 Jeffery Cromartie, Emmy Bronsema, Lars Jebjerg, and Constantinos Tavlas. *European Leveraged Super-Senior CDOs: Performance Update and Rating Stability Analysis*. DerivativeFitch, October 2007.

19 Elwyn Wong, Cian Chandler, Cristina Polizu, Stephen McCabe, Astrid Van Landschoot, Sebastian Venus, Derek Ding, and Bob Watson. *Quantitative Modeling Approach To Rating Index CPDO Structures*. Standard & Poor's, 2007.

20 Alexandre Linden, Matthias Neugebau, Stefan Bund, John Schiavetta, Jill Zelter, and Rachel Hardee. *First Generation CPDO: Case Study on Performance and Ratings*. DerivativeFitch, April 2007.

21 Anne Le Henaff and Bongani Dlamini. *Rating Actions*. Moody's Investor Service, November 2007.

22 Cian Chandler, Katrien van Acoleyen, and Cristina Polizu. *29 Ratings On Index Constant Proportion Debt Obligations Placed On CreditWatch Negative*. Standard & Poor's, December 2007.

23 Richard Hewitt. *An Introduction to Structured Investment Vehicles*. Moody's Investor Service, January 2002.

24 Stephen Wallis and Perry Inglis. *SIV Outlook 2007 - Another Bumper Year Ahead For SIVs After Assets Approach $30 Billion In 2006*. Standard & Poor's, February 2007.

25 Henry Tabe and Paul Mazataud. *Rating Actions*. Moody's Investor Service, November 2007.

26 Amit Sohal and Cian Chandler. *Ratings On Various SIV-Lites Lowered And Put On CreditWatch Negative*. Standard & Poor's, November 2007.

27 John Ferry. Lightning up. *RISK*, May 2006.

28 Henry Tabe. *SIVs: An Oasis of Calm in the Sub-prime Maelstrom*. Moody's Investor Service, July 2007.

29 Nik Khakee and Katrien van Acoleyen. *Structured Investment Vehicle Ratings Are Weathering The Current Market Disruptions*. Standard & Poor's, August 2007.

30 Tanya Azarchs. *Creditworthiness Of U.S. Banks Does Not Hinge On Their Adopting "Super-SIV"*. Standard & Poor's, October 2007.

31 Glenn Moore and Katerina Vladimirova. *SIVs Rating Performance Update - Issue 3*. DerivativeFitch, November 2007.

32 Glenn Moore, Katerina Vladimirova, and Lars Jebjerg. *SIVs Rating Performance Update - Issue 4*. DerivativeFitch, December 2007.

33 Paul Mazataud, Henry Tabe, Paul Kerlogue, and David Fanger. *Moody's Explains Rating Actions on SIVs and their Impact on Banks*. Moody's Investor Service, November 2007.

34 Jian Hu. *Structured Finance CDO Ratings Surveillance Brief*. Moody's Investor Service, August 2007.

35 Jian Hu. *Structured Finance CDO Ratings Surveillance Brief*. Moody's Investor Service, September 2007.

36 Jian Hu. *Structured Finance CDO Ratings Surveillance Brief*. Moody's Investor Service, October 2007.

37 Jian Hu. *Structured Finance CDO Ratings Surveillance Brief*. Moody's Investor Service, November 2007.

38 Rodanthy Tzani and Jack J. Chen. *Credit Derivative Product Companies*. Moody's Investor Service, March 2006.

39 Raymond E. Owens and Stacey L. Schreft. *Identifying Credit Crunches*. Federal Reserve Bank, June 1992.

40 Sheen S. Levine and Edward J. Zajac. *The Institutional Nature of Price Bubbles*, June 2007.

41 Rudiger Dornbusch. Expectations and Exchange Rate Dynamics. *Journal of Political Economy*, 1976.

42 Kenneth Rogoff. Dornbusch's Overshooting Model After Twenty-Five Years. *Mundell-Fleming Lecture, IMF Speeches*, 2001.

43 Maurice Obstfeld. Models of currency crisis with self-fulfilling features. *European Economic Review*, 40(3-5):1037–47, 1996.

44 Max Bruche and Carlos Gonzalez-Aguado. Recovery Rates, Default Probabilities and the Credit Cycle. *Working Paper*, May 2007.

45 Hyman Minsky. The Modeling of Financial Instability: An introduction. *Modelling and Simulation*, 1974.

46 Robert C. Merton. The Theory of Rational Option Pricing. *Bell Journal of Economics and Management Science*, 4:141–183, 1973.

47 Fischer Black and John C. Cox. Valuing corporate securities: Some effects of bond indenture provisions. *Journal of Finance*, 31(2):351–367, 1976.

48 Fischer Black and Myron Scholes. The Pricing of Options and Corporate Liabilities. *Journal of Political Economy*, 81(4):637–654, 1973.

Index

Credit Crises. J. Felsenheimer and P. Gisdakis
Copyright © 2008 WILEY-VCH Verlag GmbH & Co. KGaA, Weinheim
ISBN: 978-3-527-50375-9

Practical implementation of optimization strategies

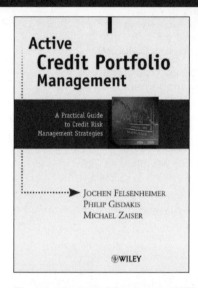

Felsenheimer, Jochen / Gisdakis, Philip / Zaiser, Michael
Active Credit Portfolio Management
A Practical Guide to Credit Risk Management Strategies

2005. 581 pages with 123 figures.
Hardcover.
EUR 119.-
ISBN: 978-3-527-50198-4

The introduction of the euro in 1999 marked the starting point of the development of a very liquid and heterogeneous EUR credit market, which exceeds EUR 350bn with respect to outstanding corporate bonds. As a result, credit risk trading and credit portfolio management gained significantly in importance. The book shows how to optimize, manage, and hedge liquid credit portfolios, i.e. applying innovative derivative instruments. Against the background of the highly complex structure of credit derivatives, the book points out how to implement portfolio optimization concepts using credit-relevant parameters, and basic Markowitz or more sophisticated modified approaches (e.g., Conditional Value at Risk, Omega optimization) to fulfill the special needs of an active credit portfolio management on a single-name and on a portfolio basis (taking default correlation within a credit risk model framework into account). This includes appropriate strategies to analyze the impact from credit-relevant newsflow (macro- and micro-fundamental news, rating actions, etc.). As credits resemble equity-linked instruments, we also highlight how to implement debt-equity strategies, which are based on a modified Merton approach.
The book is obligatory for credit portfolio managers of funds and insurance companies, as well as bank-book managers, credit traders in investment banks, cross-asset players in hedge funds, and risk controllers.

Wiley-VCH
P.O. Box 10 11 61 • D-69451 Weinheim, Germany
Fax: +49 (0)6201 606 184
e-mail: service@wiley-vch.de • www.wiley-vch.de

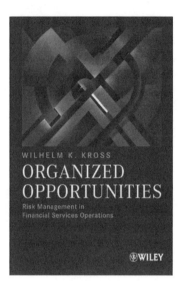